PEPPERMINT TWIST
CHRONICLES

PEPPERMINT TWIST

CHRONICLES

MY TRUE STORY OF SEX, ROCK & ROLL, JIMI HENDRIX, FIGHTING RACISM, AND THE MOB

A TELL-ALL ABOUT THE BEATLES, THE FBI, THE RASCALS,
JOE PESCI, DON RICKLES, DICK CLARK, AND MORE

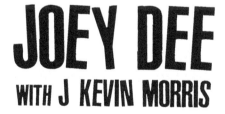

JOEY DEE

WITH J KEVIN MORRIS

ISBN: 9798536858349

Cover Design by Ronnie Dee
Cover Design © 2021 by Joseph DiNicola, Jr.

Except where otherwise noted, photographs and images are from the author's personal collection.

For my mother and my father,
Anna Orlando and Giuseppe DiNicola

A Few More Kind Words from Good Friends

I first saw Joey Dee perform at the Peppermint Lounge in 1961. I thought I was coming to see one show. I stayed for six sets in a row. There this young energetic super talented lead singer of the Starliters blew the audience away. In those six shows, I learned more about stage performance than any school of the performing arts could ever teach me. Just look at the people he mentored: Jimi Hendrix, the Brigati brothers (later of The Rascals), and a young entertainer named Tony Orlando. To the reader, I leave you with one word: Enjoy!
—Tony Orlando

Joey Dee and I were label-mates at Roulette Records during the 60s, where we experienced many of the same problems and issues with Morris Levy. But certainly one very good thing came of that sometimes difficult experience: a close personal friendship between Joey and myself. We came to know each other well—even wrote a couple of great songs together, one of which appeared on my *Nashville* album. Joey has such a great—even amazing—success story of his own that spans more than sixty years. And he's one of the nicest people you'd ever want to meet. I'm proud to call Joey Dee my friend.
—Tommy James

I've been privileged to know Joey for some fifty years. He's a dear friend and one hell of a stand-up guy. To watch Joey on stage is a thrill; a true showman, he gives an audience all he's got and then some. A professional in every sense of the word. It's an honor to know him and call him my dear friend. This book is a winner!
—Bobby Rydell

I first heard "Peppermint Twist" in1961, when I was eleven. Joey and the guys were from Passaic, NJ, and I was from Newark, so I felt a connection with them. There was real excitement in their music that made you want to dance. Joey Dee and the Starliters are part of the musical tapestry that influenced the Manhattan Transfer—and me, as a singer, performer, writer, and record producer.
—Alan Paul

I didn't know Joey during the height of his career. Our paths didn't cross till years later. But we've worked together many times, and he's a great performer even now. It's my honor and privilege to call him my friend for the last thirty years.
—Gary Puckett

Acknowledgments

Words have always intrigued me, and throughout my life I've challenged myself to learn and use as many as I could. Still, I can't seem to find the right ones to properly thank all those I've named in this book who have influenced my life for good. I trust each of you will know how deeply I appreciate you.

I acknowledge the dozens of men and women who have performed on stage and in the recording studio as Starliters or behind the scenes with me on the business end of things. You are too many to name, but please know how highly I value you, your friendship, and your talents. Together we've made good music and good memories, entertained many, and changed lives in the doing.

Through interviews and otherwise, some shared time and remembrances with me and my co-author to help make this book live. A special tip of the cap to (alphabetically): Sal Bonura, David Brigati, Jan Callanan, Joan DiNicola, Jimmy Jones, Jr., "The Amazing" Jimmi Mayes, David McLean, Mary DiNicola Mistrette, Alvin Morse, Bobby "Rod" Rodriguez, and Johnny "The Count" Van Bodegon. Still others contributed in various ways to the production of this book: Ronnie Dee, Nick DiNicola, Renee DiNicola, Dianne Morris, and my honorary Jersey boy Kevin. The book couldn't have been completed without the selfless team efforts of each of you, and I thank you.

My gratitude to all who generously lent their highly respected names in support of this work, and a special thank you to my dear friend Bruce Morrow for kindly penning the foreword—and for his support in many other ways.

With love and respect I acknowledge my parents for my very life and my brothers and sisters for sharing with me the experiences and memories of my youth and beyond; my beloved companions Joan, who is with me, and Lois, who has gone on; and my wonderful children, grands, and greats who fill my todays with everything I need and want.

Oh! One more thing. With all due respect to Florida, thank you New Jersey and New York City—for everything!

FOREWORD

The 60s—what a mind-blowing, ever-changing, earthshaking decade. And what a beginning! American U2 spy plane is shot down over Russia, and pilot Gary Powers is captured by the Reds. JFK narrowly defeats Richard Nixon for the presidency. The Pittsburgh Pirates beat the New York Yankees with a homer in Game 7 to win the World Series. And a cultural tidal wave is about to lift our tired world: A small, relatively unknown New York City night spot, the Peppermint Lounge, is about to create international headlines.

Theoretically, what happened should not and could not have happened, except, perhaps, in a black-and-white 1940s movie. Legendary film star Merle Oberon and her royal escort Prince Serge Obolensky walked into the Peppermint Lounge and created a cultural incident. The two ultra-celebs magically danced the night away. Newspapers, hungry for some good gossip, ran the story of the Prince and the Movie Queen dancing at this unknown little club. Next day, crowds and limos were lined up outside, and barricades held back the growing crowds. Overnight, the Peppermint Lounge gave birth to today's dance club. Celebrities no less than Judy Garland, John Wayne, Jackie Kennedy, and Nat King Cole waltzed—make that *Twisted*—into the club. Everybody wanted to be part of the action. Hundreds of fans lined up on 45th Street, just to gawk at the arriving celebrities.

Inside the lounge—well, it was no longer a lounge but a world-famous club—was a young musician named Joey Dee, innocently leading his band, the Starliters, to what was to become major stardom.

On the radio we were playing the music to support this new excitement—"The Twist," an amazing cover record by Chubby Checker (originally written and recorded by Hank Ballard in 1959); Fabian's "Kissin' and Twistin'"; "Dear Lady Twist," by Gary US Bonds; and "Twistin' U.S.A." by Danny and the Juniors. I also got involved, going on a promotional tour with Rod McKuen ("Oliver Twist"). And we cannot forget the iconic "Twist and Shout," originally recorded by the Top Notes and very successfully covered by the Isley Brothers and the Beatles. It seemed like I was handed a Twist record every few minutes that I was on the air.

And then it happened. Joey Dee and the Starliters released a Twist anthem: "Peppermint Twist."

The song quickly jumped up the charts and knocked Chubby Checker's "The Twist" out of the number-one spot. There had never been a more exciting and fun time for the audience. Joey Dee carried this musical phenomenon with his energy, spirit, and natural showmanship.

Was it all fun and games? NO! And cousins, get ready to read all about it. Get ready for the *Peppermint Twist Chronicles*. Joey Dee is about to tell you one heck of a story.

Bruce "Cousin Brucie" Morrow
77 WABC Music Radio
March 2021

Photo courtesy Bruce Morrow and 77 WABC

CONTENTS

Note of Explanation

Because much of what is written here relates to the role of race in rock & roll and in society, particularly in the 1950s and 1960s, we need to be clear on something right up front. In my lifetime the acceptable identifiers for people of color have evolved. The terms "colored," "Negro," "black," "Black," "African-American," "brother," and "sister" have all found use in various times, often concurrently. Sadly, the ugly, demeaning term "nigger" has been used through all those times and has somehow eluded extinction despite society's best efforts to rid itself of the vile word. The exception to its unacceptability is the Black community's adoption and in-the-loop use of the word today.

Now, I don't intend to teach a lesson in history but only explain my use of terminology that was prevalent in the times of which I write. So please—no hate mail for my use of words that were common in their respective times, nor for the occasional use of terms that were improper then and remain so now. Perhaps one day we'll be mature enough and accepting enough and wise enough to refer to people simply by their given names, without using race-based or culture-based or color-based adjectives or nouns at all. Along the way perhaps we'll learn too that an American is an American, with no need for hyphenation.

Prologue

I t was early 1965, and I was no longer in the limelight. As the founder and leader of the internationally acclaimed band, Joey Dee and the Starliters, I'd lived in that light for the past five or so years—but with the "British Invasion" fully landed, my kind of rock & roll had been carelessly tossed aside. Those of us who still played it were relegated to Holiday Inn gigs. My original Starliters were gone, and I was going through musicians like socks. In fact, it was said by some that one wasn't really a musician till he'd been a Starliter. "Everybody played for Joey Dee at one time or another," a former Starliter once said.

This was an irony as great as any you might imagine. The Starliters and I had pioneered racially integrated rock & roll and were the first Black-and-white band to have a number-one chart hit. As the house band for the Peppermint Lounge, we'd catapulted the Hell's Kitchen dive to the hottest night club in the world. I had hits at home and abroad and had sold millions of records. I'd shepherded an international dance craze. I'd played the largest, most famous, most prestigious venues in the world. I'd toured Europe twice, with my opening act at one venue having been no less than the Beatles. I'd starred in two motion pictures, launched superstars, and rubbed shoulders with café society, legendary entertainers, world leaders, European royalty, Oscar winners, Hall of Fame athletes and musicians, and Mafia crime families. With the opening of Joey Dee's Starliter, I'd been the youngest night club owner in New York City.

But there I was, out of the limelight and, on this particular day, watching Jimi Hendrix, soon to be known as the greatest guitar player in the world, being chased out of my New Jersey home, while I stood wide-eyed between him and the person giving him the bum's rush: the pissed-off mother of my children.

But this isn't really the right place to start my story. To tell it right I've got to take you back a few years and tell it all. Along the way you'll learn what brought me to this awkward moment with the legendary Mr. Hendrix—and what came after.

ONE

BROWN HAIR, BLACK ROOTS

I'm not Black. I feel certain of it. And yet I'm sometimes surprised to see a white guy staring back at me from the mirror. The basis of this confusion lies in my youth and upbringing as Joseph DiNicola, Jr., before fame and fortune found Joey Dee.

| Finding Myself |

Growing up through the 1930s, '40s, and '50s, I lived in racially and culturally mixed neighborhoods. My home town of Passaic, New Jersey, was a melting pot of Latinos, Blacks, Asians, and white first- and second-generation European immigrants from many countries. There were Catholics, Protestants, Jews. There were school-educated and street-educated.

And of course there was socioeconomic variance in Passaic. The Erie Railroad tracks that dissected Main Avenue had two sides. My family lived on the *wrong* side, in the fourth ward of the city. On the other side was Passaic Park, where stood the upscale houses of wealthy businessmen and merchants, complete with new cars out front and, sometimes, domestic help inside. Rich as Croesus, most of these people were.

My family was *not* rich as Croesus. Like most people on our side of the tracks, we were poor as Job's turkey. I'm sure we survived at times only because of the generosity and compassion of good friends and neighbors. Take the Boshnacks for example. Goldie and Abie owned the local grocery store where many in the neighborhood shopped, and Mom would send me there to get food. These good people would give me whatever Mom said we needed and then put the "purchase" in the book. The tab didn't have to be paid till Dad got paid, which was usually on Friday evening. But I don't think the bill ever got paid in full, on Friday evenings or at any other time. That's the kind of thing friends did for each other back then.

Yes, the DiNicolas were poor. But I had the great fortune of not knowing that till I was about ten years old. There's something very special about being raised by parents who worked hard to make sure their children didn't realize they were poor.

That I lived in poverty wasn't the only thing I failed to grasp. I also didn't understand that my skin color was somehow superior to other colors. Someone should have told me. I mean, I'd have been superior if only I'd known I was supposed to be. But no one at home told me. No one at church told me. No one in the community told me. No one at school told me. It just didn't make any difference to anybody. Black, white, brown, yellow, pink, purple, believer, nonbeliever, rich, poor, academic, uncultivated—it was all the same, especially to us kids. We shared the stores, the schools, the parks, the pools, the baseball teams. Where one went, we all went. What one did, we all did. Like the Little Rascals in the motion picture comedy shorts of the 30s, my young friends and I simply had no concept of segregation on the basis of skin color or culture or genealogy. We recognized differences, but different wasn't wrong. Different wasn't bad. Different was simply different.

From Washington Place—my neighborhood till I was eight years old—came the Washington Colts, my very first group. It wasn't a music group but rather a team. Or a crew. Or a gang. Actually, we were kind of like our very own Little Rascals. We were Anthony Cuva, Joe Cuva, Warren Veech, Poochie Pyron, Eddie Pyron, Mickey Hercek, Snookie Zwerin, and Joey DiNicola. We were Catholic, we were Jew. We were black, we were white, we were brown. We were Italian, Irish, Russian, German. We were poor, we were better-to-do. We were this, we were that. About the only thing we had in common was our age. And yet, we were inseparable in those youthful years. The differences between us mattered not one whit. We went to movies together, swam together, hung out together. Some of us were altar boys together. Most of all, we played sports together: baseball, basketball, football, even a little street hockey. Every sport in its season. *Together*—differences and all.

[Sadly, one of the dearest of these friends, Anthony Cuva, passed during the writing of this book. He was a beloved and respected mentor to me in so many ways throughout my life. From our childhood days till he passed, Anthony was a natural leader with a calm, soft-spoken style that was worth emulating. The leadership skills I have, I attribute to him. For more than eighty years this man and I were friends. Not many can claim the blessing of such a long-lived friendship.

But we were actually more family than friends: I'm godfather to his youngest son. When a relationship such as this is interrupted by death, a tremendous hole appears in the heart—a hole that won't be filled. Rest in peace, my friend. This Washington Colt misses you.]

We moved from Washington Place to Columbia Avenue when I was eight years old and lived there through my high school years. Woodrow Wilson Junior High School consisted of seventh, eighth, and ninth grades. When I was in ninth grade—normally the freshman year in high school—I was elected student body president. Here was another opportunity for me to see people as *people*, without regard to anything other than individual nuances of personality and interests. Ethnicity of any kind played no role in how I viewed my friends and fellow students. I was young, but I wasn't stupid; I figured out that every kid's family was trying to find its way in business, in academics, in life—and that all those families shared the simple goal of finding happiness and success in the greatest country that ever was.

And that brings me to *my* family. I was born on June 11, 1937, at Passaic General Hospital, the eighth of ten children born to Giuseppe [Joseph] and Anna Orlando DiNicola. In chronological order, my siblings are John, Nicholas the first (who died at age three years from scarlet fever), Nicholas the second, Rose, Mary, Albert, Vera, Angelina, and Joann. A close-knit family through thick and thin, we were as tight as a family could possibly be. Those of us still living remain so.

My mother and father were immigrants from Sicily (Ribera, Agrigento) and Italy (Morro D'Oro, Abruzzo), respectively. America was the land of their dreams, and they were willing to do what it took to find happiness here. They knew the value of sweat, hard work, determination, and faith. They knew how to love and serve their God, their neighbors, and their adopted country. Certainly they knew how to love and serve their family. Teaching by word as well as by example, their primary goal in life was to help each of their children become a good and honorable person. Everything they did was toward that end. To borrow and paraphrase a line from the 1953 Michael Curtiz film *Trouble Along The Way*, starring John Wayne: For my parents, family wasn't *everything*; it was the *only* thing.

My mother and father taught me countless lessons about life and people. I could fill this entire volume with only the things they taught me, but for now I'll share only this lesson: There are good people and not-so-good people. Those two kinds only. This was the single criterion to be used in determining whether you wanted to associate with a person or not. That decision, they taught, should never be based on color, culture, creed, economics, or any other such superficiality. There was good, there was bad. The end.

One June afternoon we were enjoying the warm weather, and my friends and I were creating a ruckus in the backyard. A first-floor tenant yelled at us for being too noisy, and my dad came to see what was going on. The two of them had some words that ended with Dad being punched in the stomach. I saw Dad go down and soon knew that he was hurt. I was frightened. He was transported to Beth Israel Hospital, where he was diagnosed with severe internal injuries and admitted. After several days there he wasn't improving. One night the doctor told my brother Nick, who had stood vigil with Dad that night, to return home and collect the rest of us. We all dressed, went to Dad's room, gave him a kiss, and went home. The next time I saw my father was in the Morocco Funeral Parlor.

I always felt responsible for that happening.

Dad's departure from my life was tragic and way too early. But he had taught me well, and now my sainted mother was left to carry on, solo, for the rest of her life. Whatever good I've done has been because of what I learned at their feet and at the sides of my loving, supportive siblings. Whatever regrettable thing I've done since leaving the home of Giuseppe and Anna DiNicola is on me. But because I was raised right, I believe I've gotten the big pieces right. I have faith in God. I have faith in America. I know the importance of family. I know the difference between right and wrong, even if I haven't always chosen well. I haven't a bigoted bone in my body and have thus been blessed to know and love good people of many colors and cultures.

Thank you, Mom and Dad and brothers and sisters, for teaching me that.

| Finding My Music |

I was just a child at the outset of World War II. Through those war years, when we lived on Washington Place, my older sisters Rosie and Mary spent a lot of time listening to the radio. Their favorite program was New York's 1130 WNEW broadcast of *Martin Block's Make Believe Ballroom*, so that made it my favorite program as well. With the Philco radio blaring from atop the kitchen table, we'd all listen—and dance—to the wonderful big bands of our day, including my favorite: the great Glenn Miller Orchestra. All the bands were fronted by amazing vocalists such as Frank Sinatra, Connie Haines, and Helen O'Connell. The bands often toured the country, and our Central Theatre in Passaic was a favorite stop for them. I didn't see any of those concerts, but my sisters worked odd jobs to earn enough money to attend—and they rarely missed one.

My interests expanded from big band vocalists to include singers such as Frankie Laine, Tony Bennett, Joni James, Jo Stafford, and other such talented performers. And *that*, my friend, was *music*. It became my love. More than that, it inspired me and kindled a desire to one day be in a band of my own, with singers of my own. But it was just a *thought*, mind you. Just a *thought* . . .

When we moved to Columbia Avenue when I was eight years old, I discovered a new sound. There was a little storefront church where faithful colored Christians worshiped, pastored by the father of my classmate, Kymo. Much of their worship was done in music created by an out-of-tune alto saxophone, a not-so-new piano, and drums. And voices. Oh! the gospel music created by those voices and that trio of worn-out instruments!

I loved the sounds that flowed from that church—which was a good thing, because it couldn't be avoided or ignored. See, we lived on the third floor of the building directly behind the storefront church, and members worshiped in the back of the church. When my window was open, it was as if we were all in the same room, and I was part of that wonderful congregation. And I kept that window open nearly all the time, even in the cold of winter. I sang and moved to that good gospel beat, finding myself connected to it at the soul. That sound, that feeling, that rhythm, that energy of colored gospel music would remain with me and influence my music throughout my life. But in later years I'd discover a cruel irony in the world of rock & roll. While it was based on the very sound that seeped from that storefront church, the brothers and sisters who created it would have to endure much prejudice and injustice in order to perform what they created.

On the corner of our block on Columbia Avenue stood Mr. Joe's Candy Store, run by Big Joe Piazza, Mr. Joe's son. Now, Big Joe was a mountain of a man who always wore a crisp white shirt and a huge pinky ring, and he ran a very cool joint. The juke box there was always stocked with the best records anywhere—"race" records, they were called back then. I loved listening to the juke box and watching Big Joe jitterbugging expertly with all the kids of our mixed neighborhood who shared my passion for that music. Black or white kids, green or purple kids—it made no difference.

I had one other source of race records: radio station WNJR, broadcasting from just down the road in Newark. While many stations played this music sparingly or not at all, it was the staple at WNJR, so I listened almost exclusively to that station on my little radio. The station's DJs Clint Miller, Pat the Cat, and the rest of the gang spun all my faves. If a record was good R&B, Clint and the boys spun it. And if it was anything from New Orleans, I always hoped they'd spin it twice. I got Ray Charles, B.B. King, Jimmy Reed, the Moonglows, and the Flamingos. I heard the Harptones, Fats Domino, Roy Hamilton, Ruth Brown, and Laverne Baker. These were my people.

Maybe you know, but I'll say it, to be clear: Clint Miller and the other WNJR guys were Black. They were among the many fine people who, without knowing they were doing it, persuaded me to think of myself as the same.

Between the gospel music that serenaded me at home and the music of race records coming from Mr. Joe's juke box and WNJR, I was fully converted to R&B. It was my music. It was lively. It was soulful. It was exciting. It was irresistible. And it was mostly Black. But whatever it was or wasn't, it just wouldn't let go of me. Everything I'd spend my life creating musically would be grounded in these sounds of my youth in Passaic.

| Finding the Stage |

By the fifth grade I'd discovered that music came naturally to me, and I wanted to do something with it. I found an outlet in the harmonica, which I taught myself to play. But I wanted to do more than just play music for my own amusement. I wanted to share it. I wanted to perform it.

That's where my friends Anthony "Dutchie" Sciuto and John Yanick came in. With Tony on drums, John on guitar, and myself on harmonica, my first music group was born: The Thunder Trio. We played just about any genre of music you can name, because I liked every genre. But polkas were our forte. Yes, polkas. See, I used to hang outside the Polish Peoples Home and listen to the great polka bands that played live there. I heard the best, including Bernie White Witkowski and Frank Yankovic (no relation to Weird Al, although they had musical connections). Dutchie's house, which had a grocery store downstairs, afforded us a place to practice—and practice we did. The Thunder Trio gave me my first taste of what performing felt like. My direction was set, even if I didn't yet know it.

In 1950 I "borrowed" my baby sister Joann's clarinet, which she'd gotten on loan from the school so that she could play in the band. After some lessons from Professor Moscatti, a music teacher at Clifton High School, I joined the high school marching band. Not my cup of tea. It was just too damn cold on that football field at halftime. And anyway, it seemed like a guy could become either a good marcher or a good musician; rarely did anyone become both.

I also started singing doo-wop in the early fifties with some neighborhood guys and developed a real good ear. We usually sang in front of Yippy's, a Jewish Mafia casino where my uncles and their friends played cards and bet on the ponies. As the guys left the gambling joint they'd throw us a few bucks. "Here ya go, kids," they'd tell us. "Go get some lessons."

I matriculated from the clarinet to the alto sax, an instrument much more conducive to rocking and rolling. I spent twenty bucks of my own money to buy my first horn. To hone my craft, I bought 45 rpm records of sax players such as Earl Bostic, Sam Taylor, King Curtis, and Red Prysock. I'd stack these little black seven-inch discs on my record player and play along with what I thought I heard, manually picking up and dropping the needle on the record as needed to repeat a segment of the song I was practicing. I don't know how many times I had to play each record before getting it right—without squeaks—but my mother was inducted into the Mothers Hall of Fame, nominated under the category *Listening to Saxophone Reed Squeaks Over and Above the Call of Duty*. At dinner Mom would sometimes just start squeaking inexplicably. It was pathetic, really.

But Mom and I stuck with it, and I eventually stopped squeaking and screeching. Soon enough after that, I knew it was time to let the Thunder Trio grow. To Dutchie, John, and myself I added Ralph Fazio on accordion and vocals, Tony Seragusa on upright bass, and Ernie Casini on trumpet. Dave McLean and Rogers Freeman, my first colored Starliters, were waiting just around the corner.

The band practiced and rehearsed two or three times a week, either at a bar in Wallington owned by Dutchie's cousin or in the grocery store in the Sciuto home. Now, Dutchie's family was real salt-of-the-earth people. Even though they never entertained any delusions of grandeur about our future in music, they always encouraged us to do our best and enjoy performing. And that encouragement continued right up to the day when Dutchie's father Big Dutch informed him that it was time to think about a real job. Dutchie then charted a new course that took him to Saint Peter's College, to Seton Hall University School of Law, to the rank of Captain in the US Marine Corps, and finally to twenty years on the bench of the Bergen County New Jersey Superior Court. Other than all that and remaining married to his beloved Rita—I set them up—for over fifty years, he hasn't done much with his life. Sad, really.

But I digress. The band continued to improve and was soon good enough to gig. Because I'd brought the group together, I figured the business end of things should fall to me. I took care of it. St. Anthony's hosted a regular Catholic Youth Organization (CYO) dance, and I thought that would be just the thing for us. I approached our Priest. "If you've got a good band playing at the dances," I explained, "lots of kids will be there. What better way to keep kids off the street one night every week?" The Priest bit. We were hired for the gig at ten bucks each per dance and started the next week.

Performing at that first dance, I realized something important: We didn't have a name. You can't get famous by word of mouth without a name. Hell, you can't even be *introduced* without a name. *And here they are, kids, the band you've been waiting for:* *THESE GUYS!* We had to have a name.

During a stage break I stood outside and anguished over the matter. I was willing to consider any possibilities, with only one "given": We'd be called "Joey Dee and the *Somethings*. But trying to decide on the *Somethings* was giving me indigestion. For ideas, I thought about names of groups I liked, one of those being the Moonglows with the great Bobby Lester and Harvey Fuqua. *Moon*glows. Hmm. Moon. Star. Star . . . light. Star*light*. Star*lighters*. That sounded cool to me. A little twist in spelling, and *Starliters* became our *Somethings*. Joey Dee and the Starliters. I knew who we were. Done and done.

And then came a very important break for us. My sister Mary and her husband Sam "Shuffs" Mistrette—my godfather—were the first presidents of the band's fan club, before we were anybody. Sam had great confidence in the band and submitted an application for us to play on *Ted Mack's Original Amateur Hour,* a television program that showcased amateur talent. *Amateur Hour* might be considered the original *American Idol,* with viewers calling in to vote for their favorite acts. Many great performers had graced Major Bowes's original radio version of this show, including Frank Sinatra with the Three Flashes (a.k.a. the Hoboken Four), Connie Francis, and Pat Boone. Sam's application was accepted, and we auditioned a song for Mr. Mack that I'd written. He loved it and invited us to perform on his show in August 1956. Our first-ever televised gig.

Make no mistake: We were wild. Casini held his trumpet with just one hand, and dropped to the floor. Tony hit the floor as well and lifted the bass to play it in the air. I knelt to play my sax under the upside-down bass, my head fitting nicely under the C-bout (cut-out) of the bass. Then I climbed onto the upright bull fiddle, using the C-bout for my feet as I sat and blew.

"How'd you get the idea of ridin' on that bass fiddle?" Mr. Mack asked, after we finished.

"I was the only one that could fit in the saddle," I said.

We got a lot of votes, what with all my siblings, cousins, assorted other relatives, and friends calling in, but we didn't win. We did, however, manage to come in second behind a little boy who sang the folk ballad, "Danny Boy." Hard to beat that. I guess the old vaudeville saw was right: Never follow or compete against children or animal acts.

We played the St. Anthony's CYO gig for over a year. During that time John and his guitar left us, and I hired Vinnie Corrao and David McLean on lead and rhythm guitars, respectively. I also hired Rogers "Bo" Freeman, a lead baritone singer with amazing pipes. When we met, Bo was singing with a doo-wop group called the Vibratones. But I had lots and lots of gigs lined up, so I was in a position to pay more than the Vibratones paid. That made the decision pretty easy for Bo; he jumped ship and joined the Starliters. Incredible break for us, tough break for the Vibratones.

Both of my new Starliters, David and Rogers, were Black. I'd already decided that my music wouldn't be Black OR white; it would be Black AND white. I had an idea that the combined magic of Black and white voices, rhythm, talent, creativity, and life experience would produce the sound and the performance I wanted. And it did.

I also knew that a mixed rock & roll group would be unique. Whether it's agreed or contested that we were the first truly integrated rock & roll group, certainly it's true that we were the first such band to score a number-one hit when "Peppermint Twist" hit that mark in 1962.

By the time we left St. Anthony's we considered ourselves to be in the big time. We even hired a couple of kids from nearby Lodi to help load and unload the instruments: Joe Capizzi and Frankie Scinlaro. You'll read lots more about Frankie later. Complete with roadies and a proven setlist, we were hired by policeman Joe Russo to play at the Passaic Armory every Saturday, and it wasn't long before we attracted a following. People came from all over North Jersey to hear us and dance the night away.

Joe would occasionally hire an additional group to perform with us. One of those was the Royal Teens, who had the hit record "(Who Wears) Short Shorts." The keyboardist for that group was one Bob Gaudio, who would become a member of the legendary Four Seasons, playing keyboards and writing many of their hit songs. Our paths would cross again many times in years to come.

When I say people came from all over North Jersey, I'm including chicks. I noticed them noticing me while I played, and I soon got my first lessons on the power of rock & roll to attract girls. I also learned what the back seat of a car was for. You don't learn everything you need to know at school.

We played the Armory for two years, and those were the days, my friend. Music, chicks, and money. I couldn't see how things would ever be better than that, but somehow they would be. The handwriting was on the wall.

| TIME TO MAKE A DECISION |

While I was playing gigs in 1958, I also attended Paterson State Teachers College, which had relocated to Wayne, New Jersey, from Paterson in 1951. It's now William Paterson University, a highly prestigious institute of higher learning with a grand campus. But when I studied there, Paterson State was a little house on the prairie. That didn't prevent it, however, from effectively fulfilling its mission to prepare teachers for New Jersey Schools. Despite my prodigious love for music, my goal at the time was to prepare myself to teach history and English—and band gigs such as the Armory and the Irvington House (more on that gig coming up) kept me financially solvent while I studied. I loved being in school, and I excelled in music, history (thanks Mr. Baumgartner), and English (thanks Mr. Fulton). It was there that I developed my lifelong love for history and English, but I didn't do so well in some other subjects. Take math for example. I was woeful in math, but not to worry; in later years I'd be forced by practical necessity to learn practical parts of math such as percentages. See, that's how agents and managers and record labels keep score, and I quickly learned that what I didn't know about such things *would* hurt me.

But the band became so popular that I just couldn't ignore what was staring me in the face. I dropped out of school after a year and a half to make room for the band's schedule. I gave myself a year to either get music out of my system or make it big. If I got it out of my system before I made it big, I'd return to college and finish my degree. If I made it big before I got it out of my system, I'd follow the music. It was a simple roll of the dice, and I made up my mind that I'd be fine with whatever number came up.

Of course, music's number came up, and I honored my decision to follow that course. But I have to say this: While I don't have all that many regrets, one of the biggest is not graduating college.

| Finding the Recording Studio |

The next logical step toward making it *big* was making a *record.*

There were hundreds of independent record labels in the City, and it was time for me to see what I could come up with. I soon signed with the Little Records label to record my first single. The A-side was "Lorraine," a song about an unrequited love of mine from Elizabeth, New Jersey. The B-side was "The Girl I Walked to School." I wrote the songs, and Rogers sang lead on both. Also sitting in on that session were Dutchie on drums, Vinnie on lead guitar, Dave on rhythm guitar, Ernie "Rel" Interella on keyboards, and myself on sax. The record was good. No sales to speak of, but a good record.

At the request of its principal, we played a gig at Garfield High School. Mr. Andrus had been my mechanical drawing teacher at Passaic High. Hearing of our success in Passaic, he asked us to perform for the students at his new assignment. We shared the stage that day with the Hi-Fives, a doo-wop group made up of Pete

Grieco, Ronnie Menhart, Howie Lanza, Rudy Jezerak, and David Brigati. The group had already scored a hit with "Dorothy" on the Decca label, a record which climbed high on local charts and hit number one in Hawaii. I knew the group; in fact, I'd filled in briefly for Howie. After the show I found David Brigati and talked business with him. Clearly, I wasn't above stealing talent when the opportunity presented itself. David's amazing tenor voice could have soothed any savage breast, and I wanted him as a Starliter. I wouldn't take no for an answer, and he came on board.

Now we had David Brigati who would prove to be not only an integral part of our sound and our performance but a lifelong friend as well. With the voices of Bo and David up front and the strength of the best band in Jersey behind them, we were ready to take a giant leap forward. That happened when my Passaic High School friends Shirley, Beverly, Addie, and Doris—you know these ladies better by the name Shirelles—hooked us up with Florence Greenberg at Scepter Records. We signed with the label and produced a great single in 1960: "Face of an Angel" backed with the Luther Dixon-penned "Shimmy Baby." "Angel" was written by David and my pal Chuck Jackson ("Any Day Now"), and David sang lead on the record backed up by the Shirelles and myself. Bo sang lead on "Shimmy." The songs were great, and "Face of an Angel" should have been a chart-topper. Fickle finger of fate and all that, I suppose.

But I had found myself, my music, the stage, and the recording studio. I had created an incredible team, and the course was set. The rest of it was waiting just down the road a piece.

Two

ROCK & ROLL IN
BLACK & WHITE

Quickly becoming the mixed band I'd envisioned from the beginning, Joey Dee and the Starliters showcased some of the best musicians and vocalists ever to have worked—and we always made a great sound. I sometimes ponder what we'd have been without Rogers Freeman, David McLean, Carlton Lattimore, Sam Taylor, Jr., Willie Davis, Jimi Hendrix, Jimmi Mayes, Calvin Duke, Ronnie Spector, Estelle Bennett, Nedra Talley, Shirley Owens, Doris Coley, Addi "Micki" Harris, Beverlee Lee, Charles Neville, Alvin Morse, Jimmy Jones Jr., Dennis Williams, and all the other Black vocalists and musicians that took the stage or recorded with us. On the other hand, had we not had Anthony "Dutchie" Sciuto, John Yanick, Ralph Fazio, Vinnie Corrao, Ernie Casini, Ernie Interella, David Brigati, Larry Vernieri, Billy Callanan, Tommy Davis, Eddie Brigati, Felix Cavaliere, Gene Cornish, Joe Pesci, Bobby Valli, Ronnie Grieco, Eddie Barbato, Lois Lee, Bobby Rodriguez, Eddie Martinez, and our many other white and Latino musicians and vocalists, our sound would have been equally compromised. The skin color of these men and women simply didn't matter; their talents and musicianship mattered a whole bunch.

Sadly, the Starliters and I ran into discrimination, prejudice, and outright bigoted stupidity from time to time as we performed across the country through the years. Such were the times in which we found ourselves. But to be fair, most audiences and clubs and towns showed respect to our band and appreciated our talents regardless of skin tones. Sadly, other audiences and clubs and towns stand out even now just a little too vividly in my memory for the wrong reasons. But that's life. You take the good with the bad.

I believe that music and sports are the great equalizers. They don't care about the color of a person's skin. They care only about talent. And talent will out, sooner or later. Take the man who broke the whole Black–white sports thing wide open: Jackie Robinson, the Baseball Hall of Fame legend. What he faced in the pursuit of his dream would have overwhelmed and defeated most, but he pressed on. His effort and determination were remarkable—but they could be remarkable because his talent was remarkable. And, like the proverbial cream, that talent couldn't be stopped from rising to the top. To be fully transparent, however, it's important to note that Jackie had a little help from Branch Rickey, the white president of the Brooklyn Dodgers. Rickey found Robinson, recognized his talent, signed him, defended him, respected him, supported him—not only because his talent made the sport better, but because it was right, and it was time. Together they got it done. Now, at the risk of being accused of gloating or big-noting myself, I believe that, in some small way, I was a Branch Rickey for rock & roll. And if I'm even the slightest bit justified in that claim, I feel proud. Very proud indeed. The *good* kind of proud. In fact, of all my career accomplishments none ranks higher in my mind than the contributions Joey Dee and the Starliters made to rock & roll in this important matter.

It was such an important matter, in fact, that I'll break the overall chronology of this work to share in this chapter some of the Black-and-white adventures of Joey Dee and the Starliters. The vignettes are in no particular order. Some may make you seethe, others may make you smile. One or two may even make you cheer. But I'm pretty sure none will bore you.

| PLEASE DON'T BEAT THE DAISIES |

We ran into a little trouble in 1959 at a gig at the Bankers Club, located on the Jersey side of the Hudson River, in West New York, New Jersey. Yep, *West New York New Jersey*. Sounds made up, but no. The building had been an actual bank before being converted to a club. We were playing good shows; from the applause and whistling, we figured everyone in the audience liked us. I think everyone did—except that one guy.

It seems that Rogers had gotten more than a bit chummy with a sexy white redhead who'd been sitting at the bar, nursing a beer and paying close attention to Bo. At the end of the show, he asked me if he could bring her along with us in my car. Of course I said yes. I always said yes to that kind of request. David and I climbed into the front seat of the car while Bo and Miss Lady made themselves comfy in the back seat. I was reaching for the ignition key when I heard a *tap-tap-tap* at my window. I turned to my left to find a .38 revolver pointed at my face. I'd seen guns before but never one so close to my face, held by a man who looked eager to use it. I rolled the window down. Seemed the courteous thing to do, under the circumstances.

"Ya know," the man said, "that's my girlfriend in the back of your car with that nigger."

The thug seemed to be waiting for a response from me, but I just didn't have one. "Oh?" was the best I could do.

"Yeah *OH*," he said. "Now listen here, you hot shot music bastards. You ain't shit to me. I could kill you right now. I ain't, but I could. But you show up tomorrow, me and my boys'll take care o' you good. Now get her outta there and get yourself the hell outta here, or you won't be goin' nowhere no more."

Bo let the chick out, and we took off as the guy yelled after us: "I'll be back for you tomorrow." In the rearview mirror I could see him beating the hell out of that girl. I knew we were in trouble. I'd seen this guy before; he always came in with a bunch of hard-asses.

I had a cousin named Phil Russo. Well, we weren't related by bloodlines, but we lived in the same neighborhood, and his parents and my parents were real close—so we called ourselves cousins. Phil was one tough son of a bitch, and he'd just recently gotten out of jail. Certain that the redhead's boyfriend was dead serious about his promise to us, I phoned my cousin and explained the situation to him.

"Where you playing?" Phil asked.

"Bankers Club, West New York."

"What time you go on?"

"Nine."

"We'll be there at eight."

"Okay. Thanks, man," I said. I felt a whole lot better now, knowing Phil would have my back. But I worried about him and wanted to make sure he understood how serious the situation might be. "Phil," I said, "he's coming with a lot of guys."

"Fuhgeddaboudit, Joey," he said. "We got you."

Confident that Phil would take care of any trouble, we showed up at the club and went to the stage to prepare for the show. True to his word, Phil and his guys showed up at eight, each wearing a white carnation boutonniere. All my "cousins" spread out and took seats randomly around the room. The show wouldn't begin for some time yet, so there was only a handful of customers in the room. My boys had barely gotten settled in when, right on cue, in stormed Mr. Disgruntled and his crew of about ten guys. Their clubs and bats told us they were there to do us serious harm, up to and including making us all dead. They made a bee-line for the stage, but they never made it there.

Converging on the would-be attackers from their random seats, my cousins were on those bastids in a New York minute. For the next who-knows-how-long, there was a bloody brawl. Fists and clubs flying here and landing there, bloodied and unconscious men hitting the deck, cursing and moaning filling the air. When the dust cleared, I saw that my cousins had beaten both the piss *and* the hell out of the mob. It was quite a sight, watching the bloodied, vanquished thugs help each other out of the club. They hadn't done what they came to do, but now they were glad just to be alive and able to walk, limp, or crawl away. They'd come expecting to teach the rock stars a lesson. They had no way of knowing they'd be the students, taught by a bunch of ex-cons who made their living beating people up. The redhead's boyfriend et al. had violated an age-old saw that's been respected by entertainers, speakers, and writers since the dawn of time: Always know your audience.

When it was all over, I thanked Phil and his boys. This was what family was all about—having each other's back. But I was puzzled by one thing, and I asked Phil about it.

"Hey Philly," I said, "what's with the white daisies?" A beat-down seemed an unusual occasion for floral accessories.

"Simple, Joey," Phil said. "When fists and feet and clubs are flying like that, it can be hard to know whose head you're cracking. The daisies kept us from beating ourselves up."

Should have been obvious to me, I guess. But you don't know what you don't know till you know it.

| California or Bust(ed Heads) |

In 1963 the band caravanned west in my Caddy and a van to play one of our many stretches in California. Passing through Little Rock, Arkansas, we ran into a special kind of trouble: race-targeted riots and mobs. Apparently, Governor Eugene Faubus didn't have a solid grip on things in Arkansas just then. I didn't have to strain my brain much to know that this was a dangerous situation for Willie and Carl. It was a dangerous situation for *all* of us.

At one point we could see a roadblock ahead. As far as we could tell, only white men were there, some of whom brandished weapons. We knew there'd be trouble if Carl and Willie were discovered in our company, so we pulled over some distance ahead of the roadblock to discuss what to do. It seemed a pretty safe bet that the van would be searched, so we put the guys on the back-seat floor of my Caddy and covered them with clothes and instruments. We could only hope the storm troopers wouldn't get too curious or thorough in their search of the back seat. It was demeaning, what we were asking Carl and Willie to do, and I hated to inflict such humiliation on them. But the potential alternative seemed worse.

The men at the roadblock waved us over. One of them approached me.

"Whatchy'all doin' heah in our little neck o' the woods, boys?" he said.

"On our way to California to play a little music," I said. I didn't dare tell him our name; he might know us and wonder why we were so white just then.

"California, huh? Myself, I ain't never been there," he said. "But I guess y'all gonna have a right big time on the beaches and whatnot."

As he spoke to me, another man slowly circled my Caddy like a hawk eyeing a field mouse. He paused for a moment to take a closer look at the equipment and clothes covering the back floor and seat. My heart jumped into my throat. If he decided to start poking around . . .

Eyes still fixed on the back seat for a few more steps, the man continued walking toward the van. Another man was on the way to the van as well. The two met at the driver's window and tapped on it with the barrel of a pistol. Larry rolled the window down.

"Whatchy'all got in the back?" one asked.

"Just equipment and stuff we need for our gig," Larry said.

The man grunted. "Hmmph. How 'bout we take a little look-see. Y'all don't mind." He wasn't asking.

"No sir," Larry said. "Not at all." He got out of the car and walked to the other side to open the door for the men. One of them stuck his head in and looked around. There was nothing to be seen of course. Nothing that would interest *him* anyway. They stepped away from the door. Larry closed it and returned to the driver's side to get back into the van.

The two men signaled to the men ahead and said, "We clear heah, boys."

The man talking to me took a slow step back from my window. He spat a disgusting wad of used-up chewing tobacco onto the ground, wiped his mouth with the back of his hand, and said, without making eye contact with me, "Now you fellas have yo'selves a nice day, heah?"

I've no idea what might have happened to us, had Willie and Carl been discovered in hiding. I'm just happy that we didn't find out. We didn't delay our departure, but we didn't burn rubber either. If we'd seemed too eager to leave, maybe they'd have taken another look. And now we were on our way again, all of us a little worse for the wear.

| All or Nothing at All |

In late 1957 our up-and-coming band consisted of my colored friend David McLean on rhythm guitar, Vinnie Corrao on lead guitar, Ernie Casini on trumpet, Ernie "Rel" Interella on keyboards, Anthony "Dutch" Sciuto on drums, and myself on alto saxophone. My brother Rogers Freeman hadn't yet joined us as vocalist and wouldn't, for another six months or so; till then, we were primarily a dance band, and a damn good one. We made a good sound and played lots of local and some outlying gigs. In the little New Jersey farm community of Hightstown in Versa County near Trenton, my friend Dave ran into a little difficulty.

The gig was a dance in a fire station there in Hightstown on a Saturday night. For a town this size lots of kids had turned out for some good rock & roll. The rest of us had already arrived and were setting up when Dave came in carrying his guitar and amplifier. You'd think his cargo would have made it easy to identify Dave as a guitar player, but the ability to draw conclusions based on observation apparently varies from one brain to the next.

"What are *you* doing here?!"

Dave turned to see a young man of about seventeen years—Dave's age. The boy's face showed an odd mix of smile, disdain, and surprise.

"Are you talking to me?" Dave said, glancing over his shoulder to see if someone stood behind him.

"Yeah, I'm talking to you," the boy said. "What are you doing here?"

Dave was good at returning wit for stupidity. "Well, let's see," he said. "I'm carrying a guitar and an amplifier, so yeah . . . I'm the piccolo player."

The kid didn't bat an eye. Not real quick on the uptake. "Well, you can't play here," he said. "You're a ni . . ." He didn't get the word out, but Dave heard it just as clearly as if it had been spoken. "I mean, you're colored. You can't play here."

"Seriously man? Are you serious?" Dave said. "I'm in the band."

"Doesn't matter," the kid said. "Can't play here."

Well, here was a stand-off. Dave needed to set up, but this bozo wouldn't let him pass. With a sigh of exasperation, Dave scanned the area and saw me at the front of the room. He caught my eye with a wave. I could tell he needed me there, and I trotted over. I was pretty sure what the problem was, but I asked anyway.

"What's the problem, Dave?"

"Aw, Joey, talk to this guy," Dave said, clearly a bit vexed.

I turned to the kid. "What's the problem, man?"

"This guy can't play here."

"Why not?" I asked.

"He's a . . . he's colored," the kid said. "He can't play here."

Not much in this world gets my dander up like staring stupid bigotry in the face. And that's what I was doing. I guess I could have punched the guy out, and I considered doing it; but in the end I chose a different tack.

"Okay, gotcha," I said. "Give us just a minute to get our equipment together and we'll be outta here."

"*Outta here*?! Whaddaya mean, *outta here*?!"

"Whaddaya mean, *whaddaya mean*? This is our guitar player here. He doesn't play, we don't play," I said. "You can whistle songs for your dance."

"Uhhh, wait . . . wait a minute," the guy stammered. "Just . . . just wait a minute." Processing the situation as quickly as he could, it was clear—even to him—that there'd be no dance without a band. And the band was about to leave. "Hang on," he said. "I guess it'll be okay if he plays. Yeah. It's okay if he plays." The kid's breakthrough moment of maturity didn't just solve our problem; it was good for him. Having granted his consent, he looked as though the weight of the world had been lifted from his young shoulders.

Dave set up. We played the gig. All was copacetic.

My friend David McLean left the group about a year later to pursue his education. He became an educator himself, changing and inspiring the lives of countless youngsters as a teacher and then as a principal, retiring as assistant superintendent of Passaic Public Schools, the town in which we both grew up.

| Hit the Floor! |

Near the Pep was a greasy spoon called the Peerless Diner. Many of the Pep workers often met there before work, and I'd occasionally stop in for a cup of coffee and a donut. Despite its name the joint was anything but *peerless*. It was a dump. But it was conveniently located, and that kept us at its tables.

One day in 1961 I was with some guys from Tyree Glenn's band. Tony, a Black man, was sitting next to a white girl, a Pep dancer. Suddenly they were joined by a New York redneck—yes, New York has rednecks—who objected to the mixed color at the table. I heard the nasty things he was saying with increasing volume that reached at last what I'd describe as *louder than hell*. Having heard enough, Tony stood to confront the asshole.

But the asshole suddenly became *Mister* Asshole when he pulled a handgun from his pocket. Quick on the uptake, Tony could see he was in a bad spot. Now, I'll never know why the maniac didn't just drop Tony with one shot—but he didn't. He chose instead to fire randomly in every direction. Customers hit the deck, diving for cover under tables and chairs and behind the bar as the psycho squeezed off round after round. It was chaos. It was loud. It was frightening. I didn't count the shots, but they seemed like a million. Terror can bend perception and make a single something seem legion or a moment seem forever. I presume he emptied the gun. Anyway he stopped firing.

Our good fortune was twofold. First, a pair of New York's finest was nearby and heard the shots. The two crashed into the diner, took the assailant to the floor with no mercy, cuffed him, and dragged him out of the joint. Second, this guy was the worst shot I've ever seen. Probably the safest place during his target practice was right in front of the barrel of his gun.

When the dust settled, we all went back to our coffee and conversation. Just another day in the naked city.

| The Ballad of Hendrix's Hair |

Using the name Maurice James, the great Jimi Hendrix joined the Starliters in 1965 (much more about that later). To understate it Maurice was particular about his hair. He always wanted it to look good, and it did. He liked the way Little Richard looked when he worked for Richard, and Maurice sometimes wore his hair the same way Richard wore his. He used a hair-pick first thing in the morning and carried it with him throughout the day, using it frequently. He even liked to have his hair "done."

To that end my nephew "Count" Johnny Van Bodegon and I took Maurice to a hairdresser. We found a nice place downtown and went inside to see what could be done. We wondered if there'd be any problem, given that Maurice was a man—this was a women's salon—and that he was a Negro. This was 1965, and things were what they were. Of course, there weren't many salons then that catered to men, whether colored or white, so if either of these characteristics turned out to be a problem at this salon, we were screwed.

"Ma'am," I said to the woman who approached us when we entered, "we need a little hair work done."

"Oh?" she said. She seemed perplexed by the lack of femininity among us.

"Yes ma'am." I took Maurice by the elbow and urged him front and center. "My friend here needs a little help with his hair."

"Uh, yes," the lady stammered. "Yes, I see."

I sensed a slight hesitation that sent a small shiver down my spine. Had to do something about that. The best defense is a good offense.

"Now, I know we've got a couple of things going against us here, ma'am," I said. "Yes, my friend's a man. And yes, he's a Negro, and . . . well, I don't see anyone here but white women," I said. "Is either of these issues a problem?"

The lady's face, at first a bit ghostly, eased into a grin. "No sir. Neither of those things is a problem. We do hair here. We're happy to help."

Maurice was directed courteously to a chair. "Madge!" the lady called. "Would you please? We need some help here."

Madge approached Maurice, said a friendly hello, and spun the chair so that he was facing the mirror and she was standing behind him, at an angle. She picked and pulled at his hair for several moments, taking a step backward now and again to get the overall picture. I guess she was sizing up the job.

"Now, just how did you want this done?" she asked.

"Well, ma'am, I guess just kinda all out and shaped good."

"Mmmkaaaay," she said, her eyes never leaving that head of hair. "So just rather free and shaped a bit." She gave Maurice's hair a final gentle tug.

"Yes ma'am."

"Indeed," Madge said. "Rose! Dottie! A hand here, please?"

The work began. Clearly, Maurice enjoyed the attention he was getting. Shampoo, rinse, light perm, comb-out, shape, spray. Done.

When at last Madge spun the chair around and stepped away to proudly inhale her work, Maurice was gorgeous. I thought for a moment I might ask him out, if the hairdressers didn't beat me to it. He left the salon sporting not only perfectly quaffed hair but a smile of contentment and confidence as well. My man was ready for a show or anything else that might come his way.

I've often wondered whether or not those kind and courteous ladies are still with us, and I've imagined what a pleasant surprise it would be for them to learn just whose hair they did that day.

| City of Rocks and Roses |

In 1963 we did a fly–drive tour with Chubby Checker, the Dovells, and Dee Dee Sharp. Miss Sharp had begun her career as a backup singer to Chubby, Lloyd Price, Bobby Rydell, Frankie Avalon, and Jackie Wilson—nice resume—before going on her own to record such hits as "Do the Bird," "Mashed Potato Time," and "Gravy (for My Mashed Potatoes)." Consisting at the time of Jerry Gross,

Arnie Silver, Mike Freda, and Lenny Barry, the Dovells had recorded the smash hits "Bristol Stomp" and "You Can't Sit Down." Lenny later left the group to go solo, scoring a major chart hit with the tune "1-2-3" in 1965. Also joining us on that tour was Dee Dee's mother, who didn't trust a single one of us.

Good thinking, Mom.

On one of the flights I found myself extremely nervous. The feeling seemed to come from nowhere, but it was nearly overwhelming. In order to burn some of the adrenalin pumping through my anxious body like water through a high-pressure fire hose, I began doing push-ups in the aisle. The exertion helped a little; at least it got me through the flight. Still, it was such an overpowering feeling, I decreed I'd never fly again, no matter what. And it's a documented fact that I never boarded a plane again in the next forty years. I guess whatever I had must have been contagious, because David Brigati stopped flying as well.

We played gigs along the West Coast. Our ground-travel accommodations in those days weren't quite the posh, comfortable, catered circumstances enjoyed by today's entertainers when they travel. No, it was just us in an old Greyhound tour bus, trying to find a comfortable position to sit and sleep on a well-worn seat. Somehow we managed, and our music turned out to be just as good as if we'd been traveling in the lap of luxury.

In Portland we found a bit of trouble: There was a riot at the theater where we were to perform. Apparently always looking for something to chew on, Portland has a rich history of riots, protests, and demonstrations. This particular uprising, if memory serves, was ignited by the murder of civil rights worker Medgar Evers in Mississippi. Whether I'm remembering that right or not, it was clear when we arrived at the venue that we couldn't get out of the bus just yet. We could tell from the screaming, cursing, fists, and epithets that this was an ornery crowd that meant business. But the disturbance was more than just noise; our bus was suddenly under attack, being pelted with bottles and rocks and who-knows-what-all. Before you could say *duck and cover* windows were shattered and glass shards were flying, inflicting cuts on some of the Dovells and Starliters. I managed to avoid injury by climbing up into the luggage rack, a storage area similar to a plane's carry-on compartments. I sometimes found advantages such as this in being small.

Clearly, we weren't going to make it to the dressing rooms just yet—at least not without air or artillery support and Marine boots on the ground. With horn blaring and engine revving, the bus driver got us out of there, and we stayed clear till the police restored order.

After all was said and done we made it safe and sound into the theater and played a great gig without ducking a single rock or bottle. It turned out to be just a handful of assholes that caused the problem. In my opinion this is nearly always the case. Take Israel and the West Bank for example. I think most people on both sides want to live peaceably, but a minority of voracious pot-stirrers creates all the problems. In any case we had no more trouble in Portland. Then it was on across the Canadian border to our next gig in Vancouver, British Columbia.

| Not with the White Girls, Please |

Being entrepreneurial, Clint Miller, master DJ at WNJR Radio, had a side gig hosting a dance at the Irvington House on the Garden State Parkway in Irvington, New Jersey. I knew about Irvington House, but it wasn't till the Starliters and I had made a name for ourselves as the best band in Jersey that Clint invited us to play there. Sometimes we played our own music, but most of the time we backed the big-name artists he always managed to book—artists like Frankie Avalon, Connie Francis, Bobby Rydell, Fabian, and others of that magnitude. Big hitters all, and we got to back them up. I was thrilled with this gig, as you might imagine. I remember telling Bobby Rydell that I was gonna be "one of you" one day. His response: "Joey, you and the guys are really good. I think you'll make it."

When Clint hired me, he had a few instructions for me—instructions that I was to follow to the letter.

"Joey," Clint said, "I gotta tell you this right up front, so there's no misunderstanding and no mistakes."

What the hell is this, I wondered to myself. It sounded downright ominous.

"Now Joey, you've got Freeman and McLean in your lineup," he said. "They're good. They're great. And you're a pretty smart guy, Joey, to have colored guys playing rhythm and singing. You know what makes people dance. Hell, I hired you for this gig because you're mixed and you've got the best sound out there. But," he continued—I knew there had to be a *but* hiding in there somewhere—"Rogers and David canNOT dance with the white girls."

It was 1959, after all, and things were still what things still were.

Rogers was a handsome cat—in addition to "Bo," we called him "Jungle Fever"—and girls found themselves attracted to him whether they wanted to be or not. And he was a great dancer. Whenever we performed, he got on the floor and danced with whoever was handy. This wasn't only part of the show; it was Bo's nature. White girls, pink girls, black or green. Made no difference to Rogers. He'd dance with a trailer hitch if it had rhythm. But every time he'd do his dance thing at Irvington, Clint would yell at me. "Joey," he'd say, "I told you a hundred times. The colored guys can't dance with the white girls!"

"Clint," I answered, "Bo isn't really dancing *with* the white girls. He's dancing *near* the white girls."

Clint invariably backed down. "Well . . . okay then," he'd say. "As long as he's not dancing *with* the white girls." I guess Rogers maintained acceptable social distancing, because Clint never fired us. Pardon the gloat, but he wouldn't have fired us anyway. We were the best band there was.

Clint said something every day on his radio show that I've never forgotten, and its underlying principle is as applicable today as it was then: "As you go through life, my friend, whatever be your goal, keep your eye upon the donut and not upon the hole."

| Carl's Painful Hair |

I liked to go to Harlem to visit the world's greatest boxer: the one and only "Sugar" Ray Robinson. He owned a barber shop located on the ground floor of the Hotel Theresa between West 124th and 125th Streets. Interestingly, this was the hotel that housed Fidel Castro, legendary Prime Minister then President of Cuba from 1959 to 2008, and his entourage when he was in New York for United Nations meetings.

The fact that Sugar Ray had his own barber shop may give you a hint that he liked hair and hairstyles. It's true. He did. And he's credited with having set a trend among Negro males when he began to "Marcel" his hair. He even made the cover of the September 24, 1953, edition of *Jet* magazine ["Sugar Ray Robinson: He set new trend in men's hair styles"] that explained the Marcelling process and addressed the question, "Should Negro Men Marcel Their Hair?" That issue of *Jet* also addressed the topic, "Why People Walk In Their Sleep," but who cares.

In any case our man Carlton Lattimore decided to Marcel his hair. While most men took the safe road and visited a beauty parlor to get it done, Carl decided he could do it himself. Jaybra (forgive any misspelling) was the brand name of the product he applied to his hair to get the desired effect. It had the strength to break down the protein in a Black man's coarse hair so that it could be straightened and then curled as desired. The problem with the stuff was that you couldn't get it on your scalp. If you did . . . damn!

And, of course, Carl did just that. Somewhere a Richter Scale registered an unexplained blip of notable magnitude when Carl screamed. Shrieking and yelling, he stomped and crawled around, looking to get his hands on towels to blot the acid off his head before bone was exposed. And all of this begging the question, *Is a frickin' curl worth all this pain and suffering?*

No. No, it wasn't. Not to anybody except Carl. Even with all the agony, he endured two or three more blistering hot scalp treatments before reaching the conclusion that he looked just fine without the curls.

With all due respect, damn your Marcelled hair, Sugar Ray.

| Cheap Road Labor |

We often traveled to gigs in two vehicles, as was the case in 1962. On the way to Ohio, Larry, Willie, and Carl shared one van, while David, Sam, and I shared the second. My van arrived without incident at the college venue where we were to play, but the other van didn't arrive at the same time. It wasn't uncommon for the two to get separated along the way, so I wasn't worried that we hadn't arrived together. We proceeded as usual, unloading the equipment from our van and schlepping it onto the stage to set up.

After we were set up I began to worry a bit that the other guys still hadn't arrived. But worry was all I could do; I had no way of finding out whether something had happened to them along the way, or they were just slow.

Meanwhile, somewhere on an Ohio highway . . .

Larry fell asleep at the wheel. When he awakened with a jerk, he overcompensated into a swerve, and the van lost its footing and flipped, leaving broken glass and twisted chrome in its wake as it rolled. It's hard to account for the fact that none of the three passengers was killed—or even injured. The old saying is that God protects fools, drunks, and children, but I suppose you might add *sleepy rock & roll musicians* to the list. In this case at least, it seemed to be true enough. They all emerged from the wrecked vehicle ruffled but unhurt.

Of course, a rolled-over, wrecked, smashed van in the middle of the highway is bound to draw police attention. And so it did. Several squad cars were soon gathered at the scene.

Thumbs hanging on the buckle of his gun belt as he ambled, one of the officers approached the guys. "You fellas hurt?" he asked. Not waiting for a response, he added, "Guess you boys had a little too much firewater, eh?"

"We weren't drinking, Officer," Larry said. "And no, we're not hurt."

The officer barely heard Larry; he was more interested in watching Willie and Carl. Not that they were doing anything except counting their blessings.

"Well, boys," the officer drawled out slowly, "I'm glad you ain't hurt, but you sure made a helluva mess on my highway here."

Surprised at the officer's take on things, Larry said, "Well, yeah. I guess we did. Windows sometimes break when a van rolls."

"Not right sure I like your tone, son," the officer said. "In this state we got a law against littering, and that's what you done on my highway here."

For a moment the guys waited for the punch line that surely must be coming. It never came. They were incredulous. This bozo wasn't joking.

"You're serious," Willie said.

"Serious as a heart attack, boy," the officer growled. "And I'm gonna have to run you fellas in. But first," he said, "I need you to clean up this mess."

Okay, now—there *had* to be a punch line to *that*. But when the officer went back to his car and returned with a couple of brooms in his hands, the guys stopped expecting that punch. Another officer brought a third broom from his car, and Willie, Larry, and Carl found themselves sweeping glass and gnarled chrome off the Ohio highway. It took them a good while to finish, and then, true to his word, the officer and his minions cuffed the three of them, ducked them into the back seat of a squad car, and drove toward town.

At the courthouse the guys faced some kind of kangaroo court that ended with the three of them being remanded into the custody of the county and jailed, being held on a thousand-dollar bond.

Go directly to jail. Do not pass go. Do not collect two hundred dollars.

Before the bars slammed shut on the guys, Larry used his one phone call to reach me. To this day I'm amazed that he was able to track me down at that college. I mean, there were no cell phones, no tweeting, no texting, no GPS tracking. With only the name of the college, Larry was somehow able to find a phone number that hooked him up with the right person. That someone found me and told me I was wanted on the phone; I should please follow him.

"Joey," Larry said. "Larry here."

"What the hell, man?!" I said. "Where are you guys?"

"Jail," Larry said flatly.

"Seriously, man," I said. "Where are you?"

"In jail. Seriously," Larry said. Then he sang his song of woe, giving me a condensed version of all that had happened. And he capped it off with, "We need a grand to get out of this place."

I told Larry not to worry, and hung up. I then dialed Western Union to arrange for the bail to be wired to the courthouse. A thousand frickin' dollars this cost me—not to mention the cost of a totaled van—and the incident never even made the papers.

There was a big shot there at the college who, when he learned what was going on, pulled some strings. A short time later our lost boys were delivered to us by police escort.

I like to ponder how this story might have played out today, what with smart phones with photo and video capabilities, texting, email, and so much social media. Two brothers and a white guy sweeping the highway as smiling police officers look on. A picture or a video of that moment would circle the globe in minutes, and those police officers would have hell to pay.

But that was 1962. Life was so different then. Right?

| Too Much Color for the Mob |

To understate it the Mob didn't care for colored people. In fact, had there been a *How Much Do You Hate Negroes* contest in the sixties between Mobsters and allies of South African apartheid, it surely must have ended in a dead heat.

But the Starliters were multi-colored faces from the start. That's who we were. That's who I wanted us to be. That's why we were able to produce the right sound. Sadly, we also lived in a world that included all levels of wise guys, many of whom were friends of mine and had a positive effect on my career. The challenge before me, always, was to find a way to balance these two circumstances. I was usually able to accomplish this ticklish little feat, but doing so sometimes brought me closer to the flame than I cared to be.

I was often called over to the tables of wise guys after a set. They always enjoyed our music and were generous enough to tell me so in person. But the conversation too often came around to the color of my band and how much better the Starliters would be if there were less diversity. "Got a lotta *dark* up there on the stage with you, Joey," they'd say. "What's with all the niggers? You should get rid of the niggers. You boys would sound and look a lot better. Get rid of 'em, Joey." Even if the words were spoken with a lightness and an air of friendliness, the meaning between the lines and the men who spoke them were rock-hard serious.

I couldn't have disagreed more vehemently, and it made me sick to hear such talk about my friends. But I had to respond carefully. I mean, I wasn't about to get rid of anyone, as these guys suggested, but neither could I be insulting or derisive or patronizing to them in any way. Such things could get a person dead. So I'd just laugh with careful timing, nod my head innocuously, and just generally shine them on without agreeing or disagreeing or disrespecting. They never pressed the issue to the point that we *went to the mattresses*—to use a phrase we learned in the *Godfather* films—so it always ended with hugs and handshakes instead of trouble.

One night in April, 1962, Ava Gardner, the glamourous 1940s movie star, ventured into the Peppermint Lounge. What a looker that lady was! The Creator was paying especially close attention to His work the day Ava Gardner hit the planet. On this particular night Miss Gardner was in the company of three colored men. I've no idea about the relationships; maybe she was a liberal party girl, maybe they were bodyguards. No idea. But some Mob guys expressed an opinion about what they saw—and just loudly enough.

"Look at the nigger lover," one of them said, and others at the table put forward similar points of view.

The Pep host saw and heard enough to be concerned. The last thing anyone wanted was a race riot in that particular club on that particular night. To avoid such trouble the host tucked Ava and her guests away at a nice, quiet, out-of-the-way table. Happily, the strategy worked; there was no scene.

There certainly might otherwise have been trouble—and probably would have been. See, the one thing Mobsters hated more than a colored guy was a white chick who was *with* a colored guy. More than once I saw wise guys chase such couples out of the club. Well, they didn't actually get up and run after them. They instructed the bouncers to remove them—and the bouncers always did as they were told in such matters. But this was to be a fortunate night for Miss Gardner—she wouldn't see her name besmirched in the gossip columns next day.

Interestingly, these Mobsters were showing their prejudice in New York, not in Georgia or Arkansas where such behavior might have been less surprising. Contrary to accepted myth, bigotry in the sixties wasn't confined to the Deep South. Willie was from Savannah, Georgia, and Carl hailed from Lake Butler, Florida. They knew prejudice firsthand, and they had learned that wrong thinking could pop up anytime, anywhere—not just in the South. It was all very confusing. Ironic, even. Perhaps our guy Sam Taylor, Jr., who was born in Alabama but made his adult home in New York, described that cultural enigma as well as anyone: "Up in Brooklyn where I'm from," he said, "they hated you, but they didn't tell you they hated you—so you never knew who hated you and who didn't. Down South, everybody treated you the same all the time. Good or bad, at least you always knew what to expect there."

Sam, Willie, Carl, and all the brothers who were Starliters in those days learned to keep a sharp eye on everyone. All the time. And when there was trouble, I never hesitated to lay myself down like a bridge over troubled water between it and my guys—even if the trouble was the Mob.

It was my pleasure.

| White Where White Shouldn't Be |

Once in a while the ugliness of racial prejudice surprised us by flowing from

Black to white.

Our first rehearsal after I hired Jimi Hendrix was held at my Lodi home. I met him and Jimmi Mayes at Big Wilt's Smalls Paradise Club on 135th Street and 7th Avenue in Harlem to take them there. Smalls Paradise Club had been around for many years, opened by Ed Smalls in 1925. It was sold in 1955 to Tommy Smalls (no relation) and then again a few years later to Harlem businessman Pete MacDougal and legendary NBA Hall of Fame big man, Wilt Chamberlain—which, of course, accounted for the "Big Wilt's" part of the club's new name. No place captured the real swagger of Harlem more than Big Wilt's did. Everyone there was experiencing the ups and downs and highs and lows of life, and every con game known to man came through its doors sooner or later. Here was where the younger generation developed street smarts—which reminds me of one of my "Dee-isms": Street smarts beat book smarts every time. More on Big Wilt's later.

I arrived ahead of the James boys—my collective name for Jimi and Jimmi—and navigated toward the bar, thinking to have a drink while I waited for them. As I made my way through the shoulder-to-shoulder crowd, a few heads turned and maybe there was a whisper here or there: *What's whitey doin' in here* or *He's too small to be a cop.* But I didn't sweat it. I knew I was very likely the only white guy in the place, but it certainly wouldn't have been the first time. I'd been in and out of the club many times, both by myself and with my guys Rogers and David. I understood how things were, but I knew I was welcome in Harlem bars and clubs, and I never felt uncomfortable in any of them. The regulars knew me, and I knew them.

On the way the bar I brushed between two large, angry-looking brothers who seemed to be sizing me up. I guess I looked like an easy mark for these bruisers who weren't frequent flyers at Big Wilt's, but I held my course.

At the bar I asked my friend Jerome for my usual Seagram's V.O. Whisky straight up with a water chaser. And then I saw the two men moving. I guess they'd finally adjourned their conference, having reached agreement that I was a whitey who could be strong-armed. And here they came.

The men approached and greeted me, not at all friendly. One of them grabbed my arm and sort of spun me around. "Hey! Honky!" he said. "What da fuck y'all doin' up in heah? Don't got nowheres else to go or what?" He turned to his confederate: chuckle, chuckle, skin-slap up, skin-slap down. But then, almost in unison, their postures straightened, their eyes darkened and glared, and their entire gestalts were dire and threatening. "You ain't 'pose to be in heah, honky, and you gonna hafta pay jus' a little," the second man said.

Perhaps a smarter man than I might have felt a bit more frightened in this moment than I did. Not that I wasn't at all anxious; I knew the situation had the potential for turning bad. But I was confident of my status there, and I figured my friend Jerome had my back.

He did.

Seeing and hearing the confrontation, Jerome set my drink on the bar and leaned forward over the counter. With a stout hand he grabbed one of the brothers by the collar, yanked him up eye to eye, and said calmly, "Now, you two fools done picked on the wrong mark tonight. This heah fella my friend Joey Dee, and he a'ight in heah. Now y'all bes' get yo' black asses outta my house. NOW."

With no more chuckling or skin-slapping, the two men turned and went away. And they moved like cats through a dog pound, apparently understanding the consequences for dallying. They may have been a bit socially uninformed, these two—but they weren't stupid.

Hendrix and Mayes showed up just moments after my would-be muggers vamoosed. I placed a ten-spot beneath my untouched glass of VO, exchanged friendly gestures with Jerome, and headed with the James boys toward my Caddy. I never told Hendrix or Mayes about the scene that had played out before they arrived. I didn't think it had been anything to write home about or discuss. Done, finished, forgotten.

| HOMIE DON'T PLAY THAT |

Earl "Speedo" Carroll. What a guy. You'll remember him as the front man of the Cadillacs with the hit recording, "Speedoo." Earl went on to sing with Carl Gardner and the Coasters for years, leaving them in the 1990s to bring the Cadillacs back to life.

One day my son Ronnie and I were walking on Broadway, near the Roulette Records building, when we bumped into Speedo.

"Speed!" I said. "What's happening, man?"

"Oh, you know how it is, Joey," he said with a wry smile. "Sometimes chicken, sometimes steak."

We were playing a gig in Louisville, Kentucky, with Earl, Gary "US" Bonds, and Shirley Reeves. We were all standing outside the hotel, waiting for a bus to take us to sound check. We were chatting, horsing around—generally enjoying one another's company. Speedo was dressed nicely in a suit and hat, looking a bit like he might have been a hotel employee. I mean, he was dressed for the part and stood in the right place to hail cabs for hotel patrons. I guess I wasn't the only one who thought he bore some resemblance to a doorman. The guy that popped out of the hotel clearly thought so too.

"Hey boy!" he said, slipping a couple of keys into Speedo's hand. "Here's my keys. Run down to the corner and get my Buick for me. There's a quarter in it for you. Honk when you're out front." With that the man ducked back into the hotel.

For a moment we all stood staring at one another, dumbfounded. Then Speedo broke the silence.

"Say *what?*!" Speedo was livid. I can't recall ever having seen a brother go pale, but I swear Speedo's color changed. He was that mad. He looked at the door of the hotel, then at us, then at the keys. He was incredulous.

"Who in the HELL does that cracker think I am?!" he shrieked. And with a step toward the door, he added, "Man, I'm goin' in there and yank a damn knot in that cat's tail!"

Now, Earl was just over five feet tall, and he bore some resemblance to Colonel Sanders—but it would be a mistake to underestimate the guy's grit. We could see our friend meant business here, and he was prepared to take care of it; but we didn't want that kind of trouble. We sort of wanted to get out of Kentucky alive and in one piece. Collectively, we got between Speedo and the door, trying to soothe him while lovingly blocking him from his goal of inflicting some Harlem comeuppance on the guy.

"Now, Speed," I said, "you know that guy didn't mean anything. He just thought you worked here."

"Well, hell, man," he said, "I ain't no damn butler. I'm from Harlem, and we don't play that. Homie don't play that."

"I know, man," I said. "The guy's a schmuck. Just let it go. Here now," I added, "just gimme the keys and I'll take care of it."

We hadn't done a very good job of soothing Speedo. He was still fuming, mumbling, and growling, but he handed me the keys anyway. I took them in hand and went into the hotel. Finding the man, I approached him.

"Excuse me, sir," I said. "You just ordered one of the finest musicians and performers on the planet to fetch your damn car." I chucked the keys at him. They hit him on the chest and dropped to the floor. As he stooped to pick them up, I signed off with, "Fuck you AND your Buick, you cracker bigot."

I don't know whether that guy ever got his Buick or not, but sound check went fine.

| Feel Free to Eat, But Don't Touch the Food |

Jimmy Jones was an amazing singer, songwriter, and performer. While with the

Sparks of Rhythm, a doo-wop group, Jimmy and Charles Merenstein wrote the song, "Handy Man" (you may know the 1977 James Taylor cover of the iconic hit). After he left the group to go solo, Jimmy and Otis Blackwell reworked the song, recorded it, and released it late in 1959. It reached number two on the Billboard Hot 100 in 1960. Later that year he recorded and released the Fred Tobias/Clint Ballard, Jr. tune, "Good Timin'", which reached number three on the Hot Billboard 100 and number eight on the R&B chart.

Jimmy had a son, Jimmy Jones, Jr., who became a talented keyboard player and singer in his own right, despite Jimmy's wish that he remain in school and learn a trade. But it was too late; Jimmy Jr. had caught the bug from Dad, and he'd have nothing to do with anything that wasn't music. It was his passion, and he has happily pursued it throughout his life.

And what a keyboard player he was. And *is*. When I first met Jimmy Jr. and invited him to join the Starliters, he hesitated. A very religious kid, Jimmy Jr. was playing for the church. For him church wasn't just a go-to-it-for-an-hour-on-Sunday-and-then-forget-about-it thing. For him and other faithful members, church was an every-Sunday-all-day thing. And when his congregation worshiped, it was a joyous celebration of faith, complete with clapping, dancing, saxophones, organs, and voices. The works. If church had been like that for me, I'd never have missed a Mass. Jimmy Jr.'s congregation had it right. We had it wrong.

But my son Ronnie and I wore him down. Jimmy Jones, Jr. joined the Starliters in 1993 and played with us until about 1997. We became close friends and remain so today. The years Jimmy Jr. spent with the Starliters were fun times. Well . . . except for that one gig.

It was the grand opening of a club in Leonardtown, Maryland. We would be doing the first show ever done there. At the time, Jimmy Jr. was the only Black Starliter. During rehearsal a man carried a tray covered with cheeses, crackers, and cold cuts, which he was taking over to the buffet table that had been set up for us. Having just driven up from Florida, we were all hungry. Jimmy Jr. thought he'd avoid the rush and take a little nosh right off the tray as the man carried it. But when he reached for the tray, he got something besides cheese.

"Get your monkey paw off the tray."

Wait. What?

Jimmy Jr. had no idea that the guy was serious. In fact, he thought it was funny, what he'd heard. He laughed. And when I say *laughed*, be advised that Jimmy Jr. has an incredible, gut-driven laugh that can rock the room like an earthquake. That's the kind of laugh he gave this guy, and right in his face. But after several moments of laughing, Jimmy Jr. noticed that the guy wasn't laughing with him. In that moment it dawned on him.

"You're serious?" he said. "You're serious!"

"Damn right I'm serious, nigger," the man said. "Keep your monkey paw off the tray."

Now, aside from this guy's bigotry, what made the interaction odd is that he was a performer himself, with a Bill Haley and the Comets cover group. Not only that but he actually knew Jimmy Jr.'s father, who had once given him a trailer. The problem was, the guy didn't know he'd just insulted Jimmy Jones's son. Maybe he'd have behaved differently, had he known; but it shouldn't have mattered or made a difference in his attitude.

I saw and heard it all. Jimmy Jr. was incredulous and really didn't know how to respond to this thing. I figured it was time to get involved. Rushing over to the scene, I spoke to the server. It wasn't easy to find words, because I was livid. My face must have looked like I'd been rolling in beet juice.

"This *monkey*," I said, "is my music director, you son of a bitch. Where *he* don't go, *we* don't go." Turning to the band, I said, "Okay, fellas. Pack it up."

Everyone began scurrying around, unplugging and rolling and lifting and lugging. In what seemed like a heartbeat, we were loaded into the van. By now the club manager had gotten involved and was doing his best to keep us there. But it was too late. My mind was made up. There was nothing left to say or do. We climbed into the van and took off.

At this stage of the game, such an incident wasn't new to me. And every time it happened I always responded the same way. This guy should have checked with the other guys I'd left in the lurch for disrespecting us. They'd have all told him the same thing: "Don't mess with Joey. If you do he's gonna leave." That's a nice badge to own. I'm very proud to own that badge.

I wasn't the only one upset by what had happened. All the guys had felt the pain and embarrassment Jimmy Jr. must certainly have been feeling. In fact, everyone was crying, to one degree or another—everyone, that is, except Jimmy Jr. I think he was still a bit speechless, having never before heard such vulgar epithets leveled at him.

We didn't drive straight back to the Bronx, where I was living at the time. We still hadn't eaten, and we were even hungrier now. Apparently, staving off bigotry builds a good appetite. I took the guys to the best seafood restaurant in Leonardtown, Maryland—my treat. While there I found an opportunity to pull Jimmy Jr. aside.

"Bro, I'm so very sorry about all that's happened," I said. "And I'm paying you for the gig." I handed the cash to my friend and thanked him for being a member of the group. He was visibly affected by the gesture. I was affected by his response.

Jimmy Jr. called his dad later and told him what had happened—how the band and I had stood up for him.

"You never have to worry about Joey and the guys," Jimmy said. "Joey will always take care of you."

Then Jimmy Jr. shared with his father that he'd been called nigger for the first time. His dad's response: "Son, it won't be the last time."

How I wish Jimmy Jones, Sr. had been wrong about that.

| The Food Probably Sucks Too |

When we were playing the 1962 grand opening of the Peppermint Lounge South, located on the 69th Street Causeway in Miami Beach, the great Sam and Dave were in town as well. We had a night off, so we decided to catch their show. We thought we'd enjoy a nice quiet restaurant meal prior to the show. I've forgotten the name of the restaurant we selected, and I guess it's just as well, all things considered.

I suppose I should have been struck by the preponderance of white faces inside the restaurant, but I somehow failed to take notice. Perhaps it was because I'd known from youth that many Jewish people took their winter vacations to Miami Beach—so I figured everything would be cool here.

Be that as it may, we sat and talked at our table for a good long while, not yet having been approached by a waitress. I was willing to cut a little slack; I could see that the restaurant was quite busy. But after an hour of chatting among ourselves without having heard a word from a waitress, I figured it was time to give somebody a little nudge.

"Miss? Excuse me, miss?" I said to a passing server. She stopped. "Excuse me, but we've been sitting here for over an hour. I've seen customers leaving who got here after we did."

"Yes sir?" she said snidely. "And your question?"

I didn't care for her tone. "Well, my *question*, miss, is what the hell?"

"Didn't see the sign out front, did you?" she said.

I knew what was coming next.

"We don't serve colored people here."

And there it was. Different city, same old tired story. Willie and Carl uttered the slightest sigh of aggravation. Just another helping of the same old crap pie.

There was much I could have said to this lady bigot, and perhaps I should have said at least some of it. But I simply said to the guys, "Okay, fellas. Let's go."

We left and grabbed a bite to eat elsewhere before going on to enjoy Sam and Dave. It was, of course, a fabulous performance, and we enjoyed both the show and the relaxation that came along with it. We spoke with Dave Prater after the show, and the conversation came around to the treatment we'd received at the restaurant. Dave's response was simple.

"It ain't no big thing, Joey," he said. "You gotta expect that down here."

| HEARTLAND BIGOTRY |

In the summer of 1963 we did two gigs in Indiana: one at Lake Freeman and the other at White Lake. Every show was a stand-out, and the sold-out audiences expressed their appreciation for our performance with standing ovations. Before and after the shows, it was a different story. White Lake might have been named White *Only* Lake, because the whole time we were there—except while on stage—Carl, Willie, and Sam were treated like lepers. It was the same deal at Lake Freeman, which we'd hoped would have a different vibe. I mean, the name of the lake was the name of our Rogers. Had to be a good omen. But no. We were wrong. They didn't cut our brothers any more slack than White Lake had. Yes, we're the Land of the Free, but at these gigs, *free* was the last thing Carl or Willie or Sam felt. But they did get to hear lots of racial slurs and experienced the first-ever *social distancing*. So they had that going for them.

Now, the great Louie Armstrong's band was playing the same gigs. They slept in their bus at each hotel where they were appearing. They weren't any more welcome in the hotels than we were. In such a situation, we always managed to find rooms elsewhere—*together*. Sam, Willie, and Carl were pissed off, of course, about the whole discrimination deal in general, but they seemed to be even angrier with Louie for obtusely allowing his guys to face this wrong treatment and wrong thinking without his involvement.

Now, Sammy had put his boots on the ground in Korea. And he didn't just do close-order drills there; he fought bravely for our country. He received a Purple Heart for wounds received in battle, and he survived two tail-spinning helicopter crashes. And yet, here he was, having to swallow back the bile of careless disrespect that couldn't be spat out.

| YOU NEVER SAW THIS ON BANDSTAND |

In 1963 we played a club in Wildwood, New Jersey. The week-long gig was fun, reminiscent of my early Shore gigs at the Parrot Club and he Chatterbox Club in Seaside Heights. I considered Seaside to be my summer home, even though I didn't own a house there.

On Saturday night we were treated to a surprise visit from the amazing Dick Clark and his guests. Having already made two appearances on his television show, *American Bandstand*, I had become friends with Dick. I'll write more about him and his show later. For now suffice it to say I was pleased and honored to have him visit us at the club. I was also glad he was there on a night when the place was bursting at the seams, and we were rocking the stage. The night promised to be memorable.

And memorable it would be—but not in the way I expected.

Willie was dating a white girl who was in attendance that night. The chick was a knockout, but she tended to be a little on the loud side after a few drinks. In fact, scratch *a little on the loud side* and use *louder than hell* instead. She had positioned herself at the middle of the bar in order to keep eye contact with Willie while he was on stage, which stage was directly behind the bar.

Now, on this night it seemed Miss Lady was trying to set a sorority drinking record. That meant she was extra loud and terribly indiscreet about her feelings for Willie. The bartender was an Italian kid from Philly who wasn't keen on the relationship between this white chick and our Willie. I guess he (the barkeep) must have made some snide remark to her about it, which opinion Willies girl didn't appreciate. And she told him so. Loudly.

Let the name-calling begin. One obscenity led to another, and the bartender finally got around to the ultimate slur.

"You nigger lover!" he said to her, up close and personal and easily matching the volume at which she had screamed names at him. Anyway he yelled it loudly enough to be heard on stage. Without hesitation Willie dived right onto the bartender's back, and they went at it. There was hitting, there was gouging, there was kicking. I think I even saw one or two ankle bites. It wasn't pretty, and it didn't end as quickly as we'd have liked.

I didn't come down from the stage nor did the other band members; Willie could handle himself. As I looked beyond the ruckus, I could see that the audience was understandably restless and nervous. Some were leaving. And the exodus included our surprise guest, Dick Clark. I saw him call the waitress over, pay his check, and exit the club with guests in tow. Being involved in such a fracas could do nothing but give him and his career a black eye, and he was having none of that.

To my memory, Willie won the fight.

Always a class act, Dick called me a week later to apologize for leaving the club. "I just couldn't stay, Joey. I hope you understand."

I did.

| SOUTHERN HOSPITALITY |

In 1962 my agents Jolly Joyce and Don Davis approached me. They'd been contacted by an agent in Atlanta who wanted to book us on a tour through the South. That excited me. See, Willie was from Georgia, and Carl was from Florida. This would be an opportunity for their families and friends to see them perform as Starliters.

But there was a hitch.

"Joey," Don said, "the agent wants you to replace Carl and Willie with white Starliters. No change, no tour."

"You're kidding, right?" I said.

"Nope, not kidding," Jolly said. "If you don't, Joey, they don't want you."

"Then we don't go," I said. "Either we all go, or we all *don't* go."

Willie and Carl weighed in on the matter. "It's okay, Joey," Carl said. "We can sit this one out."

"Yeah, Joey," Willie said. "You don't wanna pass on this one. It's a lot of money, man."

"It's absolutely *not* okay," I said. "We all do or we all don't. That's it."

That decision might have been a difficult one for some people. I mean, to anyone playing one-nighters for the door or drinks, nixing a tour that paid fifteen grand per week wasn't the act of a sane person. Such a payday may not sound like a life-changer in this age of dime-a-dozen billionaires, but for musicians in the early sixties, it was nearly unheard of.

We passed. Somehow word got out that we'd stuck together on principle and turned down a very lucrative tour. *Jet* magazine—a now-defunct periodical that catered primarily to Black readers—heard the buzz and ran a piece on it. I guess *Jet* had pretty good circulation in the South—Don got another call from that Atlanta agent. He wanted us badly enough to give on the issue and allow the entire band to make the tour. *Now you're talking, you cracker prick*, I thought to myself.

We got the itinerary, made travel plans, loaded my Cadillac and an oversized van, and headed south. It would be a long drive, and we'd have to take turns driving and sleeping. No problem. We'd manage. As for myself, when I got tired I could always lie on top of the organ in the van and catch some shut-eye. Once again, being small had its advantages.

We drove through Jersey, Delaware, Maryland, and on toward Dixie. As we got further away from home, I began to notice some interesting signs outside service station bathrooms and next to drinking fountains. Signs like *White Only* and *Colored Only*. Willie and Carl were hip to this language and knew how things were, but such segregation was new to the rest of us. The issue became more pointed when we tried to eat at a restaurant.

"Welcome to Johnny's Diner," we were told. "Now, I guess you fellers musta missed the sign out front," the man continued, wearing a patronizing grin, "so I'll explain it to y'all. You white fellers are good to eat here, but you colored boys are just gonna hafta go 'round back."

Here we go again, I said to myself. "If they go around back," I told the manager, "then we all go around back." The man said that was fine with him. See, he didn't want to pass up any money—he knew it was all green.

At the back of the restaurant, we found sacks of flour stacked three or four deep. We ordered our food from the cook and sat on the sacks to wait for it to be prepared. That's where we ate, with the sacks as our tables and chairs. Interestingly, the cook was Black. The hypocrisy was great enough to stop a runaway locomotive: White people were fine with Black people cooking food for them back in the kitchen, but no one of color could go through the front door. But even in the face of such discrimination, Willie would try to throw some light and understanding on the situation. "Don't be too hard on these folks, Joey," he'd say. "They just being Missuh Cholly and Miss Ann, like they was raised to be." *Mr. Cholly* and *Miss Ann* were the in-the-loop nicknames the colored community often used for white people.

This dining scenario wasn't a one-time thing. It was commonplace. And at hotels and motels it was the same story. There was always a *White Only* sign posted out front, so we just went to *Soulville*—my name for the non-white section of town—to find lodging. We stayed at some nice little hotels where everything was spic-and-span. Not only were the accommodations spot-on, but we usually got the royal treatment when the owners found out who we were. I mean, they fawned over Willie and Carl like they were puppies at a pet shop. It made my heart glad to see that. It was about time they got their rightful due.

At last we arrived at the University of Georgia in Athens to do our first show. We played to a packed house and were extremely well received. They loved us—*all* of us—and we took this as a great compliment. See, our kind of music was still blossoming in some regions of the country, and it was, of course, a break-down-the-barriers kind of sound. On top of all that we were a mixed-race band, and here we were in the heart of the Deep South. But aside from that one comment I heard during sound check, made by a young white college boy to his white girlfriend—"I'll be damned if there ain't some niggers up there"—we enjoyed this first gig very much. It kicked off an outstanding tour. The only thing we'd have changed was one demographic of the audience: It was all white. We'd find this to be the case at all ten of the one-night stands on the tour. But, ironically, we even came to feel kind of good about that. See, we understood that we were breaking ground. We were blazing trails. We were creating inroads that would be followed by others as the world of rock & roll—and, indeed, the world itself—became increasingly Black & white.

And it was simply our pleasure.

THREE

GODFATHER OF THE TWIST

The Twist dance of the early 1960s was arguably the most ubiquitous and controversial dance craze ever to command a dance floor, inspire songwriting, and drive movie production while it was in vogue. Volumes have been written about this phenomenon, but the true and complete story of the song, "The Twist," and the popularization of the dance it inspired may surprise you.

| How It Really Started |

Rogers Freeman knew all the good clubs in Newark—especially soul clubs—and visited them frequently, often taking David and me along with him. And so it was that he introduced the two of us to a joint called Ben's Cotton Club. I thought I'd just found another great place where I could enjoy the kind of music I'd always loved; but what I'd discover there would be more than that. It would be a game changer.

Now, Ben's place was excellent. It featured a hot group with a female guitar player/vocalist named Pearl Reaves, along with Lonnie Youngblood on tenor sax and Pearl's husband Paul Farrano on drums. Man, were they good! Pearl had already made recordings with the Concords, including the 1955 record "I'm Not Ashamed (Ugly Woman)" on the Harlem label. A few years later, she and Paul started their own Pearlsfar Records label and performed under the name Pearl Reaves and the Paul Farrano Trio.

At Ben's this night and every other night we visited it, Paul, David, and I were the only white people in the club. I've already mentioned that this wasn't unusual for David or me; we were often the only white guys at many of the clubs we visited. Didn't matter to us.

As a bit of an aside, Pearl had a roving eye, and she liked Bo. Of *course* she liked Bo. *Every* woman that met Bo liked him. He was handsome, smooth, and always smartly dressed. I don't know, but I guess Paul was familiar both with his spouse's wild side and Bo's reputation. I venture this guess, because he seemed to make it his business that night to know every move Pearl made. The man watched her like he was a cop on stakeout and jumped into action the moment he saw the slightest irregularity.

Ben's had a nice little jukebox, which we listened to during the band's breaks. I was always interested in checking out those machines to see what was playing around. If something played regularly on the jukebox, it was worth paying attention to. Ben's machine always had great R&B race records—my favorite kind of music. On this particular night in 1959, I heard an R&B song about a dance. The record was new to me, but I was drawn to it. I loved the beat, the feel, the sound—and I was intrigued by the dance everyone on the floor was suddenly doing. I hurried to the jukebox to find the name of the artist. It was Hank Ballard and the Midnighters. The song was "The Twist." From that moment my life was forever changed.

Mr. Hank Ballard wasn't new to me. He'd been around for years, breaking into showbiz at age sixteen when he took over a group called the Royals. I knew Hank's early recordings "Work with Me, Annie," "Sexy Ways," and "Annie Had a Baby." His songs were generally classified as "dirty music," which meant more or less that they were too hip to be played by white radio stations. That didn't matter to me; I could always listen to Hank and other great R&B artists on my favorite radio station, WNJR. Great stuff. But this *Twist* song, now. *This* was something special to me. And the people at Ben's Cotton Club that night were doing the first version of the Twist I ever saw.

I made a quick, irrevocable decision: This song would be in our repertoire. To make that happen, next day I went to a Paterson record store that sold soul records exclusively. I inquired after the record. They had it. I bought it. We learned it. Rogers sang lead, and in no time at all we had it down pat. I knew this new tune would be a great addition to our set list, and I was right; it quickly became the most popular part of our show. But I had no way of knowing that it would become my ticket to far greater success.

And Rogers did manage to pull Pearl that night at Ben's. Don't know how, but he did.

| Nation's Sensation |

Hank's recording of his own song did all right, peaking at number twenty-eight on the US pop charts and at number six on the US R&B charts. But to Dick Clark's ear this song had greater chart potential than that, and he aimed to help it achieve that potential. He believed that, re-recorded, "The Twist" would hit higher on the charts than Hank's version had done. With that goal in mind, he asked Ernest Evans—later dubbed "Chubby Checker" as a nod to "Fats Domino"—to record [read: *clone*] Hank's song and made the production arrangements himself. Now, when I call Chubby's cover of Hank's "The Twist" a *clone*, consider this as evidence: Hank once said to me, "Joey, the first time I heard Chubby's record, I thought it was me." He was justified in thinking that. The two versions are very similar indeed.

And so, with the weight of Dick Clark behind him, Chubby recorded a "cover" of Hank's song and proved Mr. Clark right: The song reached number one on the US Billboard Hot 100, remaining there for a week, and number two on the US Billboard R&B Singles.

I don't know why Dick accorded Chubby the honor of covering "The Twist." Perhaps it was because Chubby did indeed sound a good deal like Hank. Perhaps it was more complex than that. At least one writer, James Wolcott, in his article, "The Sixties—A Twist in Time," published in the November 2007 issue of *Vanity Fair* magazine, opined that Chubby was the perfect choice to revive and popularize the song and the dance:

"With his beaming smile, booming optimism, and teddy-bear huggability, Chubby . . . was the perfect racial-crossover ambassador, making the [Twist] acceptable for Dick Clark's . . . wholesome white teenagers out there . . ."

Whatever the reason for Dick's judgment, Chubby's record hit number one in September, 1960. The record was good, but it wasn't superior to Hank's original version. Better promoted, yes. But not better. And, of course, Chubby was instrumental in introducing the Twist dance to the nation's teenagers. But he and the teenagers would ride that horse only so far. And when the critter was staggering on the roadside, they climbed off it and left it to die, moving on to some fresh, new horse.

| Godfather of the Twist |

Fortunate for the dance, someone else had been covering Hank Ballard's "The Twist" for some time, even before Chubby recorded it. That would be Joey Dee and the Starliters. We had added the song and the dance to our stage performances before it was a number-one hit for Chubby. And when he (Chubby) and Dick Clark's teenagers were done with it, we weren't. We knew this horse, properly cared for, had untold miles left in its legs.

Joey Dee and the Peppermint Lounge to the rescue, bringing along with them some of the most unlikely Twist fans imaginable.

Mr. Wolcott again:

"The Twist would have died the natural death of other passing sensations if it hadn't been adopted by fairy godparents. It was when the saltshakers of the Beautiful People began to wiggle that the Twist acquired cachet and splashed into the news, becoming a cosmopolitan rage. 'In a curious anomaly, a small wreck of a bar in midtown Manhattan with an occupancy limit of 178 achieved what Clark's nationwide TV show had failed to do: make the dance into a worldwide fad,' Bill Brewster and Frank Broughton write in Last Night a DJ Saved My Life: The History of the Disc Jockey."

I'll write more about this shortly, but on a rainy night in 1961, a little group of socialites, entertainers, and columnists ducked into the Peppermint Lounge to escape the rain. There they heard Joey Dee and the Starliters riling up the house with Hank Ballard's "The Twist," and the *real* Twist craze started. Hank had written the tune and begun the dance but hadn't pursued it. Chubby had taken it for a lap around the track but was already on his way to the locker room. Joey Dee and the Starliters took it to the Beautiful People who had discovered something worth "wiggling their saltshakers" about. I could never have guessed it would be the middle-aged, fur-clad, tuxedo-wearing, stick-up-the-ass celebs and Beautiful People du jour who, sharing a tiny dance floor with the great unwashed, would help me take the baton and turn a sprint into a marathon.

Now, most columnists and reporters took a positive view of this phenomenon, but a few saw it differently. Consider the opinion of Fred and Grace Hechinger, he the education editor for *The New York Times*: "Those who are determined to find silver linings in every cloud of questionable taste, interpret Noel Coward and foreign nobility rubbing elbows or knees with duck-tailed teenagers as a sign of disappearing social barriers and class differences [but] whatever the deep psychological reasons, the example of the Twist and its history points to a new trend of society: Instead of youth growing up, adults are sliding down."

And hear this from then-President Dwight D. Eisenhower:

"I have no objection to the Twist as such, but it does represent some kind of change in our standards. What has happened to our concepts of beauty and decency and morality?"

Geez, people. It's just a frickin' dance. Enjoy it.

And what of the uppities who didn't stand in line to spank the planks at the Pep? Well, they considered the Twist an uncivilized affront to their pearl-strung necks and their manicured, bejeweled fingers, and to their hand-carved, Latakia-stuffed Meerschaums. I mean, if they had to sit all day on a straight-backed, generations-old chair, balancing a dainty teacup and a bite-sized nosh on their knees, then why should anyone else be Twistin' their rebellious asses to a raucous beat? But these sourpusses gained no traction with those who were shaking their cabooses on the dance floor. America had been promised by President John F. Kennedy that he would uncover its young energy and "get this country moving again." The band and I were doing our part to help him do just that. We would spur the Pep and its clientele toward a younger, energetic tomorrow. In an incredibly ironic *twist*, oldsters were following the lead of youngsters, much to the chagrin, I suppose, of President Eisenhower and Mr. and Mrs. Hechinger.

| THE DANCE |

The Twist was unique, but it wasn't complicated or difficult to learn. Although the now-legendary dance instructor Arthur Murray offered a six-lesson course in the dance, Twisters didn't need arrows drawn on the floor to tell them where that errant right foot should be just now. And even if you couldn't do the dance *well*, no one cared. The point of it was to have fun. You know, like golf. Except for the guys on TV every Sunday, *no one* plays golf well. But still it's enjoyable.

Yes, the Twist was the Every Man's Dance. This simple little step allowed more flexibility and range in agility than any other dance ever. Everyone on the dance floor had body parts that moved to one degree or another, or they wouldn't have been on the dance floor. And to Twist, it was necessary to move only one or two of them. However, if you were thus blessed, it wasn't illegal to move every single hinge and joint on your entire wherewithal. Yes, you could be like Marilyn Monroe who reported that she didn't do the Twist. She did the *Twister*. "I add a little something to it," she said. Did she ever.

Now, according to one-time Black Panther leader Eldridge Cleaver, white folks might have to work a little harder than Black folks at being a good Twister. This from Mr. Cleaver's memoir, *Soul on Ice*:

". . . the Twist [was] good news, to teach the whites . . . how to shake their asses again. It is a skill they surely must once have possessed but which they abandoned for puritanical dreams of escaping the corruption of the flesh, by leaving the terrors of the body to the blacks."

He may be right—in one respect. It's clear that, when it comes to shaking, not all asses are created equal. But the Twist didn't follow racial or any other lines. Black folks handled it fine. White folks handled it fine. Youngsters handled it fine. Oldsters handled it fine. Simply put, no one couldn't do the Twist. This is what people discovered about it. This is what people loved about it.

Learning the Twist was as easy as a youngster learning to use a Hula Hoop. In 1958 this toy hit the market and started a craze that lasted for several months. It's made a resurgence today as a physical conditioning aid. But in 1958 it was a child's toy; and if you threw one of those hoops over the head of a nine-year-old, the thing would hit the ground only once, maybe twice, before it was orbiting that kid's midriff effortlessly. And it wouldn't hit the ground again till the dinner bell sounded. No lessons. No instructions. Easy peasy lemon squeezy. Like the Twist.

The Twist also changed the traditional dance format—you know, where the guy and the gal faced each other, gripped hands and backs, and glided across the floor, synchronized. Even the bop or the jive—not just a stodgy old waltz—required partners to be connected at the hands somehow. But not the Twist. No touching, no synchronized gliding, no facing each other required. As a matter of fact, you didn't even need a partner. Dance with one, dance with everyone, dance with no one. It's your thing, as the Isley Brothers sang. Do what you wanna do.

For all those offended by society's alleged partiality to the male, the Twist leveled the dance floor, to paraphrase an idiom. In this dance no one led. The man wasn't in charge here. Partners were equally empowered to choose tempo, direction, footwork, embellishments—and neither had to wait for the other to make the same choice. A partner could invade the other's personal space or create distance—a little or a lot. Such flexibility this dance had!

The Twist cared nothing for social status, wealth, unemployment, job description, age, gender, or dress. Had you seen the Pep dance floor in those days, you'd know this is true. All social strata, all "castes," were represented on that little floor, and dancing was as much fun for Jackie Kennedy and Truman Capote as it was for my Hell's Kitchen roughneck crew. And this wasn't true only at the Pep. There was Twistin' at teen-age dance parties at the neighborhood pavilion, shindigs around a fire pit at the beach, and eight-year-old birthday party dances in the backyard. No one couldn't do the Twist, and no one didn't enjoy doing it—except, perhaps, a few of the stiff-upper-lip types that couldn't enjoy anything that didn't require a silver spoon or the "right" pedigree confirmed by royal historians. Everybody else under the sun had fun Twistin'. Everybody.

And consider how swiftly the Twist made its way into clubs and dance parties from coast to coast, crashed television and recording studios, and jumped the pond to international clubs. It moved as though it were alive and breathing and aiming at domination—and it accomplished all that without the help of social media or texting or email. Word of mouth and the publicity generated primarily by Joey Dee and the Starliters at the Pep made the dance an international sensation faster than any fad or craze. Ever.

Nor has it been completely abandoned. Even now, sixty-ish years later, the Twist can be seen in contemporary dance, grade school programs, high school assemblies, ice rink and other athletic competitions, and modern and period-piece movies. It lurks patiently just beneath the surface, eagerly anticipating the moment when society realizes its value in today's world.

The South may never rise again, but I bet the Twist does.

FOUR

PEPPERMINT LOUNGE: HOT SPOT OF THE UNIVERSE

O pened in 1958, the Peppermint Lounge was located in Manhattan at 128 West 45th Street. With a connecting doorway to the adjacent Knickerbocker Hotel, the lounge had been previously called the Gangplank, but its name was changed after it was bought out—or whatever—by the Mob to be used as a safe place to conduct business. The club in its early days has been described over the years with too many crummy adjectives to list, but the word *seedy* occurs just about as often as any. Having been a part of the Pep nearly from its beginning and certainly in its heyday, there's little about the club I don't know. With due humility I say Joey Dee and the Starliters put the Peppermint Lounge on the map as the international epicenter of the Twist craze and launched the little out-of-the-way bar from *seedy* into the realms of New York legend. I saw it all. I experienced it all. And if what I write here isn't everything there is to know about the Pep, everything I write is true as I remember it.

| Discovered |

In 1960 the home base for Joey Dee and the Starliters was a place on Route 46 in Lodi, New Jersey. Olivieri's Night Club it was called, and we played there three, four, maybe five nights a week. The band comprised the vocal talents of Rogers and David, Carl on keyboards, Don Martin on drums, and myself on sax.

We hadn't yet filled out our sound, but we were good. We were damn good. And the crowds at Olivieri's grew as word of mouth spread. Jeanie Olivieri, the owner, thought we were something special. And why not? When we played there the joint was packed, and the cash register was ringing: the two things that make a club owner happiest. On the other hand, had the joint been empty and the register silent, we'd have been kicking dirt clods down the road, looking for a place to play. Money didn't just *talk* to club owners; it *shouted*. And they paid very close attention to what it had to say.

We not only *sounded* good; we *looked* good. And we had our own style: white shirts, thin black ties, and form-fitting single-breasted, three-button suits with thin lapels and pant legs altered to rest two inches above the shoes. The "high-water" pants allowed the audience to see our footwork. Hollywood and Madison Avenue would soon take note of this style, and a trend would follow.

I took my dress so seriously, in fact, that, in April 1962, I would be listed among the ten best dressed men in America, by the Fashion Designers of America. Others who shared the honors in that vote were Joe DiMaggio, Henry Cabot Lodge, Senator Barry Goldwater, Troy Donahue, Shelly Berman, Colonel John H. Glenn, Robert Sarnoff, Frank Onorati, and William Gaxton. President John F. Kennedy and Dick Clark had been among previous recipients of the award. Pretty good company, if I do say so myself—and a great honor for a man who always prided himself on his attire. The band busted my balls about making the list, but I gave it right back to them. "Just work real hard," I told them. "Maybe you'll make it too." We laughed it off, but I was proud.

Olivieri's hosted a going-away party one night for Sal Bonura, who was to report to Fort Dix next day for basic training. Sal hired us to play the party, and the two of us hit it off immediately and big. This was the beginning of a lifelong friendship. Upon his return from the military a couple of years later, Sally would own a place called the Choo Choo Club next to the railroad tracks in Garfield, and it would become the hottest club in Jersey.

On another night a man approached me as we were preparing to set up.

"Mr. Dee?" he said, extending his hand.

"Yes sir. I'm Joey Dee."

As I shook the man's hand, I espied in one ear an earpiece, from which extended a wire leading to a pocket of his coat jacket. I rightly supposed that the pocket contained the power unit of the hearing aid. I didn't know it then, but this was information about Mr. Davis of which the mischievous Starliters and I would later make good use—and *funny*, at least to us.

See, for the next several years we'd take every opportunity to convince Don that his hearing aid was broken. When we'd speak to him, we'd sometimes abruptly stop vocalizing mid-sentence but continue moving our lips. Thinking his hearing aid had gone on the fritz, he'd take the unit from his pocket, shake it around, smack it against his hand or a table, wiggle the wire . . . and then we'd start vocalizing again. He'd return the unit to his pocket, satisfied that he'd fixed the problem. Other times we'd speak increasingly more softly, till we were barely audible. Again, he'd take out the unit and give it a beating till we'd bring our voices back to normal level. It's impossible to say how many hearing aids he bought or repaired because of us.

But all that fun was for tomorrow. At present, Mr. Davis and I were just getting to know each other.

"Quite a crowd brewing here tonight," he said. He'd been attracted by the great number of cars in the parking lot. "Is this how it usually is?"

"Usually. Yeah, usually," I said. "I mean, it's up and down, you know, but usually there's a real good crowd."

Nodding and looking around, the man handed me a business card. *Don Davis, Agent, New York City*, it read. "I'm Don," he said. "I'd like to stick around and hear you boys play."

"That's cool," I said. "But if you'll excuse me, I gotta get set up." I probably should have said more, but I was a bit taken aback by this man's presence there.

Mr. Davis took a seat not too near the stage, and I left to get ready to go on. I managed to find a minute to tell the guys we were being checked out by an agent from the City, and that we should do our very best to not suck.

And we didn't suck. We played a helluva set. At the break the man approached me once again. He looked pleased.

"I understand now why you draw the crowds," he said. "You're good."

"Thanks a lot," I said. "We had fun."

"I could see that," he said. "Now, a small matter of business, if you don't mind. I've got a band at the Peppermint Lounge, a little club in the City. The band needs a break. Wonder if you'd like to play there. Give the boys some time off."

A gig in the City. Yeah. Yeah, I think we'd like that. *But don't jump too fast*, I thought to myself.

"Sounds fine," I said timidly. "Have you got the dates?"

"Sure do," he said. "October 17, 20, 21, and 23. Gig pays a hundred a night, but you'll have to pay a small commission out of that."

I wanted this badly, but I thought I shouldn't appear too eager. Be cool. Be calm. Be adult. Be business. *All* business. And, for heaven's sake, *don't blurt!*

"Where do I sign?"

Damn. I blurted. Maybe the *business-all-business* calmness would come later. Next stop, the Peppermint Lounge and rock & roll history.

| Becoming the House Band |

The first time I saw the Peppermint Lounge was in the afternoon of October 14, 1960. I took a bus into the City from Hackensack, New Jersey, to meet Don Davis—now our manager—and an agent named Jolly Joyce whom Don had selected to work with us. Inside the club I was introduced to Joyce and to Ralph Saggese, a well-dressed man who seemed ambivalent about me and this meeting. Ralph was the club's owner of record—I suppose because, as a retired cop, he was able to get the liquor license without hitch or hassle. Soon I'd meet Sam "Kon" Konwiser and Louie Lombardi, the Mob-connected managers of the club—not that I knew of their connections when first we met. Don, Jolly, and I made our way through the sleazy joint that reeked of alcohol, stale tobacco, and something awful that I couldn't identify. As we sat at a table, I noticed the stage was the size of a postage stamp, and the dance floor wasn't much larger. Taking in the whole of the venue, I found myself questioning my decision to take this gig. But it was no time for second-guessing; the odds of an up-and-coming band being noticed a second time were just too long. Opportunity knocks once. You either open the door, or it walks away.

In order to sign a contract and work as a musician, one had to be a member of the American Federation of Musicians. I was a member of the Paterson Local 248 in Jersey, but that did me no good here. The Peppermint Lounge being within the jurisdiction of NYC Local 802, we had to pay a fee for working in that Local's territory. To tell the truth this whole racket was simply another scam to squeeze money from the little guy and line the pockets of the big guy.

The contract offered was for four nights, as Don had said. We would play nine-thirty p.m. to three a.m., with six 40-minute sets per night. This would be work with a capital W, not much easier than heavy construction. But it would prepare me for what was to come. Ralph signed. I signed. I got back on the bus, returned home, and called the guys. They were ecstatic. I told them we'd need to practice for the next three days, and practice hard. We simply couldn't fail; I wouldn't allow it. David, Bo, Carl, Don, and I didn't know it yet, but this was our chance of a lifetime.

And the pay? It may not sound like a lot of money today, but to us it was amazing. Four days, four hundred dollars—minus forty for Don, forty for Jolly, and eight for Local 802. Three hundred twelve bucks split by five for four nights' work. Pretty good money for 1960. And so began the high life I'd be living for the next few years.

On October 17 we wowed them. Well, when I say *them*, I mean the waitresses and bartenders. No one else was there, to speak of. But it was a good sign that the help loved us. I mean, they got to see lots of entertainers and had learned to spot talent when they saw it. Still, we went home after our shows not knowing whether the boss liked us or not. At two p.m. the mystery was solved. I got a call telling me that I should return to the City right away; Ralph wanted to sign us for six weeks, at six hundred per. Same hours. I was so happy, I couldn't speak—so I grabbed my wife Joanie and little Joey, and we all danced around our tiny apartment. "It" had happened. I could feel it.

I got back on the bus and returned to the Pep. When I entered the club this time, the smell wasn't as bad as I remembered. And I'm sure it was my imagination, but the stage seemed to have grown. The second contract had been drawn up ahead of my arrival, and I signed it. I called the guys and explained what had happened. They were ready, willing, and able.

And just like that, Joey Dee and the Starliters had become the house band for the Peppermint Lounge, the permanent replacement for Jimmy Vee and the Scamps. I guess that taught the Scamps not to ask for time off from a gig. We were in, they were out. That's showbiz. I got to meet Jimmy about two weeks into the gig. I told him I was sorry about the way things had worked out for him. He took it like a gentleman and complimented the group and me. Good guy, Jimmy.

| Cooking in Hell's Kitchen |

At the beginning of our gig, the Peppermint Lounge was a hellhole in the middle of Hell's Kitchen; but strange as it may seem, I loved its vibe. Our audience, when we had one, consisted mostly of longshoremen, hookers, and sailors—but they were perfect for us. These were real people who let you know the score before the game was played. A guy named Frank was the head of the dockworkers. He came in almost every night with six or eight others. On some nights this crew was our entire audience. Frank and his guys thought we were special, and we returned the respect. I often sat with them during breaks, and Frank appreciated that. These guys were tough and belonged to the Irish crew in Hell's Kitchen. The Pep's bouncers, Tommy "One Punch" Carcone and Tony Bello—each tougher than the Apollo Theater audience on amateur night—never mixed it up with the Hell's Kitchen crew. This was their turf; Tony and Tommy knew that.

In these early days I'd walk in the front door, no big deal. Nobody was in the club. Later, at the peak of the Pep's popularity, I'd have to sneak in through the back door just to have enough privacy to assemble my sax before going on stage.

Among the colorful customers that frequented the club in the beginning was a hooker named Terry. She was a well-liked broad there; no one judged what she did to make a living. One of Terry's legs was shorter than the other and she lilted a bit to starboard, but the sailors that came in and plunked down five or ten bucks for a ride couldn't have cared less about the leg. They didn't need her leg, and what they did need, she had.

One day Terry was sitting at the bar while we were on stage rehearsing. I don't know what she said or did to the drunken sailor sitting next to her, but something certainly upset him. I watched in surprise as he punched Terry hard in the face. She went down like a sack of doorknobs. A bad day for Terry, to be sure—but soon to be a worse one for the drunken sailor.

The Navy Shore Patrol (SP) cruised 45th regularly and frequently. The club's bouncers had no jurisdiction with military personnel who came in, so when sailors were involved in an altercation, the SP was called. In order to respond quickly, SPs had to be only a short distance from the club at any given time. And so it was on this occasion that Red, a regular SP, was called to the scene and arrived moments after Terry hit the deck. Red sized up the situation, clubbed the hell out of the guilty sailor, dragged him by the heels out of the club, and threw him unceremoniously into the paddy wagon—a van, actually—to be hauled off to the brig at the Brooklyn Naval base. Before leaving, Red came back into the club to make sure Terry was all right. He found her upright, sitting at the bar. She'd shaken it off, and the place was already returning to normal. Terry thanked Red, and he left. Within five minutes it was as if nothing had happened.

There were many fights in our early days at the Pep. I mean, you're in Hell's Kitchen among hookers and sailors and roughnecks—many of them drunk—so trouble and fisticuffs were bound to happen. Some nights it was hard to keep the tables right-side up. But the bouncers always kept it off stage. As soon as fists started flying, I grabbed the mike and called an "86" (*throw the bum out*) for Tommy. I had a great vantage point from the stage, enabling me to sometimes see trouble before it got out of hand. Sometimes I could point out the instigator to Tommy as he ran into the fray. But even when I couldn't, my man had no problem taking care of the situation. He'd simply take his best guess at who was responsible and, without warning, threat or fanfare, knock the sucker out with a single, bone-crunching blow. Ergo, "One Punch" Tommy. Of course, as soon as the guy hit the floor like a rag doll, everyone else involved in the skirmish ran for it. Case closed.

Louie and Sam got nervous as hell and ran around like a chicken with its head cut off whenever trouble brewed, but the band and I never did. At the start of any ruckus, I just called the "86" and then made the band play louder.

| Nearby Competition |

Just around the corner from the Pep was a club called the Wagon Wheel. The hippest night club in Hell's Kitchen, the Wheel was owned by Saul Cohen and his wife Shirley—who, by the way, was one tough broad. No one ever got the upper hand on Shirley. There was always a never-ending line out the door of the club, but Saul and Shirley very kindly gave the band and me carte blanche. We came and went as we pleased. I remember looking at that line of eager customers waiting to get in, and thinking to myself, *One day we'll have this crowd, and Saul and Shirley will get our overflow.*

The Wagon Wheel featured the best bands in town, and that was fine with me. I wasn't at all threatened by competition; I relied on it to make myself better. My favorite group at the Wheel was Clarence "Bad Boy" Palmer and the Jive Bombers, who had the hit record, "I'm Just a Bad Boy." Among the many things I learned from watching Clarence and the other great groups at the Wagon Wheel was that we were better. No matter who fronted any of these groups, they couldn't match our very own Rogers Freeman and David Brigati. Saul seemed to know this as well: "Joey, you're gonna make it big," he told me. A great compliment, coming from Saul Cohen. And he was right.

| My Friends, the Bouncers |

In the beginning the Pep had only Tony and Tommy to keep the peace, but other bouncers were hired as audiences grew larger and the workload for each bouncer became greater. Big Tiny, Gino and Bobby Iannozzi, and Joe Danna came on board. I got close to every single one of these men. I was little, you see, and they were big. I may have been small, but I was no fool; I knew little guys needed big guys to watch over them. And I had a special guardian angel, as Tommy was not only a bouncer but also my personal bodyguard. With such special attention I was safe as a babe in its mother's arms. Never once in all the time I worked the Pep did anyone get to me on stage—or off.

I met Bobby and Gino Iannozzi in 1961. Hailing from Brooklyn, each was over six feet tall and tough as nails. I hit it off with both of them right away, even though they were as different from each other as night from day. Bobby was calm as a lake at dawn. He kept a low profile on the job and never made mountains out of the many molehills that arose. Gino was different. He'd drink too much with the customers, and before you could say *Jekyll and Hyde*, he'd be drunk. Now, drink can make some people happy and horny—I admit it—but it affects others in different ways. Gino was affected in one of the *different* ways: He was a nasty drunk. In fact, if you google *nasty drunk*, Gino's name will pop up first on the search results list. When he was drunk, Gino would go out of his way to find trouble and pick a fight with anybody, including his brother. Sometimes he'd finagle his way into a drink with a customer and end up swinging at the guy. Other times he'd just start swinging randomly at anyone within arm's reach, causing way more trouble for the club than any of the customers. I'm sure you can guess what Louie and Sam thought of Gino's behavior. Yep, Louie fired him. Every time. But then Gino would go home, sober up, become a person again, and talk his way back onto the team. I guess Louie must have figured Gino's upside was greater than his downside. And it was true: When he was doing his job right, Gino did his job right. And he was absolutely the one you wanted to have at your back when the dam broke.

Now smile at this: Gino had a girlfriend whose body leaned a bit to the right when she walked. Not her whole body—just the top half. Weird. We all called her "Ten After Six." Think about it.

Ironically, the calmer Bobby suffered a violent death some years later when he was shot by his employer. Gino, the instigator, is still around, I think. I loved both of these guys and had some great times with them.

Another of the bouncers with whom I became close was Joe Danna. Joe was much like Bobby in temperament, but he had an additional gift. Joe was a little guy who disliked violence. Odd traits for a bouncer, I grant you, but Joe made it all work for him. Instead of breaking heads—which he could do if necessary—Joe practiced the art of diplomacy. And he practiced it better than anyone I ever saw. Without a threat or a fist he could calm the drunkest, the most belligerent, the most violent guys in the joint and deflate a situation that might otherwise have led to broken furniture and broken bones. His was a gift and a talent, plain and simple—and it was an honor just to watch him practice his art.

| BECOMING THE PEP |

I was always a house man—anything for the crowd, that was my philosophy. In the early days we played for two hours straight when we had a crowd. When it was slow, we took longer breaks. Louie and Sam left the decision to me. During the week we typically had forty to sixty people; on the weekend, we played to a hundred or more.

We started playing six nights a week. We did great shows and began to develop a following. Word of mouth quickly drew fans from all over. Because the drinking age in New York was eighteen, many kids drove from surrounding states, where the drinking age was twenty-one, to enjoy our show and a few legal drinks. My soon-to-be-friend Maynard Strickland and a few guys and gals would drive down from Connecticut. Before coming to the Pep, they'd hit a bar called the Blarney Stone—a chain franchise on the West Side—for some sixty-cent shots of Three Feathers, Four Roses, and any other rotgut the joint served. The Blarney Stone also featured a free lunch. Yep, there WAS such a thing as a free lunch. As long as you were drinking, the food was free. I often took advantage of the deal.

After getting their lights turned on at the Blarney Stone, Maynard and associates made their way to the Pep. Protecting themselves by staking the bouncers to some pretty nice tips, the bunch wouldn't buy a single drink while they were there. They simply swiped beers from tables while the guests were dancing. They never got caught, and that was a very good thing for them. They'd have had hell to pay. See, Louie knew liquor was the Pep's cash cow, and he did all he could to milk her dry. "Keep 'em dancing, Joey," Louie reminded me from time to time. "Just keep 'em dancing. The more they dance, the more they drink."

The Pep was located in the heart of the theater district in New York, so we were surrounded by parking garages that people had to walk to and from when they attended a show. One dark and rainy night—honest, it really was—in late September 1961, a group left a Broadway theater and stepped into the Peppermint Lounge to take shelter from the rain. It was about ten p.m. when they ducked in. The boys and I were kicking it on stage, and the joint was jumping. The visitors saw youngsters dancing to my music in a way they'd never seen people dance, and they were intrigued. They'd soon learn that what they were seeing on the dance floor was the Twist. They were enthralled by this interesting new whatever-it-was, and they took a table, just to watch it. Among the group of visitors were Merle Oberon, a well-known Hollywood actress; Prince Serge Obolenski, a Russian-American aristocrat, socialite, and publicist; and gossip columnist Cholly Knickerbocker. Now, "Cholly Knickerbocker" was a pseudonym used by several gossip columnists of the day, including this man whose real name was Count Igor Cassini Loiewski, brother of fashion designer Oleg Cassini. After passively enjoying a few numbers, some of the more adventuresome of the group ventured onto the dance floor, joining the kids and roughnecks and imitating them as well as they could. And *there* was a sight. Café society and teenagers and roughnecks, all Twistin' side by side. East Side meets West Side. Whoda thunk it?

Next day Cholly K wrote about that little foray into Hell's Kitchen, doing his best to describe the Twist, this novel dance that was so interesting to watch and so fun to do. Soon more "swells" came in, some in gowns and tails, and danced next to youngsters and longshoremen. Ironically—it was almost eerie—they all got along. Other columnists, such as the late, great Earl Wilson, took up the banner for the Peppermint Lounge and the Twist. And just like that, barricades were being erected outside the club to control the crowds, and beacon lights were splashing the night sky, showing the way to the action. Police officers were busy trying to manage the total gridlock created by cars and lines of eager people streaming into and from the club, hoping to head off any trouble that might threaten.

Fire regulations rated the club for a capacity 178 guests, but the demand became so great so quickly that up to four hundred at a time were being shoehorned in. This was way too many people for our little Peppermint Lounge. I mean, if you tried to scratch your ass, there was a very good chance you'd get slapped by the owner of the ass you actually scratched. Yep, fire code violations all over the place, but no one seemed to mind. Lines of people outside our doors stretched for blocks. One of the policemen who helped oversee containment was Pauly, a friend of mine. "We were trying to harness what had become an organized stampede at the Pep," Officer Pauly wrote. "We had to recruit two hundred additional officers from Queens, Brooklyn, Staten Island, and the Bronx to keep the crowds at the 'Mecca of the Twist' organized and polite. Many of us were stationed on the block," Pauly continued, " because every night was like New Year's Eve on Times Square by half. We even deployed mounted policemen to keep order."

Of course, the goal was to admit as many live bodies as possible. After all, we were talking about big money—well, not so much at first, because initially there was no cover charge and no minimum drink requirement. But this was quickly replaced by a hefty cover charge and a two-drink minimum that was aggressively enforced. And then the bucks rolled. But there was an issue perhaps even more critical than money: Included among the herds waiting in line were high-profile people of wealth and influence. It was difficult to turn away royalty and Hollywood celebrities. We did it, when we had no other option; but it wasn't easy to do. Of course, hard cold cash had a great deal to do with who made the final cut for admittance. Fins, sawbucks, and double sawskis greased the palms of cops, doormen (more on that in a moment), maître d's, bouncers. In a blink every night at the Peppermint Lounge became a Saturday night.

This new popularity created an interesting, even sad, phenomenon. When the rush first hit, the Pep audience was a nice mix of famous, unknown, young, old, sophisticated, rough. But when fame and money became the criteria for admittance, the kids and the unknowns and the roughs got pushed to the side. These had been my real audience—the faithful fans to whom I'd catered, and the ones who had made the Peppermint Lounge what it was. I was as happy as anyone for this popularity, this success; but the irony wasn't lost on me.

Perhaps you're wondering about other clubs in the neighborhood and how they fared as the Pep took front and center. Sadly, one of the collateral effects of our success was the failure of others. The night club scene in New York City changed. And it changed quickly. Places like Toots Shor's, El Morocco, and the Stork Club, which only yesterday had been overflowing with paying customers, became ghost towns. I guess the only thing in life that can be reliably counted on is change. These once-famous watering holes and others like them had to deal with the abrupt change—some for a while, others forever. It comes, it goes.

And so the legend had begun: The Peppermint Lounge became the Pep. I think it would be accurate to say that no social phenomenon ever burst onto the New York scene more explosively than the combination of Joey Dee and the Starliters' Twist and the Peppermint Lounge. We could be seen nightly on TV news programs as reporters and cameras spotlighted the celebrities and Beautiful People du jour. To me it all was like a grand dream. I hoped no one pinched me, because I simply didn't want to wake up. This was what I'd been waiting for. This was my ticket to stardom.

We'd taken New York by storm, and soon we'd have the world by the tail.

| Doorman |

After waiting in a seemingly endless line for who knows how long, a guest had to clear perhaps the most important hurdle of all to enter the hallows of the Pep: the doorman. When—if—you survived the brutal line and made it to the doorman's stanchion and velvet ropes, you had to be prepared to fork over a pretty hefty fee. Tip. Bribe. Call it what you will. And this was in addition to whatever you'd already shelled out to cops or others to get this far. The usual minimum for the doorman was twenty bucks, but if you paid more you might be remembered next time you showed up. And that would be good. It would also help you to remain inside for more than one set. See, after each set the bouncers would let the big tippers and the famous remain, but everyone else got bounced to let in fresh cash and unslaked thirsts.

Now, the doorman was nearly as entertaining as the show inside. His antics were so much fun, in fact, that I often went to the front on breaks to watch him work. Each doorman had his own way of dealing with people, and each put on his own kind of show. Take Tony Bello for example. When my man Tony was on the rope, I figured to see an Academy Award performance. I was never disappointed.

Tony Bello hated everyone. No one escaped his thinly veiled hostility. But he wasn't an uppity or a bigoted or a prejudiced man. Not at all. He'd take money from any customer who offered it, no matter the amount and regardless of his personal feelings toward that customer. But if the tip were insultingly short or if the customer annoyed him, Tony would express that annoyance. Subtly perhaps, but he'd express it. As the offending soul cleared his rope and passed in front of him, Tony launched a gigantic glob of spit to his or her back. He especially enjoyed doing this to a couple dressed to the nines in tux, fur, and finery. Tony was hilariously insidious in the doing of this vile deed, and he never got found out. He often added bonus insult to the ladies, with a warm smile and a *have a nice evening, Contessa*, heavily emphasizing the first syllable of that title. As I watched Tony hock a massive loogie onto someone's back, I'd chuckle to myself, imagining the poor schlub who'd discover the goop. I wondered whether the finder bothered to report the disgusting mess to the victim or just turned and barfed. It's a story ending I'll never know.

Sometimes, if a lady appeared to be . . . well, *worldly*, let's say, Tony would give me a heads-up by a gesture, moving his right fist back and forth between his left hand and his mouth, suggesting that this lady might like a certain kind of intimacy. He smiled as he did it, and I laughed and let the guys know.

| Pinkus |

Perhaps you can imagine the vehicle situation outside the club. The drop-offs and pick-ups were incessant, horns chirped and blared everywhere, and vehicles—if they could move at all—crawled bumper-to-bumper, backed up to who-knows-where. Cabs and limousines delivered local fares as well as out-of-towners who'd flown in just to catch the action at the Pep. These people came to be known as "jet-setters," a term that found its way into the social lexicon, thanks to the Pep. And, of course, cabs and limos weren't the only vehicles to be greeted; regular, everyday cars needed someone to open the doors, greet the guests, collect a tip, and then find a place to park the automobile.

That's where Pinkus came in.

Pinkus had no official connection to the Pep. He hadn't been hired, so he couldn't be fired. I don't know where he came from, what his real name was, or anything else of his genesis. He was the self-proclaimed greeter for cabs, limos, and cars, and he looked the part. His diminutive five-foot frame was dressed head to foot in doorman finery complete with long gray coat, epaulets, fringes, hat, gloves, and shiny, shiny shoes. He looked like he'd escaped from the Waldorf Astoria. I don't know where he got all that stuff, but out there somewhere, I bet, a naked doorman was welcoming surprised visitors to his hotel. In any case Pinkus's work paid off big time for him. I mean, he'd get a tip from pretty much everyone who exited a door he'd opened, and when he didn't get that tip . . . well, you could have hung your wash on the look he gave that poor penny-pinching soul. Now, I've always thought a simple *thank you* should suffice as payment for such a simple act of courtesy, but for Pinkus and others like him, kindness had no value until it was cashed in.

Now, Pinkus made a lot of money greeting guests and opening doors for them, but his spirit of industry and courtesy for hire wasn't limited to opening doors. After passengers exited Pinkus hopped into the car, took off with a lurch and a screech, and chugged along till he found a place somewhere in one of the nearby parking garages. While this may sound like a wonderful guest service, it changes color a bit when you know that Pinkus didn't know how to drive. Watching this Lilliputian get a car to the parking garage was like watching a pinball machine in action, except it was a car and not a steel ball that careened here and ricocheted there. Only heaven knows how many guests discovered dents and scrapes and broken headlights next morning when they got into their cars—courtesy of the one and only Pinkus.

After all the cars were parked—one way or another—Pinkus took his business inside the Pep, where he sold flowers to guests. From the stage I could see him working the room. He'd get up to twenty-five bucks a flower, depending on how drunk his mark was or how desperately a guy needed to impress his lady. On a good night—and in its heyday, *every* night at the Pep was a good night—Pinkus easily pocketed a couple hundred bucks from these sales. And this was pure profit. See, Pinkus had stolen those flowers from nearby cemeteries, taking them literally from the graves of the dear departed, to turn a profit. Little bastid.

And where were the bouncers during all this floral commerce? They did nothing to restrain Pinkus's trade, because they had a piece of the action. Had he tried to sell even one bloom in that house without their bought-and-paid-for say-so, it's a cinch Pinkus would have been kicked through the front door like a Pete Gogolak field goal. To my thinking it would have been a proper comeuppance for the little twerp.

Scruples? No. Ethics? No. Dignity? No. Scumbag? Yes. Pinkus.

| Rockin' the House |

We were a live band . . . well, of course we were alive, but you know what I mean. We were a jump-shout-knock-yourself-out (tip of the cap to Mr. Barry Manilow for that phrase) band that played live and personal rock & roll and gave the audience something to stand up and kick about. Said another way, our forte, our bread and butter, was playing to a live audience. Before we recorded our hits "Peppermint Twist," "Shout," "Hey Let's Twist" and others and added them to the play list, we were a cover band—but the best one anywhere. And make no mistake: When the Starliters and I were on stage, the joint was jumping. The joint was hopping. The joint was Twistin'. All the time.

I loved to interact with the crowd. I often jumped into the audience to do my thing with regular club patrons such as Judy Garland, Shirley MacLaine, Shelley Winters, and others. I'll write more about those and other celeb regulars; for now, suffice it to say I loved being on the floor with these folks.

Truth be told, I liked being on the floor with any guests, celebrated or not. The way I figured, we were all in this thing together, so why not enjoy each other? Of course, being on the floor had its risks, as it made me somewhat vulnerable. I had to deal with the occasional pinch or grab, which pinches and grabs sometimes targeted areas of my anatomy that weren't prepared to be pinched or grabbed at that moment. On the other hand, such gropes might be a lovely young lady's invitation, to which I later responded with vigor.

Of course, I had to be careful about committing myself to such forward women, especially if I didn't know them. If I responded favorably to them, and they were there with Mob guys, I might find myself up the proverbial creek without the proverbial paddle. I relied on the bouncers and bartenders to help me avoid such trouble, and they never let me down. One night an oh-so-fine chick sat at a table where a lot of celebrating was going on. Every time I passed her, she grabbed me right on the . . . well, she grabbed me right where you think she grabbed me. I was sizing her up for possible post-show pleasure, when my friend Joe Danna pulled my coat.

"Joey, I know what you're thinking," he said, "and you gotta forget it, man. That guy over there just got made, and that's his girl playing grab-ass with you. You wanna go home tonight with your pecker intact, lay off that chick." He added, "Hell, you may be in trouble already."

I steered clear of that table for the rest of the night and hoped against hope that the mobster hadn't seen any of his girl friend's shenanigans. Luck was with me. He was having so much fun celebrating, he could barely see the floor, let alone his girl's hand on my crotch. Thanks to Joe I went home that night with my pecker and everything else intact. After a while I could recognize such trouble and sidestep it without help. But the bouncers and bartenders always had my back, just in case some chick was hot enough to distract me from reason.

Although Joey Dee and the Starliters dominated the stage every night, we always shared it with a second group. We played forty minutes and took forty off while the other band played. In the beginning it was forty on and twenty off, nine p.m. to four a.m., seven sets a night. We were always there, because we were the house band. Other groups came and went by the dozens. When we began to spend more time on the road, Louie and Sam brought in a number of terrific acts to substitute for us, and I became good friends with most of them, especially Johnny Maestro and the Crests, from whom I shanghaied my second wife Lois Lee; Larry Chance (my lifelong friend) and the Earls; the Younger Brothers, with three killer front men, Larry, Vinny, and Paul; and the Unbeatables, featuring Gene Cornish, who later became a Starliter and then a founding member of the Rascals. All of these people were important in my life, and I was happy for their opportunities at the Pep.

The wrought-iron rail that stood between the stage and the dance floor in the Pep broke into a ninety-degree corner at each end. When I was performing, I'd sometimes jump up onto the rail and gyrate, standing with one foot on each side of that corner. Yes, it was a bit daring and more than a little precarious, dancing on that rail while wearing slippery leather-soled shoes. It's a modern-day miracle that I didn't stumble, straddle the rail, and add an octave or two to the upper range of my singing voice.

One of the waitresses, Janet Huffnagel, liked what I did on that rail and decided to give it a go herself. She set her tray down, climbed up onto the rail—that, in and of itself, was a lovely show—and planted a foot on each angle of the rail. Twistin' and gyrating, she put on a show that was appreciated by every living, breathing male in the room. I mean, her body moved in places where I didn't even know a body had places. Her customers had to wait a few minutes for their drinks while Janet did her thing on the rail, but I never heard any complaints about the delay. And so it turned out that the band and I weren't the only ones who could stir up the Pep. The waitresses were involved in what was going on, and they enjoyed—and expanded—their interaction with the guests as well.

| Peppermint Twisters |

Janet was the first Pep waitress to charge headlong into audience interaction, but she certainly wasn't the last. As the international success of the Pep grew and the girls' style evolved, the title *waitress* gave way to the titles *dancer* and *Twister*. The girls continued to serve drinks, of course, but now they were dancing on the floor and on tables to the music of Joey Dee and the Starliters. They really socked it to the guests, these beautiful, young, table-topping, rail-riding ladies wearing custom-designed, sexy outfits. And these outfits became more popular and even influential than most people know. See, an early guest at the Pep was Hugh Hefner, creator and master of the legendary Playboy empire. He must have liked what he saw that night, because the Playboy Bunny costume, which went through several revisions, ended up being quite similar to the one worn by the Peppermint Twisters. Of course, Mr. Hefner immediately patented his final version—the only patent the US Patent Office ever granted to a service uniform. I'm not accusing anyone of fashion plagiarism or improprieties. I say only that the costumes worn by the Pep Twisters seem to have been inspirational.

With their floor dancing, table-top dancing, and mesmerizing rail stunts, the Peppermint Twisters became the very first "go-go dancers." They were also the first to use strobe lights and black (ultra-violet) lights for effect. The Twisters sprayed their stiletto heels with fluorescent paint so they'd glow fiercely when house lights were turned down and black lights were turned up at the end of the show. It was magical.

At first only the waitresses Twisted and performed as they worked, to entertain customers. Soon, a stage show featured pretty, young women who only danced and didn't serve drinks. Between the floor show and the stage show, the Pep Twisters blew the audience away every night. With all this ingenuity, energy, and creativity at the height of the Twist craze, the Peppermint Twisters in the stage show were an instant success. Sudden and well-deserved notoriety led them beyond the Pep Lounge to perform at Madison Square Garden, Carnegie Hall, the Waldorf Astoria, the Plaza Hotel, and even in South America.

I struggle to remember the names of all the terrific girls who worked the Pep, but I happily list the names of the ones I remember: Marlene (the terrific lead dancer, who had a son with Vinny of the Younger Brothers), Lois Lee (my very lovely second wife), Dotty Keating, Misty (a girlfriend of David Brigati's), Janet Huffnagel, Geri Miller (who dated James Brown and later became part of the Andy Warhol entourage), Rosemary, Mary Jo, Dotty Miller, Mary Ann, Kitty Guillepot (who accompanied us on our second tour of Europe), and Lola (later, David's wife of nine years). Not to be outdone, the Y-chromosome factor joined in the fun as well. Teri Noel, Frankie Darrow, Johnny Modina, and Ray could move with the best of them. Teri would later design the interiors of my Starliter club, and Frankie took his Twistin' on the road to gain notoriety in his own right.

The girls were active in other ways as well. See, whenever a new band came to the Pep, the dancers claimed the privilege of deciding which guys in the band they would have for after-show dessert, if you know what I mean. Sometimes the dessert came before the close of the show, made possible by generous breaks and the convenience of adjoining ladies' and men's dressing rooms. Pop in, pop on, pop off, pop out, pop back on stage. Nice. Handy.

Not to be left out of the action, Sam made it a point to know when the girls were changing costumes. With perfect timing he'd open the door and say, "It's showtime!" And I bet it was, for Sam. Yeah, he was leaning more than a little toward voyeurism, but what the hell. Sam was a man, his heart was still beating, and the girls didn't care. Good on ya, Sam.

It wasn't only the new bands, of course, who sampled the girls. The Starliters and I stayed busy during our breaks too—with customers as well as dancers. Our opportunities for quickies were so plentiful that we adopted a new clothing style. It started with my man Willie Davis, this fashion—which was the free-balling, no-underwear, commando style. See, Willie learned that, if he got into a tight spot and had one shot at it, good things were more likely to happen sans jockey shorts. Myself being a quick study and not too proud to steal, I adopted the style as well. And then David joined the ranks of the well-dressed, and everything was copacetic.

| B-Girls |

One more "flavor" of girls worked at the Pep. They weren't unique; most clubs hosted such ladies. They were called "B-girls," and they had one very special function: make customers drink a lot and drink expensive. In return they got a piece of the profit. In order to do that job, the girls would flirt and coax suckers into spending big in hopes of getting lucky—which they never did. The surest marks were out-of-towners, who were easily spotted because of their brown shoes and white socks. No matter the color of the suit, the shoes were always brown and the socks were always white. Such a fashionista was a lead-pipe cinch for a veteran B-girl. Promising him whatever she thought he wanted, she'd have champagne cocktails lined up on the bar like planes stacked up at JFK. She'd even have Mr. Midwest buying entire bottles of champagne before he knew what was happening. Now, the girls could do this all night long, because they only ordered club soda for themselves. But, at some point, the mark would get drunk and have to stand down, and that's when the bill came due, if he'd been allowed to run a tab. In that case the total bill could be . . . shall we say, a *surprise* to the customer. Happy with it or not he always ended up paying the bill, one way or another. The good side of the experience for these chumps was that they got to go home and tell their bros about the dead-sexy chicks they almost had.

| THE MOB AT THE PEP |

When I first took the gig at the Peppermint Lounge, I had no idea about Mob connections there. I knew only that Sam "Kon" Konwiser, Louie Lombardi, Ralph Saggese, and Larry Grippo were on the payroll. Sam was my mentor, and, as far as I was concerned, Sam and Louie were my bosses. Certainly, they ran the place.

I soon learned that the club was used for Mob business, but I didn't know that its ownership and management had such a deep chain of command that led eventually right to the top. Only after the Pep closed and the papers came out did I learn that Matty "the Horse" Ianniello had overseen the operations of this and many other clubs for the Vito Genovese crime family. But Matty wasn't a Mob killer; he was a Mob *earner*. That's what the Mob called a guy who turned a profit and didn't cause trouble. And the Mob *loved* earners. I'd met Matty at his 49er Club, and he always treated me and all the guys with courtesy and respect.

I suppose the sudden and unexpected fame and popularity of the Pep surprised the Mob as much as it did me and everyone else. When the club was just an out-of-the-way hole-in-the-wall in Hell's Kitchen, it served Mob purposes quite well. Wise guys could quietly conduct business there without cutting a high profile. But with the reporters, notoriety, crowds, and noise that came with its new-found popularity, the Pep's value as a place to conduct Mob business waned. On the other hand it had now become a moneymaker for the boys, and that was a good thing. After all, there were other places to do business.

And with that the Pep became more a place for Mobsters' recreation, relaxation, and partying and less the place of business that it had been. Mob guys still frequented the now-popular joint, but instead of low profiles and anonymity, they were enjoying and even encouraging a higher profile. They boldly identified themselves and reveled in the attention afforded them by the club's new ambiance.

When they made a score, Mob guys liked to come to the Pep to spread it around. They'd run nightly tabs to five hundred bucks and more, tipping the waitresses and bartenders lavishly. Watching the style and bravado with which gangsters operated, I could almost understand why kids from poor neighborhoods wanted to emulate them. Whether you agreed with their business practices or not, the truth was that most Mobsters were stand-up guys, if you didn't cause trouble for them and showed them the respect they craved. If you behaved otherwise, you might find them to be less than cordial. Although I never adopted their lifestyle and never became one of them, I enjoyed many great nights because of my Mob friends. Those guys knew how to party.

I learned many things about Mobsters at the Pep and elsewhere throughout my life, one of which I share now as a "Dee-ism": The bigger a guy was in the Mob, the nicer he was.

Between prison stints and before he became the Canary Supreme, Joe Valachi often came to the Pep, always with at least one beautiful girl on his arm. One woman in particular was stunning—a redhead who, in Hollywood terms, would have been rated an eleven, with a capital E. Valachi was treated like gold there and in the neighborhood till he was flipped and spilled his guts on national television in 1963 about his intimate, firsthand knowledge of the Mafia. To say the least this made Joe persona non grata with La Cosa Nostra—the term Valachi coined for the Mafia, meaning "our thing" in Italian. The first man ever to violate the Mafia's blood code of "omertà" (silence) died in prison in 1971.

| One Brief, Shining Moment |

Some say the City is cold and unfeeling and never gives back. I disagree. During our time at the Peppermint Lounge, New York gave us lots of hugs. Of all the accolades that came with our Pep days, perhaps none was more meaningful or poignant than this heartfelt greeting from a sanitation worker, New York's strongest, who recognized and approached me as I came out of the Pep one day. "Joey, you're the greatest," he said. Now, that's big time any time of the day.

Yes, for my money New York was the greatest city in the world, and for fifteen minutes—as suggested by Andy Warhol, a frequent guest at the Pep—we were the center of the universe. Joey Dee and the Pep became so popular and famous together that you couldn't say one name without saying the other. See, we had become one and the same as we shared a glorious ride into rock & roll history. For that fifteen minutes the Peppermint Lounge and Joey Dee and the Starliters were the brightest lights on Broadway. Not bad for a seedy little Hell's Kitchen bar and a handful of mischievous Jersey boys looking to find a gig.

But now all the excitement of the Pep had died down, and its novelty had worn off. It had enjoyed a four-year run—unheard of in the ever-changing landscape of New York night clubs. With the fading spotlight came other problems. When the FBI learned of the club's Mob connections, the State Liquor Authority (SLA) scrutinized its operations and revoked its liquor license in 1965 for mismanagement and insufficient record-keeping. A trumped-up charge, I'm sure—but who you gonna call? And no matter what was or wasn't true or what did or didn't happen, it all turned out the same: The 28th of December 1965 heard the death knell of the Peppermint Lounge—the most famous night club in history.

But damn! We made a run at it when times were good, and the Pep and Joey Dee and the Starliters did some beautiful things together. We picked up the gauntlet that had been thrown down and deserted by Hank Ballard and Chubby Checker and transformed the Twist into an international sensation. We made some of the best rock & roll music ever heard, helped launch future superstars, and changed the landscape of music-and-dance clubs in the City. Like steel to magnet, we drew in legendary personalities from stage, screen, music, and the arts; newspaper columnists and noted authors; Beautiful People and high-profile café society; national and world leaders; infamous Mobsters from soldier to boss; and characters, oddballs, and unique spirits such as never were known. We made a bazillion dollars for ourselves and the club and—sadly—spent just a little more than that on sex, booze, and rock & roll. We created the concept of go-go girls and taught the future psychedelic scene and disco world about strobes and black lights. We added words to the social lexicon. We sparked men's and women's fashion trends. We brought the well-heeled, the powerful, the fur-and-finery-clad café society, the roughneck, and the youngster together on the dance floor, all of them Twistin' their collective ass off. We left a footprint in the sands of rock & roll history that may be covered for a time by ebbing tides but can never be erased.

Oddly, the club that took the world by storm and lit it up like a fiery comet faded and disappeared without fanfare. Perhaps only those who truly knew the Pep in its glory days even noticed the small piece in the newspaper chronicling its demise. A small, humble obit for such a world-shaking soul.

And when the Pep stopped, a part of Joey Dee stopped. It could be no other way. The two of us were one.

FIVE

PEOPLE AT THE PEP

Before the celebrated Beautiful People found the Pep, there were the *real* people, some of whom I've mentioned elsewhere. These were my friends. These were the people who hung out in a two-bit Hell's Kitchen hole in the wall because they liked an unknown Joey Dee and his music. Things changed for them when the Pep began to throw up spotlights onto the night sky and draw in the "cream" of society and entertainment. There seemed to less room for these people who pioneered the place but never made the society columns or attracted reporters or cameras. I loved them, and I missed them. And even at the peak of the Pep's popularity, I sometimes just had to have my dose of them. Some nights I'd opt against hanky-panky and networking and go instead to a hotel room to play poker with some of my Hell's Kitchen guys. I've never forgotten them or the important role they played in my life.

But yes . . . I loved to hobnob too. And a continuous stream of high-profile personalities made that possible for me.

Performing at the "Mecca" of rock & roll had its perks. Great perks. Celebrities and dignitaries and world shakers were all over the place. You couldn't swing a bottle of gin without putting a knot on the head of a look-who-that-is. Should I try to list and identify every celebrity who walked through the doors of the Pep and sat at a table or spanked the planks on the dance floor, this would be the book's solitary chapter. And I'm referring only to the ones I saw and/or met. Many of the celebrated people who visited the Pep did so while the band and I were on the road. Some of these, such as the Beatles, I've mentioned elsewhere.

But I didn't miss Nat King Cole—Mr. Class himself. I made the acquaintance of Greta Garbo, who didn't want to be alone that night. And how could I ever forget meeting The Duke, the great and legendary John Wayne. The bouncers brought me to the Duke's table and introduced me to him. When we shook hands, mine was completely swallowed up in his. What an indescribable moment that was for me. I found myself also in the presence of royalty, such as the Duke and Duchess of Bedford and assorted princes and princesses. And even though this great nation has no *royalty* per se, we had President John and First Lady Jackie Kennedy, and that was pretty close. I never had the honor of meeting Mr. Kennedy, but Jackie visited the Pep, as did her brother-in-law Ted Kennedy. Jackie loved the Pep. And she loved the Twist. She even took her "version" of the Peppermint Lounge and the Twist to the White House for a "Peppermint Lounge Night." The youthful First Lady happily and energetically taught guests to Twist while the President, I'm told, observed the goings-on with smiles of delight. I regret that we weren't invited to help instruct the guests. It would have been one of the great honors of my life to have met Mr. Kennedy.

So, yes. Many high profiles enjoyed the Pep. Some I met, some I missed. While I can't list them all, a handful of notables cry out for special mention.

| LIBERACE AND SAL MINEO |

I usually closed with the raucous "Shout." We got the crowd so pumped up during that song, all hell would break loose. This wasn't a bad thing, mind you. In fact, I encouraged audience participation of any and every kind. I jumped down into the audience, selected someone, and prodded him or her to sing along with the band while I Twisted right along side them.

One night in December, 1961, I discovered that we'd been honored by the presence of two of the best-known celebrities of the time. Liberace was arguably the greatest pure entertainer of all and certainly the most flamboyant, outrageous personality in show business. His furs, striking jewelry, sequined and bejeweled outfits, ultra-bedazzled Baldwin grand piano with golden candelabra atop it . . . All this and more gave every member of every audience a never-to-be-forgotten experience. And his stage presence was like no other—ever. I don't know whether Lee, as he was known to friends, was the first openly and easily identifiable gay entertainer; if not, certainly he was among the pioneers. And what a smile! I'm convinced the man actually had more teeth in his mouth than should have been there. Now, all this is just about the great Liberace's stage presence. His genius talent on the keyboard of that gold- and mirror-plated grand would put the audience's collective jaw on the floor. More important than all this, Liberace was my mother's favorite entertainer. I wonder whether that should bother me or not.

Sal Mineo, the great star of film and television, hailed from the Bronx. I'd been a dedicated fan of Sal since I saw him crush the big screen in *Rebel Without a Cause*, which also starred, ironically, James Dean and Natalie Wood. The *ironically* refers to the way-too-early and tragic deaths of all three of these larger-than-life stars of the cinema. Mr. Dean was taken in an automobile crash in 1955, at the age of twenty-four. Miss Wood died by drowning under investigated circumstances in 1981 at age forty-three. A victim of robbery, my friend Sal was brutally and senselessly stabbed to death in 1976, as he was returning home from rehearsals. Sal was only thirty-seven years old. Flowers of my youth, too soon gone.

But on this night in 1961 both Sal and Lee were very much alive and actively involved in my closing number. I jumped onto the floor, got between the two, and danced with them. The crowd exploded. Although I can't say modern technology is always my cup of tea, here's where I'd have given anything to have smart phones scattered among the audience, to capture the excitement that the three of us, along with the Starliters, generated that night.

The three of us gyrated our boogaloos for nearly half an hour amidst the Pep crowd. Now, you must understand something. In those days the average length of a record was about two minutes. It wasn't at all common for any group to push a number to the extent Lee, Sal, and I pushed this one. Singing and dancing nonstop for such a long time was . . . well, perhaps you might try it some time. But have your finger on the speed dial for 9-1-1, just in case.

And it wasn't just us on the floor, Twistin' and shouting through this marathon. All the guests on the floor were Twistin' to beat the band, hanging in there with us. You couldn't identify partners, but who cared?

The three of us were soaking wet with sweat and sucking wind like a vacuum cleaner, but the crowd showed no mercy. It wanted more. And I believe I had enough left in my tank to have kept going, but we had to clear the stage for the guest band. I don't remember the band, but I pity it. Liberace, Sal Mineo, the Starliters, and I were a hard act to follow that night.

Lee took a fancy to David and me, and we were invited to his place. We enjoyed sandwiches and coffee—and his very special company. Of course, we knew Lee was gay. Not wanting to get in too deep to keep our feet on the bottom, we let our host know that guys weren't our thing, but we appreciated his hospitality. With that great, magnificent smile and those twinkling eyes, he said, "No problem. I still love you boys."

We returned the love, and then we split.

Liberace in a word: elegant.

| Lenny Bruce |

Of all the people—celebrated or just plain folk—who ever came into the Peppermint Lounge, Lenny Bruce was one of my favorites. This raunchy, earthy, forthright comic was always and without question the cockiest, coolest, hippest guy in the joint. If you aren't familiar with Lenny or his work, I suggest you find one of his early records—vinyl, of course—and take a listen. Here was a man on the cutting edge of sixties comedy. He had a genius gift for taking ordinary, everyday circumstances and turning them upside down and inside out. His comedy was simply hilarious—and it was usually as bawdy as it was funny.

If you were looking for "politically correct," you weren't looking for Lenny Bruce. When Lenny performed stand-up, he took no prisoners. He went after everyone and everything. He did have favorite targets, however, including politicians, government, and Las Vegas. His entire take on Vegas shows was tits and asses. This was Lenny Bruce in a nutshell.

I met Lenny Bruce one night when he was sitting alone, and I recognized him. After the set I went over to his table and introduced myself. We hit it off as fast as a Jack Nicklaus tee shot and soon were hanging out regularly. We double dated several times with Broadway dancers, including two who were appearing in the musical, *Subways Are for Sleeping*. Ah, Broadway dancers. If there exists one who isn't beautiful and who doesn't have amazing legs and a heart-stopping body, I haven't yet met her or her sister. Lenny and I would often take the girls into the adjoining Knickerbocker Hotel to *entertain* them.

One night I was hanging with Lenny during my break, having a few laughs. All at once his face became somber, and his mood changed. He looked me in the eye and said, "Joey, you gotta help me." He looked distraught.

"Hell yeah man. Anything," I said.

"Well, my mom's going out with this scumbag bartender in Vegas," he said. "I want you to take her away from him." To say the least, I was puzzled. And then, with a straight face that could have bluffed any poker pot, he said, "If you do this for me, I'll let you bang my mother."

Wait. What? Was he serious? Was he kidding? With Lenny there was simply no way to know. But I'm guessing he was serious as a heart attack. I'll never know, though, because it never happened. I never even met his mom. Nor did I see Lenny again. After that he got involved in a lot of scrapes with the law and ended up spending his entire fortune trying to extricate himself from the harsh realities of having been a pioneer on the cutting edge of comedy. Profanity, lewdness, and being misunderstood were high crimes in the early sixties, especially if you had a microphone and an opinion. How ironic it is that in today's comedy market, where anything—and I mean *anything*—goes, Lenny would be considered tame.

Lenny Bruce was the best there was, and I truly miss him.

| Miles Davis and King Curtis |

Now, if you claim to be a fan or student of any kind of music, I dare you to tell me you don't know the names Miles Davis and King Curtis. If you can do so with a straight face, then I still won't believe you.

Miles Davis could play jazz trumpet like none other. Not that there weren't other greats, but no one had this man's style. His music personality was born from early experience with Dizzy Gillespie, Charlie "Bird" Parker, and other greats, as well as a stint at the famed Juilliard School. To listen to him play is to watch a slow, red-and-yellow sunrise. Also a gifted composer and prominent bandleader, Miles earned eight Grammy Awards during his career.

And King Curtis. Being a sax player myself, I can tell you that this man could blow. If you've heard the classic horn riffs in "Yakety Yak," by the Coasters or the great Aretha Franklin's "Respect," then you have a taste of King Curtis's greatness. He traveled and recorded with the Coasters so regularly that he was considered to be a member of that trend-setting group. And rightly so. I mean, his solos and backing were every bit as integral to the group's recordings—and as memorable—as were the melodies and the lyrics. And while I admired King's talent, I treasured his friendship even more—a friendship that came from many shared gigs and personal experiences.

Knowing all this perhaps you'll understand the thrill it was for me to have these two men join us on the Pep stage. Actually, *thrill* is too soft a word. Let's try *privilege*, or *honor*, or . . . well, I can't seem to find one strong enough. This was music royalty on stage with me. I was so star-struck, it's a wonder I was even able to soak my reed. Miles and King had just come from a gig, and I guess they'd had in mind to join us, so they had their instruments with them. When they came on stage ready to play, I thought to myself, *All right, this is a joke, right? This can't be happening.* But it happened. Miles and King "traded fours" with us, meaning we alternated four-measure solos. I'm talking about *Miles Davis* and *King Curtis* trading fours with *Joey Dee and the Starliters.* Think the people in our audience that night got their money's worth? Yes, they did—and they knew it. They went nuts as we regaled them with a song called, "Things Ain't What They Used To Be," which I'd learned from Carl, our very own keyboardist and musicologist.

Man! how I love music.

| Judy Garland and Shirley MacLaine |

Just as the entire world had, I'd already come to know Miss Garland from her many incredible motion pictures, including the timeless classic, *The Wizard Of Oz*. She was a great actress—yes, in those days, men were *actors* and women were *actresses*—and, of course, her voice was magnificent. She received nominations for Academy, Emmy, Grammy, and Tony Awards. And she could command an audience like no one else. In my humble opinion she was the greatest female entertainer of all time.

Judy was a strikingly beautiful woman with a bit of pixie in her eyes, but there was also a waifish pathos about her that always struck me. I'm not saying she didn't have fun at the Pep; she did. In fact, I often jumped from the stage to dance with her, and I think we both enjoyed that. Still, there was *something* about Judy that always got to me. To this day I regret not following my instincts, which would have led me to spend a little extra time with her; to put my arms around her as a friend and tell her everything would be all right. Don't misunderstand; I'm not so vain as to think I could have healed the unhappiness she was experiencing or prevent the tragedy that waited for her in the wings. I say only that I wish I'd tried to do some good for her.

Shirley MacLaine was a highly acclaimed actress when I hung with her at the Pep. She'd already struck an Oscar pace after debuting in Alfred Hitchcock's 1958 film, *The Trouble with Harry*, and from there it was Oscar nominations all over the place. Her Oscar came at last in 1983 for a grand performance in the film, *Terms of Endearment*.

Shirley was at the Pep nearly every night, enjoying its vibe and music and Twistin' her gorgeous ass off. I often abandoned the stage to dance with her. Let me tell you, it was a thrill for me to Twist in her general vicinity. See, I secretly had the warm scorchies for Shirley. I felt somehow connected to her, as if we'd perhaps met in another life. Hmm. I mean, I had a real big thing for her. I'm sad to say she never got to see it. Ahem.

| Shelley Winters |

Shelley Winters was her very own story. I'd admired her work in motion pictures and television, and she was a beautiful, sexy woman—not the same flavor of beautiful or sexy as, say, Liz, Ava, or Marilyn, but gorgeous all the same. And she had a certain *je ne sais quoi*. A little spice, a little extra *oompf*. She was sultry, sensuous, raucous, ribald, and always ready for action. Now, she wasn't as slim and sleek as she'd been a few years earlier; she'd gained some weight. But to my eyes she was still in shape. After all, *round* is still a *shape*, and on Shelley it looked terrific.

Usually, Shelley was already tipsy when she arrived at the Pep, and she built from there. But she didn't need any help to be the center of attention; her *sober* personality was enough for that. I mean, this was a real broad—meant as a compliment—and everything I saw her do, she did with gusto. There was nothing fake about Shelley. She had this kind of barroom laugh that could be heard clear into the next county when she let loose—or at least from one end of the bar to the other. And she could curse like a sailor. Now, to all that add about a fifth of whiskey, and you've got yourself a party girl.

Shelley loved to be on the dance floor and would dance with anyone and everyone. But being less than petite and drunker than Dean Martin on New Year's Eve, she sometimes bumped—accidentally and friendly—into other dancers. Some of these bumpees had prunes up their asses and would complain to a bouncer, putting Shelley at risk of being escorted from the Pep, especially if Frank Rocco happened to be the bouncer who fielded the complaint. If Shelley were lucky enough to draw my friend and diplomatic bouncer Joe Danna, then she had a chance. Joe would take the time to apply some emotional salve to the offended hoi polloi, grant forgiveness to our happy-hearted drunk, and allow her to stay in the club to keep right on bumping merrily into others. Joe could always fix such situations to everyone's satisfaction. It was his gift.

Shelley gave me the eye every night, but I was usually just one of the many recipients of her "eye." On one night, however, she singled me out. As I was leaving the stage, she grabbed my arm and said she'd like to get it on with me and my friend Chuckie Daniels, a good-looking kid from Newark who'd also been given the "eye." Shelley had caught me on a good night; I'd made no plans. Glancing over at Chuckie, I could see that he was keen on the idea. Well, I presumed it, anyway, based on his smile that could have spanned a small canyon. We agreed that he'd take her upstairs, and I'd be along in a few.

I finished the last set, said good night to a few people, packed my sax, and went up to the room, ready for whatever was coming. I'd often seen Shelley leave her table after a show—and even *during* a show—only to return with a big smile on her face and looking a bit disheveled. I knew what she'd been up to, but all I could do was smile about it. After all, she was just doing what I always did. Funny thing about public perception of promiscuity in those days: A guy who got lots of action was lauded as some kind of conqueror, but a girl who did the same was a ho. I never saw it that way.

By the time I was in the room, I'd nearly undressed. Chuckie and Shelley were lying on the bed, making out. This being my first ménage è trois, I didn't know standard operating procedure or ethics here, so I just bull-in-the-china-shop-ed it. Rolling Chuckie aside, I took my turn. Then Chuckie took a second turn. Then we swapped out again, and again and . . . Well, I didn't count the swaps, but I can tell you one thing for sure: It was a good thing I was young. When we were finished, Shelley said, "You two were wonderful, and we need to do this again." It had been fun, to be sure; but I had so many other bodies to climb, I knew I'd probably never be with her again.

I was right.

| Salvador Dali |

Without question one of the most controversial and talented artists to venture into the Pep was the world-renowned Salvador Dali. I'd heard of him, of course, but I never thought our circles would intersect. But he often visited the Pep during its heyday, and I did get to know him. Unique, flamboyant soul that he was, Dali rocked that trademark waxed handlebar moustache. It was thin and stiff and pointy enough to put out an eye, if you passed carelessly close to him. Yes, it was a l-o-n-g moustache. That gold-tipped cane commanded a bit of attention as well. And he was attended always by an entourage that zigged when he zigged and zagged when he zagged.

Waitresses and bartenders always had the skinny, or info, on the who, what, when, where, and why of all the important customers. So, I have it on good authority that the legendary Salvador Dali was tighter than a bullfrog's ass, and we all know that's waterproof. According to the waitresses, Dali never paid the tab. For anything. Ever. It was always paid by one of his lackeys—and never with Dali's money.

One night a member of Dali's entourage handed me a note inviting me to join Dali at his apartment after the show. When I saw the note, we still had one more set to play. I sidled up to David, told him about the invitation, and asked him to go with me. He agreed. We both thought this would be something not to be missed, especially when the man was surrounded by so many heart-stopping honeys. We were sure to get lucky, we thought—although luck had little to do with it when you fronted the hottest group in New York City.

David and I were stylin' in my new Caddy as we followed directions to Dali's apartment. Parking was never a problem in those days. We located the address, parked a few doors away, and walked to his building. We rang the doorbell. Somehow I expected the bell to sound like something from an episode of *The Addams Family*, but it was the ordinary Avon ding-dong. When the door opened—again, where were the creaks?—a gigantic dude greeted and ushered us in, saying that we were expected. As we stood in the anteroom, or foyer, a chick offered us togas. I looked at David. David looked at me. *What the hell*, we thought, as we dropped our pants and removed our jackets, shirts, and ties and handed them to the young lady waiting to collect them, and then donned the togas. Wearing the required garb, we were escorted into a massive room devoid of furniture save for a mantle atop a great fireplace. In the center of the floor was spread a massive, fully opened parachute, presumably of the type used to deliver heavy equipment from airplanes. Around the chute sat twenty or so cross-legged, toga-clad souls awaiting who-knows-what.

These were all ultra-hipsters, the kind I'd expect to be with the master. David and I plopped onto the floor next to a couple of cute chicks, unsure what to do or what to expect. There was some talking, but not at the level you'd normally expect at a party. But I didn't know whether this even *was* a party. The air was thick with smoke, and it took only a moment for me to realize it wasn't coming from Cuban cigars. It was the devil weed. The "perimeter people" were taking turns sucking on a big ol' joint and then passing it along. But I didn't need to have a pull from that weed; I was already enjoying what potheads sometimes call a "contact high" from all the smoke enveloping us.

Now, to remind you, David and I didn't do marijuana. We didn't do any kind of drugs. Alcohol? Hell yeah. I could do a quart of V.O. during a night at the Pep and sweat it off on stage. Amazingly, thanks to a steel liver and a high tolerance for the stuff, booze actually seemed to work in my favor when I performed. But this was drugs. I didn't do drugs. The great jazz trumpeter Dizzy Gillespie once told me, "Joey, don't ever pick up anything you can't put down." So, when the little smokey fella came around to David and me, we passed as politely as possible. With one look at each other, we knew it was time to go. If we stayed and the band ever found out about it, we'd be screwed, blued, and tattooed. And laughed out of town. We found our street clothes, dressed, thanked our host for the kind invite, and rushed to fresh air.

The great Salvador Dali never again invited us to one of his soirées, but that's life in the fast lane. Either you're in or you're out. Credit Dali with an error for thinking we were potheads. And credit David and me with an error for thinking we'd get lucky that night.

| Tommy Hunt |

Among the entertainers who filled in for the Starliters and me while we were enjoying lucrative gigs on the road was a fabulous singer named Tommy Hunt. Before going out on his own, Tommy had been with the famed Flamingos, with hit records such as the iconic, "I Only Have Eyes For You."

Tommy was—and still is—a handsome and talented singer with a voice like slow-melting butter. His first solo recording was "Human," which was intended to be the B-side to the Bacharach/David tune, "I Just Don't Know What to Do with Myself"; however, a DJ named Jocko Henderson mistakenly played and promoted "Human," which eventually became Tommy's biggest seller. The B-side song still became a hit, covered later by Dusty Springfield, Dionne Warwick, and Gary Puckett.

Tommy was a big attraction at the Pep after I left. The man sang his heart out and put on a great show. And his alter-ego, "Herkemiah Scruggles," was funny and bright and kept things flowing. I later booked Tommy to play at my Starliter club, and he always knocked 'em dead. We became good friends and remain so today.

There was another side to Tommy.

A madam named Marie had befriended Tommy. By today's standards she might have been seen as a stalker. I don't know. But I do know she was Tommy's number-one fan. She indulged him with whatever his heart desired, buying him cars, diamonds, and other gifts as lavish as you might imagine. Marie wasn't a young woman, but the girls who worked for her were, and I guess they must have been as good as they were young. Lots of money. *Lots* of money, they earned. It filled the bags that Marie handed to Tommy at the Pep from time to time.

I don't know the extent or depth of Tommy's involvement with the business. Maybe he just liked being around Marie and her girls. I know only that Marie appeared to be one helluva sugar mama, and I'm guessing the girls were good friends of his, one way or another.

| Chubby Checker |

We were having more live success playing "The Twist" and bringing the house down with the dance than Chubby ever had. Joey Dee and the Starliters had turned the Pep into the epicenter of the Twist craze, and everyone in the music and entertainment industry knew it. The earthquake of publicity rumbling from our little club shook every nook and cranny of the industry; even Chubby himself couldn't ignore the shock waves clear down in Philly. He decided he'd better take a run into the City and get the skinny on things firsthand. On a night in November, 1961, Chubby entered the Pep, his manager and entourage in tow. I wasn't aware that he was in the audience when we took the stage. But it didn't take long for me to find out.

We were in the middle of "The Twist," and I had just melodically invited the little miss to come on and do the Twist. I guess Chubby took that as his cue, because he jumped right up onto the stage and started singing over me. I couldn't have been more surprised. Somewhere there exists a picture of Chubby and me on stage at that moment. The look on my face tells it all. I wasn't happy. But, ever the professional, I saw the song through to the end. With that the set was finished. I made a beeline to the office, where I found Ralph doing whatever it was Ralph did in the office. I was agitated.

"Ralph," I said, "I've gotta talk to you and Sam and Louie. Right now."

Ordinarily, I might have gotten a bit of resistance or at least some questions from Ralph. Not this time. I guess the tone of my voice and my body language gave him the answers to any unspoken questions. He stood and left the office, returning momentarily with Sam and Louie.

"Okay, Joey," Ralph said. "Say what you gotta say."

"What the hell was that just now?!" I asked. "I mean, what the *hell*?"

"Whaddaya mean, Joey?" Ralph asked.

"I think he's talking about Chubby's stage visit just now," Sam said. He'd seen the unwelcome intrusion, as had Louie. Ralph was oblivious. As usual.

"Hell yeah that's what I'm talking about!" I said. "What the hell?!"

Ralph was annoyed. "Joey," he snapped. "Don't bother me with this bullshit. I got things to do."

This was typical of Ralph. He couldn't care less about such trivial things as friendship, commitment, empathy . . . stuff like that. And loyalty meant nothing to him in business. I was wrong, I guess, ever to expect such things from the button-down ex-cop.

But Sam and Louie had class, and they were willing to listen.

I explained. "I put my heart, sweat, and guts into this joint, and this guy's gonna jump up onto the stage, take over my show like he owns me and the stage and the Pep and the Twist, and try to take credit for what I've done here? No! *Hell* no!"

"Now, Joey," Sam said, "you know we didn't know Chubby was gonna do what he did."

"Doesn't matter," I said. "He did what he did. And if he stays, the boys and I are gone."

Sam and Louie knew I meant what I said. They looked at each other, perhaps wondering who should take the lead here. Ralph was still unconscious.

Sam spoke. "You're right, Joey. You're right. We know that, and you know how we appreciate what you've done for us and the Pep. You know that."

"Absolutely. You *are* the Pep, Joey," Louie said. "Don't worry. We'll take care of it."

"Yes, we will," Sam said. "We'll make sure Chubby stays off the stage while he's here."

With that the meeting was over. I still wasn't jumping for joy, but as long as they kept the guy away from me while I was performing, I'd be okay. Sam and Louie left the office, told some of the bouncers what was going on, and gave them instructions. There were no more impromptu duets.

I've always been about respect and loyalty. I knew whose song I was performing every time we played "The Twist." It wasn't Chubby Checker's. It wasn't Joey Dee's. It was Hank Ballard's, and I always credited Hank and his song for making me and the Pep famous. Hank appreciated that. Once, he said to me, "You know Joey, Chubby never mentioned my name, not once. Like he wrote the song and was the first and only man to record it."

But the irony was so thick you could have taken a picture of it. Because of the popularity of the Twist dance at the Pep, Chubby's recording of "The Twist" was re-released—and it reached number one again. That was the first time a song ever hit the number one position on Billboard's Hot 100 twice. The Pep gave him that gift. This time the record would remain for two weeks in the top position. But its replacement—I'll get to that shortly—would hold the spot for three weeks and linger longer on the charts.

Fast forward to 1988. I was on the road, watching the halftime show of Super Bowl XXII on a television at a restaurant. To my surprise Chubby appeared on that screen, singing about doing the Twist again like we did last summer. That was hard enough for me to take, but then a stake was driven right into my heart when he segued from his song into—guess what—my "Peppermint Twist." The words were doctored to make it the "Super Bowl Twist," but it was our song. *Our* song, written by Henry Glover and Joey Dee, taken to number one on the charts by Joey Dee and the Starliters. And there was Chubby, performing it in front of who knows how many people. I couldn't help feeling that it should have been me down there singing my own song. I'll never know why I didn't get the shot.

I guess I was pretty visibly upset about what I'd seen and heard. The guys in the band tried to console me: "At least it was your song being played down there." I did find a bit of consolation there, and I appreciated their effort. I had to admit it was a compliment that my song was performed at the Super Bowl. But through the years, Chubby's never mentioned having done my song that day. He's never acknowledged the role the Pep and I played in reviving the Twist dance and turning it into an international craze and making his re-released version of Hank Ballard's song a second-time-around hit for him. And it's not like he never had opportunity; we subsequently did shows together and even went on tour together. He'd sometimes say hello, sometimes not. But I'm sure his gratitude for everything is hidden way down deep in his heart.

Don't mention it, Chubby.

Six

THE MOB:
SWIMMING WITH CROCODILES

Where I grew up and lived most of my years, the Mob was a simple fact of life. If you were friendly with it, you got breaks and blessings. If you were unfriendly with it, you got . . . other things. I understood from the beginning that the influence of the Mob was ubiquitous—bars, restaurants, politics, construction, clubs—but for a long time I didn't know just how deep that influence and control extended into the recording industry. Early in my career I heard things, of course, and there was the occasional newspaper piece that implied or even accused. But none of this seemed real to me—at first. But with a little experience, I lost the naivete. And once I'd lost it, it was gone. It was gone forever.

I was recently asked how I could coexist through so many years with such lifestyle, business, influence, and intrigue without becoming personally connected with the society. "It must have been like swimming across a crocodile-infested river," the questioner added. "How is it you didn't get bitten?"

I've no explanation for that turn of events, really. I just did my thing, respected others around me, avoided causing trouble that would have to be dealt with (although I sometimes came close to screwing the pooch on this one), and tried not to judge. In any case I never got bitten. Still, the swim across the river wasn't without a close call and a nip or two, and heaven knows I saw enough to know what a crocodile could do.

JOEY DEE

| Food Fights, Fur Coats, and Big Carmine |

As any band musician will tell you, a house gig is primo. It's regular work, and you don't have to worry about where the next gig is coming from—at least for the term of the house gig. Not only that, but you can leave your equipment at the venue every day, with at least some assurance that you'll find it there when you return. This saves on budget-busting medical bills for treatment of spinal injuries and hernias from schlepping all that heavy, awkward equipment to and from the van every day. Any legit road musician will understand and appreciate what I'm writing here.

Thanks to club manager Vincent "Vinny" DiNapoli—a distant cousin of my soon-to-be second wife Lois Lee—I got such a house gig at the Robin Hoy on Westchester Avenue in the Bronx in 1966. The place was packed every night, because all my Bronx guys showed up: Joey Gee, Joe Sport, Tony Horse, Bobby Trinchi, and all their friends who had enjoyed seeing us perform at the Jokers Wild on Pelham Parkway.

My band and I had the stage at Robin Hoy three nights a week, and it was another hot band I had put together. Ronnie Grieco—who was like family to me, because his older sibling and I had grown up together—played sax. On drums, Gregg Diamond. Jimmy Gumson played bass. Jimmy and Greg were a package deal and key to the cohesiveness of our sound. Joey "Dippy" Duvol, a handsome guy from Washington Heights, who was a good musician with a good voice, played trumpet. Dippy got us Ricky, a Latino keyboardist, also from Washington Heights. David Lavender handled guitar duty—another handsome guy who could really play. As important as our sound was to me, I never thought it hurt to have two or three real "lookers" among us. See, good-looking musicians attracted chicks, and chicks attracted guys. Good formula. I topped off our organization with "Little" Frankie Guerra, my valet or roadie or whatever you wanted to call him.

Little Frankie had dwarfism. While dwarfism can take many forms among little people (LPs), in Little Frankie it presented with short arms and short legs but typical-sized trunk and head. Interestingly, when Frankie and I were both sitting, he appeared to be as tall as I was. And, of course, in those days there was no way he wouldn't have to face a nickname. That's just how it was. But I guess "Little Frankie" wasn't enough, though, because Sam Taylor assigned a second moniker to him: "Lead Pipe," because that's how tough the little sucker was. Sam was great at giving nicknames, and they always stuck.

Whatever you called him, Frankie and I were about to get in real trouble.

The owner of the Robin Hoy was Big Carmine, a Mobster who controlled the

Bronx at the time. He was no man to be trifled with, and it was always a good idea to walk softly around him. Whenever Carmine was in the club, everybody, and I mean *everybody*, behaved and didn't get loud or rowdy. For this reason Carmine didn't come into the club on Saturdays.

See, Saturday night at the club was "cumare night" for the Mob, meaning wise guys took out their girlfriends and left their wives at home. Things were usually looser in the club on Saturday; the guys would make a score and then want to party and let their hair down. Vinny handled the club on cumare night, and he let the boys have a good time.

Nobody had a better sense of humor than wise guys, in the proper situations. Perhaps this gift served a purpose for them, as it often did for Jewish people and other ethnic minorities; that is, when you're always close to the edge, you use humor to get you through. But wise guys could choose to respond to a given situation with humor, or not. You had to be careful. Take for instance that awkward moment between Little Frankie and Big Carmine. Things could've gone either way.

Big Carmine sat at a table, where he'd been doing some light work for a time and enjoying listening to us rehearse. The guys and I were taking a break when Little Frankie, acting on some inexplicable impulse, approached Carmine. Looking the boss straight in the eye, Little Frankie said, "Carmine, this town ain't big enough for the both of us, so I think you'd better leave."

Wait. What?

I couldn't have been more surprised if a frickin' camel had walked into the room. I knew it would be a matter of mere moments before Little Frankie got the slap that was most certainly coming his way.

The big guy glared at Frankie for what seemed an eternity. Unbowed and unintimidated, Little Frankie stood fast, returning Carmine's stare. And then the big guy laughed. He laughed hard and with every part of his body. He laughed in a way only an in-charge guy like Carmine could laugh. And then he spoke.

"Kid, you got balls," he said through his laughter. "Balls the size of an elephant's you got. Come. Sit. Have a drink!"

Little Frankie—he of elephant balls—sat at the table with Big Carmine and drank, talked, and laughed. I was supremely impressed that Little Frankie survived the moment. On this I'd never have bet. But survive he did. In fact this was the beginning of a friendship. After that little episode Carmine would come into the club just to see Little Frankie. Yep, they became pals, and all was copacetic.

For a couple of weeks. And then came that Sunday night, when everything hit the proverbial fan.

So, Saturday night at the club was for the guys and their girlfriends; Sunday, on the other hand, was wives' night out, and Carmine would usually show up for that. On one particular Sunday the band and I were playing, and playing well. Everyone in the club was having a good time and behaving, and it was a nice evening out for the ladies. Between numbers someone handed me a written note informing me that the wife of a made guy was celebrating her birthday. We played a couple bars of "Happy Birthday to You," and then I made an announcement.

"Ladies and Gentlemen," I said. "It's my pleasure to announce that today is Teresa's birthday. Please join us in wishing her a happy birthday."

As the house sang "Happy Birthday to You," Little Frankie emerged from the kitchen, carrying a custom-created cake for Teresa. As he passed me, that sometimes-irresistible urge for mischief hit me. I scraped a bit of the cake's frosting onto my finger and smeared it on Frankie's face. Well, there was simply nothing else for the little guy to do but retaliate. In a blink I had a dab of sweet frosting on the tip of my nose. I hit him with the stuff again, and he again returned the favor. Not to be outdone, the rest of the band joined in, and, before you could say *Larry Moe and Curly* the stage became a battleground—the scene of an all-out food fight. Cake flying here, frosting splattering there—and all of us on stage laughing like kids at the park.

But we were the only ones laughing.

That the wives didn't participate in the food fight per se doesn't mean they weren't *involved*. See, flying pastry found its way into the audience, hitting some ladies who'd rather not have been hit. Now, most Mob guys' wives wore fur. Fur coats, fur stoles, fur collars, fur whatever. Not the cheap fake crap most people wear today, but real fur. Costly, *valuable* fur. Fur and cake icing do not mix in a happy way—that you can believe. Never have, never will.

The next voice I heard was Vinny's, who had made his way to the stage.

"What the hell, Joey?!" he said. "You got any idea what you've done here?"

The question and the look on Vinny's face catapulted me back into reality and stopped our laughter in its tracks. Looking around I could see what we'd done, and it wasn't pretty.

"Get off the stage, Joey," Vinny said. "Get off the stage NOW!"

We left the stage, and the show was over. *Both* shows were over.

Vinny said nothing else to us. As we were preparing to leave the club, I said to Vinny, "Tonight's pay night, Vinny."

"Pay night?!" he said. "You're worried about getting paid? I'm worried about you getting killed!" He continued, "Come back here tomorrow morning. Carmine wants a sit-down with you and the little guy. Be here at eleven sharp."

Well, shit. This couldn't be good. In fact, it was downright serious, and I knew it. Yep, we'd ballsed it up this time. The night wasn't restful for me; I practically shredded the sheets, tossing and turning through the night, dreading what was sure to come with the morning.

Little Frankie and I arrived at the club a little after ten. Given the trouble we were already in, we couldn't risk being even a single tick-tock tardy. Vinny was already there, waiting—and we sensed a near-stifling eeriness. Little Frankie and I were both shaking in our boots as we waited for Carmine to show up. I mean, we were so tense, you couldn't have gotten a greased BB up our butts. Then the man arrived and called us into his office. When we were all seated, Carmine spoke.

"Boys, I don't like what you did here last night," he began. "It wasn't a good thing, what you did."

I wasn't sure when—or if—I should speak, but I had to let Carmine know how we felt.

"Carmine," I said, "we're really sorry for what we did. I don't know why we did it, but I guarantee you it won't happen again."

"Oh, I know that, Joey," Carmine said flatly. "I know it won't happen again. But see, it shouldn't have happened the first time. You guys hit some important customers with that shit, not to mention messin' up some fur coats." He continued, "I think something's gotta be done. Whaddaya think I should do?"

My first impulse was to say simply, *please just let us leave here in one piece*, but then I thought it might be better to take a more positive approach.

"You don't have to pay us, Carmine. Just don't pay us," I stammered. "Don't pay us."

Carmine thought for a moment, never taking his eyes off me. "No, Joey. I like you boys, and I'm gonna pay you. But let me make something real clear," he said. "If anything like this happens again, it's over. Now get outta here."

We didn't have to be told twice. Vinny handed me an envelope with our money in it, and we were the wind.

Outside, Little Frankie and I looked at each other, knowing we'd dodged a bullet—certainly metaphorically and possibly literally, had things gone sideways. This was an envelope against which we could never push again. We'd caught some break. We couldn't count on the same good fortune a second time.

| MATTY THE HORSE |

David and I met Cheri and her friend Lillian in our early days at the Pep. They asked us to join them at their table, and it was with them that I took my first drink.

I now know it was a screwdriver, but, at the time, I didn't know what the hell I was drinking. That changed quickly. Too quickly. I soon graduated to V.O. straight up in a pony glass, with a water chaser, and I was guzzling with the best of them. I'd go on stage, have a good set, then come off and drink five or six shots before taking the stage again. I could handle lots of booze, but at times it got a little much, even for me. See, the bartenders would pour my drinks into a rocks glass and fill it to the top every time someone bought me a drink. "You guys are gonna kill me," I told them. "Everybody buys me drinks, and I can't drink 'em all. Just tap the bottle on my glass."

After this first encounter with the girls, they came back several nights in a row and teased the hell out of us, if you know what I mean. I convinced them at last to take us to their room at Hotel America on West 47th. This was a historic event for me: the first—but, sadly, not the last—time I didn't go home to Joanie.

Now, these chicks wore the trendy mile-high beehive hairdos and high heels, and they towered over us. We must have looked like two Lilliputians chasing after two Amazons. But we weren't intimidated. We accepted the challenge before us.

In the morning Cheri made a nice breakfast for me. Well, maybe it was more of a brunch, given that she served it to me around noon. Whatever it was, she served it to me, then gave me a kiss and a note with the name and address of a club scribbled on it. "Meet me here when you're up and about," she said and left for work. David and I usually didn't have all cylinders firing till about two p.m., and that's when we left for the 49er Club on West 49th.

When we arrived at the address, we found a place called the 49er Club. Now the address made perfect sense. The girls made a fuss over us when we came in. Their doting caught the attention of a large man sitting at a table, who firmly suggested to the girls that they should attend to their drink-buying customers. "That's what you're being paid for," he told them. After that he called David and me over to his table.

"Boys, I'm Matty. I own the place," he said. "I see you've taken a liking to two of my girls. Cheri, Lillian—nice girls." He continued, "Sit. Please, sit."

"Thank you," David and I stammered out together. We sat at the table, feeling a bit timid. Hard to know what was coming next.

"Who are you boys?" Matty asked.

"Joey DiNicola and David Brigati," I said. "We play at the Pep."

"The Pep? You play at the Pep?!" he said, and then he paused thoughtfully for a moment. "You Joey Dee and the Starliters?"

"Yes sir. That's us," I said.

"Good things," Matty said. "Good things I hear about you boys. You got all those crowds and lines going on over there. You boys should visit us here more often," he continued. "You're welcome at my place anytime. Anytime."

"Thanks, Matty," I said. "We appreciate that."

This man was Matthew "Matty the Horse" Ianniello, an associate—and later to be acting boss—of the Genovese crime family. Matty would die in 2012 after a storied history with the Mob. To us he was always kind and gracious and respectful, and we were, in fact, always welcome at his club. Thanks, Matty.

| Sam by the Tie |

The band and I were on stage at the Pep one night in 1962. I heard a ruckus on the floor. I looked to see two guys, one on either side of him, lifting Sam by the arms and walking him from the front door toward the office. The bouncers stood their ground; they knew these were Genovese boys, and they knew better than to get involved. After Sam and his escorts disappeared into the office behind a closed door, I jumped from the stage to see what I could do to help my boss and friend.

Standing at the closed door, I heard slapping and moaning coming from inside the office. The sound was ominous, and I considered for a moment that I shouldn't butt in. Biting my lip and choking back more than a little trepidation, I pushed the door open to see these two mugs holding Sam up in the air—by his tie. He was hanging there, red-faced and bloody, being slapped, hit, and kicked by those goons. They saw me at the door and stopped their beating long enough to tell me to get the hell out. It didn't take any special people skills to see that they meant business; still, I hesitated just a beat.

"Please, Joey," Sam gasped. "Please leave." I closed the door. The beating resumed. I returned to the stage, hoping against hope that my friend and boss wouldn't be killed.

Sam survived the beating. Apparently, he'd just been given his first warning. I'm sure it was a *first* warning, because the Mob never gave more than one. I'll never know the reason for the beat-down. Sam never told me, and no one ever discussed the incident. I presume Sam got the message.

| Kill Jimi |

In December, 1965, we played a place called the Beach Ball in Revere, Massachusetts, a beach town with a strip of night clubs right across the street from the Atlantic Ocean. Connected to the Patriarca crime family, the Beach Ball had been previously known as the Ebb Tide Lounge. Its connection to the Mob was generally known, and certainly more than one hit was coordinated at its tables. The business conducted at the lounge got blatant enough at some point that people thought twice about going there, and then they *didn't* go there. At that point the name was changed to Beach Ball in hopes of improving its public image and strengthening its bottom line. But it still wasn't pure as the driven snow. In fact, while we were playing there, we became involved in more than just music.

I got my first hint that trouble was afoot when I left the club one night and went to the parking lot. Maurice (Jimi Hendrix) was there too—not with me, but in the parking lot. Headed straight for him at a brisk pace was a young white guy dressed in a suit. Two things about the guy caused me concern. First, his face wore a look of fierce anger and determination. Not a good combination. Second, he was brandishing a handgun. Ordinarily, either the look *or* the gun would be enough to get my attention, but this fella had both. And he was taking them to Maurice.

Now, I've never considered myself to be a suicidal type, but what I did in the next few moments could be used in a court of law to prove the contrary.

Rushing toward the gun-totin' villain, I knew I had to do something to stop what I was sure would end with a chalk outline on the parking lot. Without thinking too deeply about what I was doing, I set myself directly between Maurice and his assailant. Channeling my inner Henry Kissinger—sans accent—I threw up my hands toward Mr. Gun Brandisher like I was directing traffic, and spoke.

"Okay man, just hang on," I said hurriedly. "Just wait, dammit! Just wait."

The guy slowed a bit but didn't lower the weapon. It was still pointed at my man, but now the damn bullet would have to go through me to get to him. Not a happy thought.

"Okay," I said. "Let's all just cool off a little and see what's going on here. Talk to me, man."

"This sorry nigger's banging my lady," the guy said. "I'm gonna blow his black head off. Get the hell outta the way."

I replied as quickly as my anxious tongue would allow. "Wait man. Wait! We can figure something out here. No need for this. Just wait."

The guy lowered the gun just a little, and that was certainly a good sign. I encouraged him. "Yeah man. Just put that thing down. Nice and easy does it. That's it." His arm was now hanging at his side.

"Okay," the guy said. "But you better just keep this son of a bitch away from my girl and away from me." He slipped the gun under his coat and returned to the club.

I tried to discuss the situation with Maurice, but he wasn't in a mood to talk. I had a feeling that this thing wasn't over yet, but for the moment, at least, we were both still vertical.

I discussed the matter with my road manager Isadore "Sy" Mitchell. It wasn't news to him. He'd already heard some buzz about Maurice. In fact he'd heard a couple of guys talking about hurting him, and it sounded like something had already been set up. *Hurt*, in Mob parlance, could mean anything from busting a guy's kneecaps to breaking his fingers to making him dead. You just couldn't be sure. It was certain, though, that the parking lot gunslinger wasn't gonna stand for such behavior, especially from what he considered to be a no-account guitar player—and a Black one at that.

I decided I'd better do something about this. As I'd often done in matters involving Maurice, I sought out my go-to man: Jimmi Mayes, his best friend.

"Jimmi, we've got a problem," I said. "You've gotta talk to your pal and tell him to quit banging that girl. He's just gotta knock that shit off."

Mayes seemed taken aback by my request, but, as always, he was stand-up. "Do what I can, Joey," Jimmi said. "But don't expect too much. Maurice go his own way."

Jimmi was right to caution me. Sure enough, Maurice wouldn't listen to him. When it came to women, Maurice listened only to his pecker.

Things started getting a little warmer at the joint, and it was clear that more trouble was imminent. Sy and I decided we'd better have a talk with management to see if we could make reason prevail. We spoke with the guys in the basement, where a pistol range had been set up for target practice. I guess every night club should have one of those.

"No disrespect, Joey, but I've been told to hurt the son of a bitch," the boss told me. I could see it wouldn't be an easy thing, changing this guy's mind. I'd have to tap dance—or Twist—just a smidgen.

"Guys, listen," I said. "I need this guy to finish the gig. The bum owes me money. If he finishes the gig, I can pay him and then take the money back, and then we can work out something in New York to take care of him."

The boss was quiet, then spoke. "No. I'm gonna hurt the son of a bitch."

"Look, man. I know how you feel. But if you hurt him now," I said, "I won't get my money. Just let me finish this gig and take my money back from him, and then we'll have him taken care of in the City."

Of course, everything I said was bullshit, but what's a little white lie to save the life of a friend? The guys reluctantly agreed to my compromise. At the very least, I'd bought a little time. We finished the gig and got the hell out of Dodge.

I don't know what would have happened to Maurice had we not gotten the break. Maybe they'd have killed him, maybe they'd have broken his hands. Hard to say. Anyway it wouldn't have been good, what they'd have done—and our man

Maurice James might never have become Jimi Hendrix.

I didn't tell the band about what was going on. I didn't want them to be constantly looking over their shoulders or to become too afraid to play on stage. Of course, Mayes knew something was up, but I never gave him details. He knew only that Maurice was in trouble because of a woman, and that wasn't anything new. If any of the band noticed the speed with which we packed up and left Revere Beach, they didn't say.

| Don't Bet on It, George |

When I was shopping for a label for our first recording in 1958, I visited the offices of Gone Records and End Records, both owned by George Goldner. George was on the cutting edge of doo-wop, and his long career would include important contributions to music and the recording industry. The Gone and End labels weren't his first nor would they be his last; he began with Tico in 1951 and ended with Firebird in 1970. At this time he was recording Little Anthony and the Imperials, the Chantels, Jo Ann Campbell, the Dubs, and the Channels.

Whenever I visited George in his office, I inevitably found him listening not to music records but to baseball games on the radio. He loved betting on baseball and on the ponies. He invariably lost, as all gamblers do who challenge the odds one time too many—and every time is one time too many. The only people who win in the gambling game are the bookie and the house. After all, great casinos don't get so beautifully appointed by giving their money to gamblers. They get that way by *taking* money *from* gamblers. I always get a kick out of people who brag that they got free airfare to their favorite gambling cities, free rooms at their favorite hotels, and free gourmet food during their stay. If you ask these high rollers how they made out while they were there, you'll hear, "Ehh, down about ten Gs." Yeah. That's a good deal, schmuck. But who am I to talk? I myself had a weakness for shooting craps, playing poker, and betting the horses. My Jersey friend Gary Nardino once told me that the only people who made money on the horses were Roy Rogers and Gene Autry. My connected Uncle John Lamela knew I gambled now and then, and he told me time and again to stop being a sucker. I should've listened to him. But there's something irresistible about gambling. For all I know, some of us have a *like-to-gamble* gene in our DNA strands.

But even George had to pay the piper. He was betting heavily with a Mob-connected book, and things went sideways. He lost everything. This is how the Mob worked: Get a guy hooked on the book, wait till his losses put him in deep debt, and then take over the guy's business or life or whatever. That's the way the

Mob infiltrated legitimate businesses. George had to sell his labels Gone and End to Morris Levy, and the labels were subsumed into Roulette Records. Coincidentally, George had sold his labels Tico, Gee, and Rama to Levy in 1957, along with his (George's) interest in Roulette.

George would be back in the label business in 1964, when he partnered with Jerry Leiber and Mike Stoller to form Red Bird Record Company.

| All in the Family |

From time to time, wise guys would ask me to come over and sing when they celebrated a communion, graduation, or other family event. Such an invitation I never declined; it was a sign of their respect for me, and one just couldn't refuse an opportunity to build respect and trust with these guys. And I did it because I enjoyed the gigs. I usually performed alone and a cappella, because the guys in the bands that played those gigs typically hated rock & roll. They'd play only Sinatra or various Italian songs. But I never minded singing without backup.

Inevitably, someone would try to put a roll of bills in my hand after I sang. I always politely declined the payment. See, taking the money would have made me beholden to them in ways I didn't want to be. I didn't want that kind of misunderstanding. And accepting their invitations to perform and politely refusing payment for it earned their gratitude and respect.

And make no mistake: With these guys it was all about respect—and respect for women was the most important of all. Wives, mothers, sisters, daughters, nieces. Respect. If you wanted to date the daughter of a wise guy, it was hands off unless your intentions were honorable—as in, you planned to marry her—and the guy approved of you and the whole situation. Many guys got badly hurt or killed for disrespecting a made guy's family or for proceeding in the wrong order to establish a relationship with a daughter.

Another show of respect was attending a funeral. I attended the funerals for several wise guys to pay my respects, and at each one the feds were looking in on us. I could see them taking pictures of my car, my license plates, and me. I never worried about this, because I was always legit—they knew it, and I knew they knew it. So, screw the photographers *and* J. Edgar.

At funerals there was visiting, hugging, kissing, and even business dealings. Mob business was a little like Jell-O: There was always room for it. My friend Joe Lipari told me once that he and a guy were standing in front of the deceased's coffin, carrying out some important business even as they viewed the man.

"Where's the four grand you owe me?" Joe asked his friend.

"Whaddaya talkin', Joe?" the friend said. "I paid that money back."

"Well, I ain't got it," Joe said. "Who'd you pay it to?"

The guy paused, looked down at the deceased man in the casket, and pointed. "I paid it to him, Joe."

Joe told me he didn't for a moment believe his friend's story, but he liked his creativity so much and got such a good laugh, he let the guy off the hook.

| Playing the Odds |

Bookies rarely respected their client gamblers, but they sure worried about them and tried to make sure they stayed healthy. *Can I get you a raincoat, Frankie? What about a heavy sweater—it's chilly out there.* Yeah, the bookies took real good care of the gamblers. See, if the gambler died, the bookie was out whatever he was owed. This personal concern wasn't reciprocated by the gamblers, however. They hoped the bookies would die or get Alzheimer's, so they wouldn't have to pay their losses. One's all about dying, the other's all about living. But if both stayed healthy, you could be sure the bookie would get paid. If he didn't . . . well, out came the baseball bat, and there went the patella. When a guy needed a lesson but didn't warrant being killed, it was always those kneecaps—a broken kneecap was a limp forever. Whenever a neighborhood guy walked with a limp, and he wasn't born that way, chances are he forgot to pay the bill.

In the book business, as in all other aspects of its business, the Mob liked things to be low-key and quiet. Smooth. Routine. *Just give us the money, okay*—that was the attitude. When guys would fail to give a right count or break off some of the money he was supposed to turn over to the Mob . . . well, it wasn't good. See, if you were an earner, you were in good shape. But even earners had to make sure the count was right. If you didn't take care of the *count*, someone would take care of *you*. Simple as that.

Take Joe Piazza for example, the guy that owned Mr. Joe's candy store in Passaic, where I lived on Columbia as a boy. Joe also made book on the side. Maybe he spent too much time counting his candy and too little time counting his book, because he was whacked. It made me sad; Joe was always very kind to me. But he miscounted, and that's what happened when you miscounted.

The same fate befell a bookmaker named Whitey, a regular at my Starliter club in 1964. He shorted the Mob and got his warning while in the club one night. But Whitey didn't listen any better to his warning than Joe listened to his. To paraphrase a *Godfather* line: We didn't see Whitey no more.

So, from gambler to bookie to boss, it was just as it was in the sea: The little fish got eaten by the big fish. This was a vital lesson that had to be learned well and quickly, if you were a part of that lifestyle, because there were only two kinds of people in Mob business: the quick and the dead.

| FROM VEAL TO JAIL |

At his death in 2019 Joe Lipari and I had been friends since we were five years old. His father Jack—and then Joe—owned a Passaic butcher's shop called King Veal (run today by Joe's children). Childhood friendships are often tossed carelessly aside or forgotten, but not so for Joe and me—even if he did get a bit closer to the Mob lifestyle than I. Yes, he was "half a wise guy" and liked to play the game. He was making a fortune as a butcher, so he didn't *need* any of that. But it was his lifestyle. He liked the lifestyle.

Sometimes called Joe "Butch," my friend often hung with Mob guys at Trude Heller's in the City, playing cards and whatnot. There was a server who waited Joe's table every day, and Joe always gave the guy a very generous twenty-dollar tip. One day that tip was only ten bucks, and the confused waiter returned to the table.

"Excuse me, Mr. Lipari," the waiter said, "but I think there's been a mistake. This is a ten-dollar bill."

Joe gazed silently at the guy for a moment then said, "Oh, I'm sorry about that. Here, gimme the ten-spot." The guy handed him the bill, fully expecting, I'm sure, a replacement double sawski. "Now whaddaya got?" Joe asked.

"Well," the waiter said, looking a bit perplexed, "now I've got nothing."

"Nothing. That's right," Joe said. "And that's what you're staying with."

Maybe the waiter learned his lesson, maybe not.

In the early seventies, Joe and I often went to Yonkers Raceway to watch the ponies run and bet a few bucks. I never had money to put on anyone's nose except the bill collector's, but Joe always helped me out. He could pick horses like he had a crystal ball, and, when he won, he halved his winnings with me. Heaven knows Joe didn't need the money; hitting a couple hundred on a race was pocket money to him. Still, he didn't have to give me any of it.

Splitting track winnings wasn't all Joe did for me. When my family struggled through tough times, Joe always made sure we were never without meat. King Veal's cutlets, steaks—the best. He was one of the angels that crossed my path throughout my life. Frankly, without such good friends, I've no idea how—or if—I'd have made it at times. What value can you place on such a friend?

Joe was a big-time card player. Fearless he was, with huevos the size of cantaloupes. He'd often take me with him to floating card games in the City. Every week the game was held at a different place—hence the *floating*—so cops wouldn't disrupt their fun. They'd mostly play the Italian game of "Ziginette." To put the game in a nutshell, players try to win money when the dealer matches his card before they match theirs. A banker is selected from among the players at a table—and Joe always liked to be the bank. More money to be won there. And he'd always have the capital—maybe ten grand, twenty grand—to risk big and, therefore, win big. Once in a long while he'd go home in the red, but nearly always he'd go home a winner. A *big* winner. I never had the cash to join in. I mean, I was a two-dollar gambler, while Joe was a thousand-dollar gambler. But I helped Joe by being his "out" when he'd won enough for the night. He'd give me a nod when his till was full, and I'd say, "Okay, Joe. We gotta go now. We got that thing."

Joe was elected mayor of Passaic in 1983, in which office he served till he resigned in 1992 following conviction for tax evasion and extortion. As I understand it Joe had something to do with a towing contractor who cornered the towing business in the City. And things went sideways. None of it made sense to me. I mean, Joe's bases were already loaded, money-wise—and he was above the salt socially and politically. And still, things turned out like they turned out. He was sentenced to forty-two months in prison.

But my friend Joe Lipari was remembered fondly by Passaic, and he was, from start to finish, a good friend to me and my family.

| DiNapoli Sit-Down |

In 1968 things were bad for me and getting and worse. I was really stretching to make a buck. To help keep it all together, my wife Lois took a job on Wall Street, working as a secretary at a firm there. Neither she nor I wanted her to be there—we were entertainers, not paper filers.

DiNapoli was a popular last name in the Bronx, and some DiNapolis were Lois's cousins. You've already been introduced to one of them: Vinny DiNapoli, of the Robin Hoy birthday cake fiasco. Now meet Gene DiNapoli, another cousin. Gene approached me one day.

"Joey," he said, "why don't we put on our own concerts? We might make a buck or two. What have we got to lose?"

I thought about it and discussed it with Lois. It sounded like a good idea. My phone wasn't exactly ringing off the hook with offers, so I figured we might as well take a shot. What's the worst that could happen—no one would show up? That wouldn't be any worse than how things were already going for us.

So, we organized and promoted a show, and it worked out nicely. We were doing what we loved and did best, and we made a few bucks. And if it worked once, it ought to work again. We made arrangements for concert number two.

Now meet another DiNapoli: Joey, Vinny's brother. "Joey," DiNapoli said to me on the phone, "I need to meet with you and Gene at the club on the Bronx River Parkway."

This could be very good, I thought. See, I'd played that club, and I figured Joey was going to offer me another booking. Exactly what I needed just then. But I was a little puzzled about why he wanted me to bring Gene along with me.

The meeting was arranged, and Gene and I arrived at the club at the appointed time. Finding Joey alone at a table, we approached him. He gestured for us to sit. I didn't really like the look on the man's face. I'd seen such a stern look before, but not in a meeting to discuss the terms of a booking.

"So, you're a promoter now, Joey?" DiNapoli said, piercing my eyes with his. "You're promoting concerts now, Joey?"

With those questions I knew the meeting wasn't about a booking. It was a good, old-fashioned sit-down. We wouldn't be discussing gigs today. Damn. My first impression had been right. I always hate when I'm right about things like this.

"Well, Joey," I said, "we just thought we'd . . ."

I didn't get the sentence out. "I don't give a fuck what you thought," Joey said. "You ain't no fuckin' promoter. That ain't what you do, capiche?"

I knew I had to be careful here. I didn't want to be disrespectful, that's for sure. I timidly replied, "No, Joey, I'm not a promoter. That's right."

"Fuckin' right, that's right," he said. "Now, I got this friend who *is* a promoter. That's his job. But he can't do his job, Joey, and you know why?"

If eyes could literally drill holes into a person, I guess I'd have had a couple of nice ones clear through my head, courtesy of Joey DiNapoli.

"I don't know, Joey," I said.

"He can't do his job 'cause you're taking it away from him. You're in his house, and you're taking it away from him."

"Sorry, Joey. I just didn't know," I said.

"Now here's how it's gonna be, you two," he said. "You're gonna give my friend a taste of what you've already done. And you ain't gonna do no more concerts in the Bronx." His voice had gotten increasingly louder as he spoke, and it hit full volume when he clearly and slowly enunciated his final thoughts on the matter: "Do. You. Understand. Me?!?" He didn't wait for an answer; he knew what it had to be. "Now get outta here."

And with that the meeting was over—as were my days of concert promotion. In the Bronx anyway.

Seven

PEPPERMINT TWIST: MAKING A NUMBER-ONE HIT

In my early days of playing in the City, I often saw a neon sign at 1631 Broadway, advertising Roulette Records. In those bright lights I saw the names Count Basie and Maynard Ferguson, as well as the names of other jazz and Latino recording artists that meant something to me. I determined that I'd see my name in lights on that Broadway sign some day.

And I did.

| No Record, No Career |

In 1961 I had a recording contract with Scepter Records, the label that recorded my friends Shirley, Beverly, Addie, and Doris—the Shirelles. Good friends that they were, the girls spoke with Florence Greenberg, the label's owner, and persuaded her to give me a chance. For that, I'll always be grateful to my very good friends.

Brigati wrote a great song with my pal Chuck Jackson called "Face of an Angel." We recorded it with David singing lead while the Shirelles and I sang backup. The flip side was "Shimmy Baby," featuring Rogers on lead. Scepter released the record, and it was a good one. I always thought it should have made it big, but it stalled and never found its way up the charts.

The Pep was on fire. I knew it was time to make a record that would reflect all that was happening there—and the sooner, the better. I met with Florence.

"Florence," I said, "there's something special happening at the Pep right now.

To get a jump on this Twist fever, we need to be in the studio right now. Come on out to the club," I continued. "See for yourself what's happening."

"Joey," Florence said, "I can't get too worked up about that right now. I just don't see the need." She added, "Don't forget, Joey. Your record with us kinda bombed, you know."

I was surprised by her response, but I wasn't discouraged about my plan. I knew I was on the cusp of a once-in-a-lifetime phenomenon, and I was determined to own it. So, even though I was still under contract with Scepter, I started soliciting offers from other labels. The most important consideration in selecting a label was timeliness. I knew this had to be an expeditious release, or else a thousand clones would have Twist records on the market before we did, and we might get lost in the field.

I arranged to have representatives from the record labels Atlantic, Capitol, and Roulette come to the Pep and see what was going on. They all liked what they saw and heard. Ahmet Ertegun from Atlantic said he'd need a month to get a record on the shelves—but a month, when you're dealing with a hot commodity, could be a lifetime. I passed on Atlantic. Nick Venet from Capitol said he was interested and would try to make it happen. Again, the lackluster response told me Capitol might take more time than I was willing to wait. I passed on Capitol. Morris Levy, known to his friends in the industry as Moishe, from Roulette had a different assessment of the situation.

"Kid, I'll have the record out in two weeks," he said. He talked fast, and his voice was gruff and raspy—more a growl than speech. Clearly, this was a tough guy who expected to be in control; when he was speaking, you paid attention.

I liked his style. I knew time was of the essence, and Morris was speaking my language. I accepted his offer, having no idea that the camel had just stuck his nose into the tent. As it turned out this would be the only time Morris ever kept his word to me.

"One stipulation," Morris told me. "You've gotta get rid of the big nigger. He doesn't fit. Get another white kid," he continued, "to front with you and Brigati." The man was referring to my good friend and long-time Starliter Rogers Freeman. He was okay with Carl on keyboards and Willie on drums, but he didn't want a Black man up front.

Whenever Morris was in the presence of Mobsters in the office, he referred to Black clients, entertainers, and brothers in general as niggers. It didn't matter if he was talking about Count Basie, a friend, or a stranger. If they were Black, that's what he called them. Interestingly, when he talked to his attorneys, he used the term "Schwartzes." I frequently heard him use both derogatory terms. Every time, it was fingernails on a chalkboard. Perhaps you're thinking Mr. Levy was a bigot. Perhaps you're absolutely correct.

This ultimatum from Morris—that I had to fire Bo—hit me like a ton of bricks. It broke my heart to think about letting my good friend go. But I had a voracious desire for stardom, and I would do what had to be done.

"Bo, here's the deal," I explained. "Morris thinks we need a different voice up front with David and me. No change, no record. No record, no career. I'm in a tight spot here."

Bo was clearly affected by what I said. I mean, he'd been dreaming of success right along with the rest of us. This was a low blow, but Rogers Freeman was a stand-up guy. Even when he was getting screwed.

"I understand, Joey," he said. "It's not you, I know that. And you know I ain't about to stand in the way now. Good luck, man."

What I did in that moment has remained in my memory and in my soul as one of the greatest regrets of my life. Where was my loyalty? Up my ass, that's where it was. But I rationalized and moved on, bringing Larry Vernieri on board to replace Bo. I'd met Larry a short time before, when my friend Joe Pesci brought him to the Pep to hear us play. Now he was a Starliter.

| Moishe Trumps Florence |

Throwing myself into the record deal, I went to Roulette's offices to discuss our contract. I saw a bunch of characters hanging around. I knew they were Mob guys, because . . . well, because I was from the streets of Jersey, and I'd been around. I even knew some of the guys personally, and they were always nice to me. But I knew why they were there. See, in the seminal days of rock & roll and doo-wop music, there was a great deal of money to be made. And where money was, the Mob wasn't far behind. These guys were around to take care of business. This was one of my first clues that Morris was connected with the Mob, but for a long time I had no idea just how far up he was connected. Being a Jew, he could never be made of course. But he was a great earner for the Mob, and the Mob took care of any good earner. That was a goose that laid golden eggs.

Anyway, in Morris's office I signed a contract that was, to say the least, not in my favor. Too late I'd find that the contract—not to mention the deck—was stacked against me. Among other terrors of the contract, it gave Morris my publishing rights to "Peppermint Twist." But I wasn't the first recording artist to get ripped off by a label, and I wouldn't be the last.

Signing contracts was part of daily business for businessmen. Morris was a businessman, and when the contract was put before me, he had a definite and powerful edge. I came from a blue-collar family, and I had no one to give me counsel during these contract negotiations. Moishe talked and acted fast. He discouraged me from having anyone review the documents. "It's unnecessary and a waste of our time," he told me, "and we don't have time to waste. All you need to do is trust me."

What was I to say? I knew of a guy who was reluctant to sign a contract but ended up signing it after one of Morris's boys hung him by his ankles outside a window, nine stories off the ground.

I signed the papers without reading them.

[suck·er /'səkər/ 1. informal: a gullible or easily deceived person. *See also* Joey Dee.]

To further distract me from the screw job I was getting, Morris had a guy buy me a Selmer Mark VI alto saxophone—the Cadillac of saxes—at Manny's Music. He also threw in a set of Slingerland drums for Willie.

Shiny toys and strategic flattery.

Everything was set for us to record. Everything, that is, except for one little detail: I was still under contract with Scepter Records. I reminded Morris of this.

"Fuhgeddaboudit, Joey," Morris told me. "I'll take care of everything."

He called Florence Greenberg.

"Florence," he said, "Morris here. I just signed Joey Dee and his boys, and I'm gonna record them. If they become popular, you can release whatever you have on them and make some money that way. And if they don't," he continued, "it won't matter one way or the other."

"Well, that's quite a proposition," Florence said. "Anyway I *guess* it's a proposition. Sounds a little like a done deal, Moishe."

"It's not a proposition, Florence," Morris said. "It's simply the way it is." And then an injunction: "Don't make any trouble for me on this, Florence."

Florence knew what that meant. She knew what consequences she'd face if she ignored the not-so-veiled threat.

"I understand, Moishe," she said simply. "We'll make it work."

| WRITING IT |

Now it was time to get down to business. On a Sunday afternoon in October, 1961, David and I met in the back of the Pep with Henry Glover, the Roulette producer assigned to work with us. A barely tuned piano stood there, and paper pads and pencils lay on a nearby table. Such was the humble beginning of the iconic, internationally renowned "Peppermint Twist."

Henry and I commenced writing our hit song. Finding our inspiration wasn't difficult. Henry had produced some of the great Hank Ballard's early hit records. And we all knew Hank's 1959 recording of "The Twist"; we'd played the song and danced the dance on stage for some time. The Twist wasn't our entire show, but it was a big part of it. Knowing that, Henry offered a thoughtful suggestion.

"Joey," he said, "let's make ours a little funky. You know—change up the rhythm pattern a little."

"Whaddaya got in mind?" I asked.

"Give a listen," he said.

Sitting at the piano, Henry knocked out a piece of the rhythm pattern he heard in his head. He made those old eighty-eights come to life, and the sound was funky. Real funky. To me it sounded just right. With no more discussion I grabbed a pencil and one of the pads and wrote the words, "Meet me baby down on 45th Street." From there we split words and melody lines: I did one, then Henry did one. We played off each other like we were playing ping pong. The song evolved naturally, spilling out of us like it had already been written and was now finding its voice. David threw in the *bop-shoo-bops*, and there it was. In two hours we had it. We all knew it was special and destined to be heard in lots of homes, dance halls, and cars. We were proud of it already, much like a parent is instantly proud of an infant at birth.

It was not only a *good* song; it was a *fun* song. The lyrics described the dance, and the dance wasn't complicated. *Up and down, round and round, one-two-three kick, one-two-three jump.* Today, having performed the song too many times to count, I still kick and jump—and have fun doing it. Of course, I don't grab quite as much air with the jumps as I did on this day of composition, but I still clear the floor.

| Recording It |

Next day Henry taught our song to Carl and Willie. As always they were quick on the uptake. Done and done. Henry then booked some studio time at Bell Sound located up Broadway, not far from us. At that moment, anyway, it didn't *seem* far from us. But there was a bit of a situation. The deal was that the studio had no organ, and we needed an organ. No problem, though, really. I mean, we *had* one. We just had to get it to the studio.

Again, no problem. We were young. We were healthy. We were strong. And we had a frickin' dolly. After closing the show at four a.m., we loaded our Lowery organ and Leslie speaker onto that bad boy, and pushed it and its precious cargo up Broadway. That may sound like nothing at all to you, but we had to push that thing nine blocks. *Nine blocks* we pushed it. Uphill, both ways. Okay, well . . . that line never worked with my kids either; but it was, in fact, uphill *from* the Pep. And allow me to remind you: It was four o'clock in the morning. Even in the City, grown men pushing an organ and speaker up Broadway on a dolly at four in the morning is a sight that gets attention. But no amount of embarrassment or cardiac arrhythmia would stop us. We were on a mission.

Move along, folks. Nothing to see here.

With the trusty keyboards in place, it was time to make sure we had the rest of our sound filled out. Henry added some great musicians to do just that. He brought in Sammy "Sticks" Evans to play drums along with our Willie Davis. A bit unusual to have two drummers, true. But Willie was a field drummer and prone to picking up the tempo a bit now and again. Great for performing live at the Pep; not so good for recording. Sticks brought the stability we needed for the recording. Jerome Richardson provided the baritone sax, and we were joined also by a gentleman who played the upright bass, but I can't recall his name. And Henry managed to capture Billy Butler, who played a mean guitar. To say the least.

Please allow me a brief sidebar on Billy Butler here.

A sixteen-year-old guitar player named Vinnie Corrao approached me once in the early days, asking if he could join my band. As I would do for so many others throughout my career, I gave this young man a chance to show his stuff. Handing him a recording of the great Bill Doggett's "Honky Tonk," I made him an offer.

"Vinnie, if you can learn the guitar part in this song and play it for me at our next rehearsal," I told him, "then I'll hire you."

I'll be damned if that kid didn't learn the entire bit and play it for me, note-for-note perfect. I hired him.

Now, here's the coincidence. The amazingly gifted guitarist on Bill Doggett's "Honky Tonk" was a man named Billy Butler. The very same Billy Butler who, working as a studio musician, played guitar for us on our recording of "Peppermint Twist." Odd, how paths cross in coincidence. And Vinnie? He played with our band at our Passaic armory gigs long after, even joining me for my second tour of Europe—where his mistake nearly got us executed (or at least arrested) as spies in East Berlin. More on that later. Vinnie Corrao went on to an amazing lifelong career as a jazz/blues guitarist, backing no less than Ella Fitzgerald and numerous other musicians of fame and great talent. But Vinnie wasn't always a sideman; his talent stood alone. He even managed to find his way to Carnegie Hall. And, as far as I know, his trio is still at it.

All the musicians Henry put together for this and my other Roulette recordings were virtuosi. Henry never brought in anyone but the best.

And now it was time to decide who would sing lead on the recording. David and Larry had both learned the song, and Henry asked David to take the first crack at it. After the take Henry offered an unusual complaint. "Your voice is too good," he told David.

Now it was Larry's turn, and he belted out his best rendition.

"Still not feeling it," Henry said. "Joey, why don't you take a stab at it?"

I was surprised by Henry's request. "Henry," I said, "I'm not a lead singer. I'm a backup singer. David and Larry—they're the pros."

Henry offered a friendly argument. "I know that, Joey. But sometimes the song's writer can put different inflections and a unique feeling into the sound." He urged me: "Just try it."

I reluctantly agreed, made my way into the studio, and donned the headphones. The sound coming through the phones was the band playing live—no tape for this. On cue, I started singing. "*Well, they got a new dance, and it goes like this . . .*"

Wrapping up my effort, I looked up to see Henry smiling at me through the glass. He pushed the button and spoke to me over the loudspeaker in the studio. It seemed to be no less than heaven talking to me. He said simply, "That's exactly what I wanted, Joey."

With David and Larry providing the *bop-shoo-bops*, we prepared for the first take. Henry gave us a last-minute instruction.

"Now, guys," he said, "don't stop playing. Just loop it. We're doing part one and part two in a take."

I didn't think much of it at the time, but I later understood the instruction. By doing it this way we didn't need another song for the flip side. This saved time and money for Morris, who always knew and played all the angles. And "Peppermint Twist – Part One," the finished side A—which we nailed in just two takes—ran for precisely one minute, fifty-nine seconds. In those days a song that ran longer than two minutes had a hard time getting airplay. Henry knew that. Of *course* Henry knew that.

And it was a wrap.

| Hearing It |

A week or so after we recorded in studio, Roulette released "Peppermint Twist." Someone at Roulette called to tell me I needed to stop by. There I was given a box of promotional, or "promo," copies of the 45 rpm disk, each of which sported a plain white label imprinted with *Not For Sale. Promotional Copy Only*. What a sight it was. Although this wasn't my first writing credit on a label, seeing *Dee–Glover* on the label as writers practically took me to my knees. I don't remember how many copies I was given, but I had no trouble finding a home for every single one of them, happily gifting them to family and friends till the well ran dry. The record hadn't even been played over the air yet.

Leaving the Pep after work one morning, I returned home by way of the Lincoln Tunnel, as usual. I paid the twenty-five-cent toll and went on my way. When I exited the tunnel on the Jersey side, my radio reception changed from static to sound—and I was hearing a familiar sound. *Bop-shoo-bop-bop-a-bop-a-shoo-bop*. I couldn't believe it. It was my song. I'd heard my music on the radio before, but this felt like something special. I was overwhelmed to the point that it wasn't safe for me to drive, so I pulled over to the side of the road and tried to take in the enormity of it all. I choked up and didn't even try to fight back the tears that were puddling in my eyes. I wanted so badly to say to someone, "Did you hear that?!" I even considered jumping out of the car, waving down a passing car, and tuning in his radio to my song. But that would have just been weird, plus I might have been run over or shot. So I sat alone in my car, listening to "Peppermint Twist" to its final *shoo-bop*. I don't know—maybe it was better that way. Maybe it was right that I enjoyed this first listen alone.

I knew this was it. We were on our way.

| Promoting It |

After the release of "Peppermint Twist," Morris called me.

"What'd I tell you, kid?" Morris said. "What'd I say? I said we'd get the record out. Did I say we'd get the record out? And we got a hit," he continued. "A hit we got. A bona fide hit we got here. Come on up to the office, and I'll tell you what you gotta do."

I went to 1650 Broadway and up to Roulette Records. There I found the usual cast of muscle and another guy to whom Morris introduced me. He was Red Schwartz, promotional director for Roulette. I liked Red right away, and I could see he liked me as well.

"Joey, I'm gonna send you, Red, and a couple of girls to promote our record," Morris said, "and I guarantee you a number one."

Guarantee is a strong word, and I liked hearing it. And I especially liked hearing *a number one*.

"You're gonna ride with them to break out Pittsburgh, Philly, Cleveland, and

Detroit," Morris told me. "You go out for a week and meet and greet DJs and PDs. Red's gonna take care of the rest."

Red drove, I rode shotgun, and two great-looking girls made themselves comfy in the back seat of Red's brand new black Caddy. First stop, Philly—about a hundred miles away. At a radio station Red and I went inside to meet the program director (PD). I said my hellos and shook the required hands, and Red handed the PD an envelope. Yes, the envelope contained just what you think it contained. Only Morris, Red, and the PD knew how much of it was in there.

"Morris wants you to play this kid's record," Red explained, "and then you'll meet us at our hotel. I've got another surprise for you there."

And *that's* where the girls came in.

Now, once a PD had accepted the cash, he knew the score. He promised to play the record at least every half hour. But given Morris's reputation, the station usually ended up playing it more like five or six times every hour. And heaven help the man who took the money, made the promise, and failed to deliver. That's when the baseball bats came out. Or worse.

If you think every record that got played by DJs in those days was strictly because it was a good recording of a good song . . . Well, you simply don't understand how business was done back then. Of course, many records were, in fact, good enough to get airplay on their own merits and charted because listeners liked and wanted to hear and buy them. I hold "Peppermint Twist" to be such a record. And some PDs were stand-up guys that went their own way with no outside influence. But there were business strategies in play behind the scenes that often influenced PDs and ensured that certain records got enough play to hit it big and fill the Mob's bags. For a long while such strategies weren't even illegal.

And now I had learned how you break a record. This one was easy, because we had a great record, and the Pep's popularity and publicity had the whole world chomping at the bit for it. Next stops: Pittsburgh, Detroit, and finally Cleveland, on the way back to the City. Every stop was the same routine.

After the Cleveland business we went back to the hotel and had a few drinks with the broads. Eventually, the conversation came around to the girls' job descriptions, and they asked us if we'd like a free ride. *Of course* we would. We took them up to our room and paired off. My girl was, how should I put it . . . *experienced*, and she took me around the world. Not only experienced, the girl was also cute—but I never kissed her. I knew where her mouth had been, only a few hours earlier.

We went back to the City, and the race to number one was on.

| FINISHING IT |

Except for the studio cut of "Peppermint Twist"—which would be the first track—the album was to be recorded live at the Pep. Henry made all the arrangements for that. He brought in an engineer named Doug to set up his surprisingly unimpressive master recording equipment in the dressing room at the back of the club. Henry explained to us what was going to happen.

"We're going to record all your sets for two days," he said, "and I'll edit them later, and we'll have an album, boys. We'll have a *great* album."

With Henry overseeing it all Doug hung a single mike from the ceiling at downstage center. The recording required only one mike, because everything in those days was recorded in monophonic ("mono") sound. High fidelity ("hi-fi") and stereophonic ("stereo") sound had yet to come down the pike.

"Just sing into the house mikes," Henry said, "and don't worry about the recording mike. Doug and I will take care of everything from the recording unit." I knew Henry was the one with experience, and we put our complete trust in him. But, come on! *Don't worry about the recording mike* was a lot easier for Henry to say than for the band to do. I mean, just tell somebody not to think about zebras and ask what he's thinking about. It'll be zebras. And thinking about this damn zebra that was recording us caused us to play the first set like it was the first time any of us had seen a musical instrument of any kind or sung into a microphone or been in front of people.

By the second set we'd settled down and were paying no attention to the zebra. We were back in the groove and getting our high from the electricity of the audience. We continued to play under the mike for two nights, and the genius of Henry Glover translated all those sets into one magic live album.

And was it ever a special album! *Doin' the Twist Recorded Live at the Peppermint Lounge* was a monster record. A beautiful white cover with a peppermint cane superimposed on it made the record look downright appetizing—a nice metaphor for the amazing flavor of the songs contained on it. Of course, the chart-topping studio version of "Peppermint Twist" was there, having hit the coveted top of the charts, where it would remain for three weeks and on the charts for sixteen weeks. But that wasn't the only hit track on this album. There was "Shout – Part One," the only version of the Isley Brothers tune—including their recording of it—to chart on Billboard's Elite Top Ten. It reached number six and remained on the charts for nine weeks. "Hot Pastrami with Mashed Potatoes," with Brigati doing the work, cracked the charts at number 36. Our version of "Ya Ya" charted at number one in Europe. When the dust had cleared, this album nearly led the pack in sales, second only to the soundtrack album from the Elvis Presley movie *Blue Hawaii*. Our album contained more hits than any previous album had contained, and it remained on the best-selling album charts for over a year.

Rock & roll heaven, my friend. Rock & roll heaven.

| Meanwhile, Back at Scepter... |

As Morris had suggested when he hi-jacked us from Scepter Records, Florence Greenberg released a Joey Dee and the Starliters album of her own. It consisted of unreleased recordings we'd done while under contract with her, along with several other unidentifiable cuts that we didn't record. She added sound effects to some of the tracks, like glasses tinkling and people talking, to give the illusion that they were live recordings. It was awful. Our music was good, as always, but the recording, the product . . . well, that was something else again. But bad or good, I'm sure Ms. Greenberg made a couple of bucks from the release. Can't say for sure, because she never paid me any royalties on it.

Eight

ROULETTE WITH MORRIS LEVY AND THE MOB

From the moment we met, Morris Levy and I were plagued by a give-and-take relationship that mostly saw me giving and him taking. He was the major player in my recording career, but he turned screwing me into his favorite pastime. Although I reference Morris and the Mob throughout this book (his connection with the Mob's involvement in the record industry is a matter of record), I've reserved this chapter just for him. I think you'll see why.

| What Price Glory |

With the success of "Peppermint Twist" here and abroad and the album built around it, I began counting my chickens. Artists routinely saw no royalties until a few months after the release of a record, so I knew it would take a minute for me to get paid. But I figured the check that was coming would vault me into the world of the millionaire. After three months there it was: my first royalties statement from Roulette. I tore into the envelope, certain that it contained a check for at least six figures, with more payments to come.

Please allow me to refer you to my previous dictionary citation:

[suck·er /'səkər/ 1. informal: a gullible or easily deceived person. *See also* Joey Dee.]

The envelope contained no check for six figures. It contained no check for five figures or four figures or even three figures. The envelope contained no check whatsoever. It did, however, contain a statement informing me that I owed Roulette Records eight grand.

Wait. What?

Yep. I *owed* Roulette Records. Eight. Thousand. Freaking. Dollars.

The balance sheet showed the expenses that had been charged against royalties due me—things such as thirty-five thousand for recording sessions, both live and in-studio. Other amounts were charged for returns of albums from stores because of damages or no sale or whatnot. Still other charges were made for promotional expenses. I guess that would have included the hookers and, probably, the cost of Red's shiny new black Cadillac. I think there was even a charge for Morris's damn cat's food and a dry cleaning bill. To my dismay the total statement balance was a big RED eight thousand dollars. That's what I had to pay for the privilege of writing and recording the song that charted number one in most of the world and sent an album to number two for the year. Now, Henry and I shared royalties paid by Broadcast Music, Inc. (BMI) for public performances of the song we'd written, and Morris couldn't get his claws on that money. But that didn't lessen the insult of that royalties statement from Roulette.

What I was holding in my hand was the first—but not the last—evidence that I was dealing with a big-time swindler. Morris Levy didn't play nicely with others, and now I knew it. Firsthand.

| Heeeere's Jolly! |

I knew guys who knew guys, and I was told Morris had a record plant in Jersey that pressed vinyl twenty-four-seven. Going out in truckloads, all the products were invisible to me and other Roulette recording artists—and to Uncle Sam, I presume. And since the records didn't exist, the sales were never accounted for in the numbers used to tabulate sales and calculate artists' royalties. What a racket Morris had going, and what a piece of shit he was. Not even the decency to give me a lousy crumb from the huge cake I baked for him. But knowing what was going on didn't help me resolve the problem. I mean, if I'd confronted him about it, I probably wouldn't be writing this book. Anybody who got in the way of this money-making machine was hurt—some perhaps even killed. I personally know of a couple of cases where guys with whom I'd done business had words with Morris, and next day they had .22 caliber bullets ricocheting around inside their skulls. As good a way as any, I guess, to die—but I could do without it. Whether Morris was involved or not, it made no sense to poke the rattlesnake by myself.

I needed reinforcements.

I called my manager Don Davis and my agent Jolly Joyce and explained the situation. They were incredulous. Surely, they suggested, I must have made a mistake. I read the statement wrong, or it wasn't a current statement, or the office failed to include the check. I assured the both of them that I could read and understand a royalties statement—and that I certainly could see and understand the bottom line of *minus* eight thousand clams.

"Don't worry, Joey," Jolly said. "I'll call Morris. We'll get your money."

Jolly called Morris immediately and made an appointment to meet the next afternoon at one of Morris's apartments at midtown.

"You're coming with me, Joey," Jolly said.

"No, Jolly. Unh-uh. I'm not comfortable with that," I said. "You go."

Jolly insisted, and I went along with him.

Now, Jolly was an interesting individual, appearance-wise. He was shorter than I, if such a thing is possible, and he reminded me of a leprechaun. Sprightly, agile, and always ready to sign a contract, Jolly once had me sign on the dotted line while we were in a moving car—and he was driving. He had two sons, Norman and Vanny, and they all booked me at one time or another through the years. Norman died young, but Vanny and I are friends to this day. Jolly handled some of the biggest names in show biz: Johnny Cash, Bill Haley, Bobby Darin, even the Three Stooges—and, of course, Joey Dee and the Starliters. Pretty impressive.

At the building Jolly and I took the elevator to an upper floor. We found Morris's apartment, and Jolly knocked on the door. Hard and loud, he knocked on the door. When one of Morris's lackeys opened the door, Jolly shot right through. No *hello*, no *how you doing*—just straight through and right to the point with Morris.

"The royalties," Jolly said. "Pay up."

A couple of Morris's boys began to move menacingly toward us. With a raised hand Morris stopped them in their tracks.

"Jolly, keep your mouth shut," Morris growled, "or you're gonna get hurt."

I'll give Mobsters credit for one thing: They'd nearly always give you a warning. *Don't do that!* they'd say. And that's all they'd say. Now, if you didn't get it the first time, you'd definitely get it the second time.

But Jolly ignored the threat.

"Moishe, we made a helluva lot of money for you," Jolly said. "We're not leaving till you pay us. And if you don't pay us," he continued, "I'm going to the DA. You choose."

Jolly was using an interesting strategy that seemed certain to get him hurt or killed, if it went sideways. But I could see it was working. Clearly, the little guy wasn't bluffing, and he wasn't intimidated by Morris or his thugs. He was fearless, and he was determined. Morris's choice was to kill us or pay us.

"Now hold on, Jolly," Morris said, throwing up a stop sign with his hand. "Just take it easy. I'm gonna give you a check for eight grand now, and we'll talk tomorrow. Okay?"

As Jolly and I stood our ground, Morris cut the check and handed it to Jolly. We left without trouble. I later received one more payment of five thousand, making the sum total of my royalties from Morris a paltry thirteen grand. If not for Jolly, I'd never have received a penny. One way or another Morris would have dodged me till one of us had shuffled off this mortal coil.

Not many people got to walk away after talking to Morris the way Jolly did. I believe Morris admired the old man—as much as he could admire anyone. I didn't say a word during the meeting. I wanted to; Morris was a scumbag and I wanted to tell him so. But I wasn't dumb enough to say such a thing to his face. It wouldn't have worked out for me like it did for Jolly. Just as Benny the Jet did in David Mickey Evans's 1993 film *The Sandlot*, Jolly had *pickled the beast*, and he lived to tell about it. Now it was official and incontestable: Jolly Joyce had brass balls.

| Slapping Stars in Brooklyn |

In 1962 Morris staged an amazing Christmas show at the Brooklyn Fox Theater. The ten-day music marathon featured Murray "the K" Kaufman, popular DJ and star of the radio show *Swingin' Soirée*, as emcee. The star-studded line-up of entertainers read like a who's who of recording artists at the time: Jackie Wilson (my idol), Johnny Mathis, Johnny Maestro and the Crests, Larry Chance and the Earls, the Four Seasons, Dion and the Belmonts, the Dovells, the Shirelles, the Isley Brothers, Dionne Warwick, and, of course, Joey Dee and the Starliters. These were the very acts I'd have hired had I been in charge. Every act was a headliner. It's unlikely that such a spectacle could be duplicated today, because the cost of hiring eleven groups with top-ten Billboard chart hits would be astronomical. As it would turn out, this was the greatest show I ever played.

We did six shows a day for ten days, starting at ten each morning and ending at midnight. Thousands of people attended each show, and from the theater's upstairs windows we could see throngs of people waiting in snaking lines to get into the next show. The action was non-stop from open to close. Even between shows there was a short movie for the fans to enjoy while they waited for the next curtain to go up.

Jersey was well represented by the Four Seasons, the Shirelles, and us. Of course, the Shirelles were my dear friends, and sharing the stage with them was wonderful. I'd gotten to know Bob Gaudio of the Four Seasons when he was with the Royal Teens, and he introduced me to the rest of the guys: Frankie Valli, Nicky Massey, and Tommy DeVito. Tommy was tough, but he was also a good-looking ladies' man. We became fast friends, and we remained so until his recent death on September 21, 2020. A very bad day for me.

All the entertainers just killed it for ten days. When the Seasons sang "Sherry," and Frankie hit that matchless falsetto, it was lights out. When the Isley Brothers did "Shout," it was electrifying. They pulled out all the stops. And we pulled out the same stops when we played our version of that iconic hit. The crowds went nuts. Jackie "Mr. Entertainment" Wilson slayed them with "Lonely Teardrops" and other soon-to-be classics, and Johnny Mathis left no doubt of his superstar status when he effortlessly crushed "Chances Are" and other hits. Jackie and Johnny took turns closing the shows.

It was all magical, to be sure, and all the acts got along great. But remember: We were competitors. As my friend Ralphie used to say at Chuck's Bar in the Bronx, on stage it's every man for himself. Back then everyone had special stage outfits and all kinds of stage gimmicks designed to outperform, outsing, and outdress one another. Only "old school" acts dress like that today. I miss that. Yep, we gave everything we had and left it all on the stage. Each show was more frantic than the one before. It's a good thing we were all young; older people would have been down for the count before everything was sung and done.

And New York audiences were the best. I had an extra long mike cord attached to my short mike, and I jumped into the audience. I don't know if that was the first stage dive ever, but it was *my* first—and it was interesting, to say the least. I was grabbed, groped, and kissed, all at the same time. I guess I liked it, because I did more dives through the years. Some time later I broke my wrist when I dived into a crowd at the St. Paul Auditorium in Minnesota.

As for the girls . . . well, they were as plentiful as you might imagine. And we had our picks of the many beautiful girls in Brooklyn, not to mention those visitors from the other Burroughs.

And, yes, there were shenanigans from time to time. The Isley Brothers were Ronnie, Rudolph, and O'Kelly. Sam Taylor was an ex-pug (boxer), and he and O'Kelly would spar and slap each other around for laughs. Every night before showtime they'd trade free punches to the chest. The sound of those blows was amazing—like two longhorn rams butting heads. Any of those punches would have crushed my chest, but they just shook it off and went about their business. The Crests (sans Johnny Maestro) would run bare-assed into our dressing room. We nicknamed them the "Danglers." Johnny would come by, see this, and just shake his head and smile. Johnny Maestro was always a class act, and he'd never have done something like that.

There was a downside to this fabulous production: We all were paid paltry sums—except for Mathis and Wilson, probably. I strongly doubt they'd have worked for scale. But no matter who did or didn't make money, one thing was certain: Morris got—no, *took*—the lion's share of every dollar that rolled in.

On the last day of the gig, I went into a room to be paid. There I found Morris and a few of his henchmen. As one of the thugs mutely handed me my envelope, Murray the K walked in. He looked unhappy.

"Moishe," Murray said, "we broke every record known to man with this show, and I think I should get more money than I got."

Big mistake, Murray.

With a poker face that belied his burgeoning anger, Morris looked up at Murray and said, "You want more, Murray? More? You want more?" And then he added, "Come'ere," and waved for Murray to approach him.

Murray stepped toward Morris. I don't know, but I'm guessing he thought he was about to be handed another envelope. I mean, this was *Murray the K*. Surely Morris would acknowledge his status with a little bigger piece of the gate. But Murray didn't get another envelope. He got a hard slap across the face. Morris bitch-slapped him like he was some worn-out ho who'd gotten wise and talked back to her pimp. Morris was a tough guy in his own right and only asked for help from his "muscle" when he wasn't sure he could handle a guy. This wasn't one of those times. Murray was a pushover for him.

If Murray didn't know enough to stop himself from asking for more money, he knew enough to take the slap without back talk.

"You want more money, Murray?" Morris asked again.

"No, Moishe," Murray answered. "I got enough."

One of Morris's boys picked up a duffel bag stuffed full with cash, and they all left without saying anything more. Murray looked at me sheepishly, clearly embarrassed—and I felt sorry for him. I was totally chagrined by what had happened, and, in a way, I wished I hadn't been there to witness it.

"I won't say anything to anybody," I told him. "Not to anybody."

And Murray's secret was safe with me. Before now, I've never told anyone about this. I think enough years and lives have passed now, and I think Murray won't mind.

Morris knew how to make and keep money. You had to hand it to him. And if you *didn't* hand it to him, he'd take it anyway. Who you gonna call?

| Same Tune, Different City |

The Peppermint Lounge in Manhattan quickly reached a level of popularity and fame that was a dream come true for most of us connected with it, but the situation was viewed differently by the Mob. The Pep had been a low-key place where wise guys could meet to do business under the dark cloak of anonymity and invisibility. With spotlights shining on the club every night and police officers outside to control the crowds, this business environment had become corrupted. But it was earning money—and if it worked in the City, it should work elsewhere.

Enter the Peppermint Lounge Miami.

In 1962 Mob boss Johnny Biello opened a companion club in Miami, on the 69th Street Causeway. Biello was also an up-the-line Mob owner of the New York Peppermint Lounge, even though Ralph Saggese was the owner of record and the club was run by my pals Sam Konwiser and Louie Lombardi. I'm not sure whether my friend Matty the Horse fell between Biello and the top or between Biello and the club. In any case the Miami Peppermint Lounge was expected to be another cash cow, and the boys and I were booked along with the Ronettes to play the grand opening of the "Pep South." When I arrived in Miami, I made a beeline for the beach. I mean, it was eighty frickin' degrees, in January. Totally boss chicks rockin' bikinis everywhere I looked. At that moment I decided I'd live in Florida one day.

We had good times during that gig. Aunt Helen was there, of course, to chaperone Ronnie, Estelle, and Nedra (more about Aunt Helen and the girls later), but we still had fun swimming and just hanging. Best of all, we made great money and great music—on a real stage with a legit sound system.

And I discovered that the long, rotten arm of Morris Levy could find me and choke me, even hundreds of miles from home. While I was there in Miami, a young couple named Pegs and Maria asked if I'd sign my new album for them. New album? I didn't know I'd made one. But there it was, right there in Maria's hands: *Back at the Peppermint Lounge in Miami.* I couldn't believe my eyes. The sound man played some cuts from the album for me, and I discovered that the record contained material that had been recorded at the New York Pep but not released on our first album. He'd done it to us again. This was the most egregious thing Morris had done to us yet. Bastid.

Despite the unexpected frustration, it was good to get away from the City for a while. We spent a couple of very enjoyable weeks helping to establish the Pep South, then headed north for a plethora of paying engagements.

| Last Chances with Morris |

Morris and I began to drift apart, but in 1966 I took another plunge with him. He hired my good friend Mikey Petrillo to produce some songs for me. Mike had written a hit song for the Four Seasons called "Tell It to the Rain." We worked hard together to produce a good record, but the songs turned out to be just so-so. It wasn't Mikey's fault; the band and I just couldn't capture the magic that happens when all the pieces fall into place. The same thing happened that year when Trade Martin got me a deal with Jubilee Records. Trade had been a performer with Johnny (Power) and the Jokers and, in 1962, started up the Rome Records label, signing the Earls, Del & the Escorts, and the Glens. He wanted to update and re-record "What Kind of Love Is This," because he thought it could be a hit again. We never did that re-recording, but we made an album with a title song called "Feel Good About It," in the Stevie Wonder vein. That album, *Hitsville*, also included covers of hits such as Neil Diamond's "Cherry Cherry," Sam and Dave's, "Hold On! I'm A Comin'," and the Four Tops tune, "Reach Out (I'll Be There)." Although it's a good record it wasn't what we needed it to be. Okay . . . it was a bomb. Once again we failed to capture lightning in the bottle. Funny how that works. It seems there's just no reliable formula for making a hit record.

I had my last shot at a legitimate hit record with Morris in 1969. I got a call from him. I hadn't heard from Morris in a couple of years.

"Joey," he said, "I got a hit for you. Come on down to Miami Beach. I'll give you a copy of the song, and we'll talk about it."

Come on down to Miami Beach, he said. Like it was nothing. But for Lois and me, it wasn't *nothing*. It was a great big *something*. We were stone-cold broke. But here was a chance for me to get back into the game in a big way, so we begged, borrowed, and cajoled our way down to meet once again with the great Morris Levy. Lois's parents lent us the money, which we never paid back. Harriet Lee and Lou Bart had been known as the "Sweethearts of Broadway" during the vaudeville years, and they entertained our family and friends for as long as they lived. They were a great act. They were great people.

Leaving the children in my mother's care, Lois and I drove to Miami in Lou's Nash Rambler. In a *Rambler*. In a *borrowed* Rambler.

How the mighty had fallen.

You can bet Morris didn't make the trip down to Miami—or anywhere else—in a little Nash Rambler. He went by rail, in his own comfortable, custom-built train car. Morris was aerophobic and wouldn't fly, so he followed the lead of TV and move star Jackie "The Great One" Gleason and went in his own special car up and down the coast between New York and Miami. He'd just hook up with a train when he needed to travel, and—just like Gleason—away he'd go.

We checked in to a two-dollar fleabag in Miami, and I called Morris. He asked us to meet him for lunch by the pool. Not OUR pool. Of course not; our humble little hotel didn't have such amenities. It barely had furniture. Morris stayed at the Fontainebleu, complete with his luxurious poolside cabana. That's where we met. Arriving there, I couldn't help thinking Morris was living high on my royalties—and you can bet I was right.

The three of us enjoyed a lavish lunch with all the trimmings, washed down with Dr. Brown's Cream Soda, my fave. While I sat in a lounge chair, Morris disappeared into his cabana and returned with an LP in hand.

"You heard 'Crimson and Clover'?" he asked.

"Yeah, sure," I answered. "Tommy James. Number-one record."

"There's another can't-fail smash on this album, Joey," he said, "and I'll give it to you complete. We'll kill Tommy's voice on the track and overdub yours. Good, right?"

Hmm. Interesting strategy. But it just didn't sound right to me.

"Tommy's all right with that?" I asked.

"Tommy's got nothing to say about this, Joey," Morris said flatly. "Take the record with you and listen to the track tonight. Call me tomorrow."

Lois and I listened to the record over and over that night. As much as I wanted to hear my voice singing the tune Morris had selected, I just couldn't seem to get my head around it. I called Morris the next day and told him we'd listened to the song.

"Great, right?!" he said. "Did I tell you it was great?!"

"Yeah, Morris," I said, "it's a great tune. But somehow I just don't hear it for me. Gonna have to pass."

And that was it. Even now I don't know whether Morris knew I was hurting and felt sorry for me or just had a hard-on for Tommy. Either way, if I'd recorded the song, he'd have found a way to screw me out of any royalties for it. Still, it breaks my heart to know I passed on the opportunity. Morris had a great ear, and he was probably right to offer it to me. When I think of what a hit record would have done for me at that point in my life, everything since that day becomes one great big what-if.

And I know the song would have been a hit. I know, because it was. The track was released as the second single from the album *Crimson and Clover*, with Tommy's voice intact, and it reached number one in Canada, number two on the US Cash Box Top 100, and number twelve on the US Billboard Hot 100.

The song was "Crystal Blue Persuasion." Perhaps you've heard of it.

Lois and I checked out of the hotel and drove back to Lodi in our borrowed Nash Rambler, another week older and deeper in debt, having sunken further into my professional and financial abyss.

That was the last time I ever saw or spoke to Morris Levy.

| What Goes Around... |

The following is excerpted from a September 24, 1986, *New York Times* article by staff writer William K. Knoedelseder, Jr., with contributions from *Times* researcher Tony Robinson, titled, "Head of N.Y. Record Firm Charged With Extortion; 16 Others Arrested in Sweep":

"After a two-year probe of alleged mob infiltration of the record business, FBI agents . . . arrested the president of a New York City record company and 16 other people on charges ranging from cocaine and heroin trafficking to extortion.

"Among those seized in a dawn sweep were Morris Levy, president of New York City-based Roulette Records; Howard Fisher, Roulette's controller; and Dominick Canterino, reputedly a leader in New York's Genovese crime family.

". . . FBI agents fanned out across metropolitan New York and New Jersey to make the arrests. The agents were acting on a 117-count indictment handed up Friday by a federal grand jury in Newark.

". . . Levy, Fisher and six alleged organized crime figures . . . were 'charged with conspiring to use extortionate means to collect a $1.25-million debt . . . from a [record] distributorship . . .

"Levy and Fisher face a maximum 60 years in prison if convicted . . . Levy was arrested . . . [and] posted $500,000 bail . . .'"

And things just went from bad to worse for Morris. The following is excerpted from a follow-up *New York Times* article by Mr. Knoedelseder on October 29, 1988, titled, "Morris Levy Gets 10-Year Sentence: Roulette Records Chief Fined $200,000 in Extortion Case":

"Morris Levy—longtime president of New York-based Roulette Records and one of the most . . . influential figures in the U.S. record industry—was sentenced to 10 years . . . and fined $200,000 for conspiring to extort a customer . . .

"The sentence [came after] a daylong hearing which saw . . . Levy described by his attorney as a devoted father and socially conscious philanthropist, and by the prosecution team as a heroin-trafficking tool of organized crime."

After his conviction was appealed and upheld in October 1989, Morris petitioned to have his sentence commuted because of his poor health. He was granted only a ninety-day stay to put things in order. He was to report to jail on July 16 but died on May 20.

Morris Levy was a prick, and I don't give him a pass just because he's dead now. Don't speak ill of the dead, I'm told. I call bullshit on that. If you're a scumbag in life, in my eyes you're still a scumbag after you die. But when I try to think objectively about Morris and consider all my experiences with him over the years, I find myself emotionally torn. I feel gratitude, yes. Appreciation, yes. Respect, sort of, in a distorted kind of way. Fear, *hell* yes. Hate, yes—in varying degrees and for various reasons. I guess I saw every side to of the man there was to see, at one time or another. Morris was perhaps the most dishonest, self-serving bully I've ever known, but he was a genius in his business. Ironically, he'd have been a success in that or any other business without being the vicious man he chose to be. One thing I can say in Morris's favor, however, is that he did keep his word to me one time: He promised he'd have "Peppermint Twist" out in two weeks, and he did it. And even though it was a single instance of integrity among so many displays of immorality, that single deed changed my life forever.

So I guess, in the end, we just don't do well when we try to judge others. I've had my weaknesses and foibles to overcome, just as Morris had—as does every human that has lived or will live on Earth. It's impossible for me to know how much of Morris resulted from his own life choices and how much was foisted on him by his environment and the luck of the draw. It can tire a person out, just thinking about those kinds of things. But I know this: Morris Levy had a profound impact on my life, and I can never forget him.

NINE

TAKING AMERICAN BANDSTAND BY STORM

The Pep audience on that night in September, 1961, was only maybe half the house, but we were rockin'. Looking at the crowd, I saw something that nearly took my breath away. I mean, I couldn't believe my eyes. Walking to a table were Dick Clark, Tony Orlando, Glen Campbell, Jo Ann Campbell (no relation), and another woman I didn't recognize. Tony called me over to their table after the set and introduced me to everyone—not that any but one of them needed any introduction at all. I knew who they were.

| Rock & Roll Royalty |

Dick Clark was, of course, a face and a name recognized by anyone in the music or television industries—and the public. His ABC network dance program *American Bandstand* was a star-maker show. Every teenager in America watched it, and the records and performers Dick showcased every week would inevitably be the records and the artists that the youngsters would thumbs-up. As famous as Dick was in 1961, it was nothing compared to the legendary status he'd reach in the decades to follow. His larger-than-life persona wouldn't be diminished even by a major stroke in 2004. Without regard to its effects on his speech and body, he'd stay in the public eye, especially as the host of Dick Clark's New Year's Rockin' Eve on ABC, right up to his death in 2012. Frankly, Dick Clark's career was just too amazing and too broad to cover here, nor do I need to do so. Suffice it to say he was influential, a genius, and America's oldest teenager. Most important, he was my dear friend.

Glen Campbell was a legend in the making. When I met him, he'd already done backup work with the famed Wrecking Crew, a group of backing musicians that played on records behind too many artists to name here. He'd go on to be one of the greatest country/pop crossover artists of all time as well as a major star of television and motion pictures. His passing in 2017 at age eighty-one years from complications of Alzheimer's disease was an unkind death, and too soon.

Jo Ann Campbell was on every Alan Freed show ever produced, or so it seemed. She was the original blonde bombshell, and she looked fantastic. A regular guest on American Bandstand, Jo Ann was a talented singer and actress—and our paths would cross again in 1962, when she co-starred with me in *Hey Let's Twist!*, my first feature motion picture. Jo Ann was making the late night talk show rounds at that time, appearing with Jack Paar, Johnny Carson, and Dick Cavett, and she would soon become a regular guest in 1965 on the TV dance show *Where The Action Is*, a Dick Clark production for ABC.

And, of course, there was Tony Orlando. Although meeting for the first time, Tony talked to me as if we were longtime friends. At age fifteen he'd organized the doo-wop group the Five Gents in 1959, and the demos he produced with them caught the attention of famed publisher and producer Don Kirshner. Now, in 1961, at the age of seventeen years, Tony had his first hit with "Ding Dong" on the Milo record label, and Kirshner hired him to write songs alongside Carole King, Neil Sedaka, Barry Mann, Cynthia Weil, Bobby Darin, and Connie Francis at Manhattan's legendary Brill Building at 1619 Broadway. When I met him, Tony had scored chart hits with "Bless You" and the Jerry Goffin/Carole King song "Halfway to Paradise," and there would be many more great records before the end of the decade. In the 1970s Tony would team with the backing group Dawn to record the hits "Candida," "Knock Three Times," "Tie a Yellow Ribbon Round the Old Oak Tree," and others. Tony's career would span a lifetime, and he's still hard at work today, reminding us of just how good *good* music was back then—and still is today. Tony was my dear friend then, and he remains so today.

The woman whom I hadn't recognized was Loretta, Jo Ann's secretary.

As I chatted with my new friends, I hoped the sound of my knees knocking together wasn't too great a distraction for anyone. I'd never met show biz royalty before, except for my girls the Shirelles; but now I'd rubbed shoulders with stardom personified. I seriously liked the feeling, and I knew I wanted in. I couldn't hog all this enjoyment for myself though; I called the rest of the band over to meet everyone.

Since it was already about midnight when we met, I figured my four new friends would leave after our chat. After all, these were busy, in-demand people. Surely they had better and more important things to do than stay and listen to Joey Dee and the Starliters for another three hours. Not so. They were there at three to close the joint. I guess they liked us.

I had no way of knowing that meeting these giants on this night was a portent of things to come, but I felt as though our paths would cross again. I was right. And I intersected again with one of them sooner than I expected.

| The Invitation |

The fame and notoriety we'd gained at the Pep and the airplay we were getting on radio stations—thanks to Morris and Red at Roulette—had given us a high profile. High enough, in fact, that in November, only two months after I met him at the Pep, we were accorded the ultimate compliment: Dick Clark invited us to appear on *American Bandstand*. It simply didn't get better than that, and the guys and I were beside ourselves with excitement.

Rogers Freeman, David Brigati, Willie Davis, Sam Taylor, Jr, Billy Callanan, and I prepared to travel to Philly. It was about a two-hour drive from our rendezvous point in Jersey to 4548 Market Street in West Philadelphia, where *American Bandstand* was broadcast from Studio B of the ABC affiliate station, WFIL. Like the other guys, I felt . . . well, I'm not sure what I felt. I was apprehensive, anxious, nervous, excited. Maybe a combination of all that and more. Anyway I could practically taste the adrenalin. Yes, we'd gotten a leg up on this day by meeting Dick Clark at the Pep, but that meeting couldn't put to rest all our anxieties and nerves as we faced our first national TV broadcast. Could we compete with the talent we'd share the stage with and with all the talent that had taken that stage for years? I mean, I'd watched my music heroes perform on *Bandstand*. And now we'd be on that same stage. My dream was coming true. If only we didn't screw up somehow and blow the opportunity!

| Taking It All In |

At the studio I quickly learned that Dick Clark was organized, meticulous, and attentive to every detail of the show. No part of production was unimportant to him. As staff unloaded our gear, Mr. Clark greeted us warmly at the door, inviting me to accompany him to his office, where the two of us sat and talked. I reminded him of our previous meeting at the Pep, which he remembered well. As it turned out, he'd begun dating Jo Ann Campbell's secretary, Loretta, shortly after that night, and she became his second wife.

Walking into Studio B, I felt something akin to the feeling of awe that would later strike me as I entered the Apollo Theater. This was the experience of experiences for me, and I cherished every second of it. I looked forward even to meeting the studio dancers, most of whom were show regulars and stars in their own right. I even knew the names of most of them. These kids had their own fan mail and even their own agents. Go figure. All of "teendom" watched age-peers dance live on TV, dreaming of dancing on that floor themselves. But it was an exclusive club. Seems no one had a chance to fulfill that dream unless (s)he attended a school in the Philly area.

We set up in Studio B, which seemed tiny to me. In fact it measured only 80 by 42 by 24 feet and appeared even smaller due to props, cameras, and risers used for the show. Never mind its size. Big, small, in between—didn't matter. The Pep was even smaller, and we did great things there.

With instruments set up the boys and I stirred aimlessly around the stage area, anticipating what would come next. Dick walked into the studio.

"You boys ready for this?" he asked, flashing that warm Dick Clark smile. I hoped my voice didn't quiver noticeably as I answered.

"Dick, we've been ready for this for a long time." Imagine me calling this man Dick instead of Mr. Clark. But he insisted on it. He was so down to earth.

"Good," he said. "It's all pretty simple. You'll be lip-syncing to your record, "Peppermint Twist." There'll be mikes in front of you, but they're not live. Just move your lips along with the words of the song. All right?"

"Sure, Dick," I said. "Think we got it."

"Now, when the show is finished," Dick continued, putting his hand on my shoulder, "I wonder if you'd be good enough to sit at the autograph table for a few minutes and sign for the kids on the show."

"It will be our pleasure, Dick," I said—but, as far as I was concerned, I'd have gladly swapped autographs with them. They were stars themselves.

The guys and I dressed and wished each other good luck with a *break a leg* as the show began. We heard the familiar Charles Albertine-penned theme, "Bandstand Boogie," recorded by Les Elgart. You know the tune—everybody does. And away we go!

We were scheduled to go on midway through the show. The wait seemed interminable. At last we were told to hit our marks for Dick's introduction. I wished the guys luck once more and told them to make believe we were performing live, 'cause that's what we did best. This was our chance of a lifetime, and we simply weren't gonna blow it.

| And That's a Wrap |

"We're on in five, four, three . . . And then, Dick's voice: "Ladies and gentlemen, please welcome Joey Dee and the Starliters!" I heard the intro to "Peppermint Twist," and I was at home, cool as the center seed of a cucumber. We lip-synced our hearts out as the kids danced, genuinely enjoying our record and our performance. When it was over, the applause was deafening and continued till the show cut to commercial. During the break Dick approached us, extending his hands toward us and clapping as he walked.

"Boys, that was fabulous!" he said. "Absolutely fabulous. And let me tell you something else. You'll be back here when that record hits number one."

Hmm. "Peppermint Twist" number one. Had a good ring to it. Morris had said the same thing to me, but this was *Dick Clark*. To my thinking, that closed the book on the issue. It *would be* number one. After all, this was the record guru. This was the guy who seemingly knew everything there was to know about rock & roll and records. As far as I know, he may well have had an actual crystal ball in his office. Whether that's true or not, one thing was certain: If Dick Clark played your song on *American Bandstand*, kids from everywhere would go out and buy it.

We hung around for the rest of the show, and I think every kid there asked for and got our autographs. It was an experience you dream about. When the show was over, Dick said farewell to the studio and television audiences with his trademark salute, and then he came over to thank us. We responded in kind, made sure our instruments had been loaded into the van, and hit the road for home. We were like giddy little school boys all the way back to Jersey. We sensed that the legend had begun, and we were feeling pretty damn cocky.

Hey, we were from Jersey. You shouldn't expect otherwise.

| Drums Along the Highway |

"Peppermint Twist" hit number one in Feb 1962 and, true to his word, Dick Clark invited us back to *Bandstand* in March. Rogers, David, Willie, Sam, Billy, and I prepared for the greatest return gig of our lives.

We loaded the gear into our NEW van. It was a sweetheart. The Lowery organ, Leslie speaker, guitar, and amplifier were loaded into the van with us, but the drums simply wouldn't fit in. No problem. We strapped them snugly onto the roof of the van. Done and done. No sweat.

We pointed the van toward Philly and hunkered down for the trip. It would be a nice, tight, cozy two-hour drive. Despite the cramped quarters, we were enjoying the ride. With this bunch of guys there was never a dull moment, even when conversation was the only thing going on. As we talked and laughed down the Jersey Turnpike, a car driving alongside us caught our attention. Well, it wasn't the car so much as the people inside it that we noticed. They were waving their arms and pointing. Maybe we thought it was cool that someone recognized us, even in the van. I don't know. But we just waved back and smiled. Only moments later people in another car caught our eye, and for the same reason. These guys were yelling something, waving even more frantically and pointing back down the highway we'd just traveled. Now we were curious. We pulled to the side of the road, got out, and looked behind us to see Willie's drums strewn along the highway. Not a happy sight. I guess the kit wasn't as tight and snug up there as we'd thought. We walked the distance back, gathered up the mischievous instruments, and secured them once again to the roof. You can bet they got strapped down good and proper this time. Going nowhere.

| Winners, Losers, and Face-Plants |

About halfway to Philly and despite the stimulating conversation we were enjoying, I felt a need for a little something extra. If you haven't learned it already, you will know it by the end of your read: I've always been prone to instigation. I'm not sure that inciting others to mischief and trouble is a spiritual gift, but if it is, I've got it.

"I bet Billy can outrun Sam," I said.

Everyone became quiet. I mean, this was a random, out-of-the-blue comment that both confused and intrigued.

"Say what!?" Sam said.

"I bet Billy can outrun you."

"Yo mama," Sam said. "No way."

"Let's just see about that," I said. "Here's what we'll do. You guys get out, and I'll drive up the road about a hundred yards," I continued. "You guys race, and the van's the finish line."

There seemed to be some interest, so I pulled to the side of the road to let Sam and Billy out of the van. To my surprise David wanted a piece of the action, so he climbed out too.

"I don't wanna tell y'all this," Willie said smugly, "but I can beat all y'all."

That did it. The gauntlet was down. Everyone except Rogers and me got out of the van and prepared for the race. But David had a warning for me.

"Joey, you better not leave us, dammit," he said. "I know you. Don't you even *think* about driving off and leaving us here."

He did know me. Under other circumstances I might have done that very thing. But we were on our way to do *American Bandstand*. There would be no skulduggery from me today—well, not such serious skulduggery anyway.

Now, we had all bought new suits for this gig. Mustard-brown suits they were, with our trademark high-water pant legs that hovered two inches above the shoes to let the audience catch our footwork. And we were wearing said suits and shoes, having changed into them before leaving. Yep, we were properly costumed for a footrace on dirt and gravel, no doubt about that.

"Okay, boys," I said. "I'm gonna drive up the road and stop. When you see my brake lights flash, you start."

I drove, I stopped, I flashed the brake lights. Aaaaand, they're off!

David and Sam took the early lead, with Sam nudging ahead by a whisker. Coming up from behind and closing fast were Bill and Willy. Billy was stretching it out now, coming up fast on David and Sam. Willy was trailing the field, but not by much, and David, Sam, and Billy jockeyed for the front spot. There was a lot of heavy panting and wind-sucking going on now, but the finish line was just ahead. It was anybody's race. And then . . . boom! Willy shifted gears and passed the others like they were waiting at a bus stop. He was the wind. Left 'em in the dust, crossed the finish line, and waited casually for the rest to come home.

In his final effort to win, Sam ran so fast that his legs came right out from under him. He face-planted and skidded about ten feet in the hard dirt and gravel of the roadside. He didn't stay down, but he tore the sleeve on his new mustard-brown suit and gashed his arm, making a nice splotch of blood to accent the lovely color of his suit. He doggedly continued to the finish line, where he was greeted, as the other losers had been, by a pompous Willie.

"I said I could beat all y'all," was the victory cry of Willie the winner.

Into the van they all climbed, and away we went, bloodied but unbowed.

I've often wondered what people in passing cars thought as they saw the boys racing toward *something*, wearing mustard-brown suits, ties, and oxford shoes. If any of them recognized us as Joey Dee and the Starliters and knew anything about us, they weren't a bit surprised by what they saw. If they didn't know us, they probably put the pedal to the metal.

| Lights! Camera! Action! |

At the studio we were treated to the same courtesy and assistance we'd enjoyed during our first gig. As we prepared for the moment, Dick leaned in close to explain that we were about to become the first band in the history of *American*

Bandstand to perform live coast to coast. The first live performance by a band on *American Bandstand*, and Dick Clark, The Man Himself, had granted us the honor. It made perfect sense to me, though, because live performance was what we did. We were the right band for this.

And now we were set to play "Peppermint Twist," just as Dick had promised we would do. But first, another surprise. After we hit our spots and were introduced, Dick came out and presented us with a gold record from Roulette Records, representing a million record sales. What an honor to receive such recognition at the hands of Dick Clark! But I later learned something about the award that surprised me. Not to sound unappreciative, but the commemorative record I received wasn't solid gold but only plated. Naive? Yes, I was. And I should have known it wouldn't be gold, even without being told. Not from Morris Levy. That kind of authenticity just wasn't in his nature.

With the business out of the way, we played. Cameramen snaked between and around us to get all the right angles. Rogers, David, Willie, Sam, Billy, and I were now part of rock & roll history—and we knew it.

| Through the Years with Dick Clark |

I appeared on *American Bandstand* many times through the sixties and into the seventies. In 1971 I appeared on Dick's salute to rock & roll of the fifties and sixties. Chuck Berry also appeared on that program, and he was interested in my opinion of his new shirt. "You like my new shirt, Joey?" he asked.

I didn't. It was awful. But it wasn't a good time for him to get upset, right before performing. So I said, "Uh, yeah, Chuck. It's nice. It's real nice."

"Thanks, man," he said. "I just went out and bought it a few minutes ago. K-Mart. Five bucks. You believe that?"

I believed that.

After my performances on *American Bandstand* and his other productions, Dick and I remained friends throughout his life and even worked together on community projects such as the *Starlight Starbright Foundation for the Love of Rock & Roll*, in 1987. Under the auspices of the American Music Foundation, *Starlight Starbright* would create a sanctuary for down-on-their-luck singers and musicians, much as the Actors Home in Los Angeles served actors. Dick, Dr. Allen and Judith Haimes, my wife Lois Lee, and I envisioned this charitable project and worked hard to raise money for it. It breaks my heart to say we weren't able to acquire the necessary funding, and our dream never materialized. Even with the help of Gloria Pennington, who was selected by Dick to serve as our CEO, things just didn't come together as I thought they would. I'd imagined multitudes of movers and shakers from the entertainment and record industries roaring in with huge donations to make this noble dream a reality. It never happened.

I enjoyed interviews with Dick on several occasions through the years, including one for the ABC Dick Clark TV production of *The Rock & Roll Years* in 1973. Dick was always kind and thoughtful in his interviews. He never let the audience forget that Joey Dee and the Starliters helped shape rock & roll—from the ground up.

Thanks, Dick. For everything.

TEN

STAR TREATMENT
AT THE COPA

I wish I'd always been the man I should have been for my wife Joanie, but, sadly, my committed, loving side showed up only sporadically in those younger times. But as thoughtlessly and unkindly as I too often treated her, once in a while I got it right. On one special night in 1962, cosmic forces were resting peacefully, all the stars aligned, and I treated Joanie for one evening the way she deserved to be treated always.

| Absolutely No Reservations |

"Get your mother to watch the boys," I told Joanie. "We're going out."

"Going out?" Joanie asked. "Going out to do what?"

"I was thinking about taking in Bobby Darin's show at the Copa."

"What?! The Copa?!" She was surprised, to say the least. "We'll never get in, unless . . . do you have tickets and reservations? We can't get in otherwise."

"Don't worry about it. Got it covered," I said.

I didn't have it covered. Not really. I mean, I had no tickets, no reservations. But I had something much better than either of those things. I was Joey Dee. Being as full of myself back then as a person can be and not explode, I figured that would be enough to get us in.

With the boys taken care of and the two of us dressed to the nines, Joanie and I climbed into the new Caddy convertible and pointed it down the highway. A short hour later we arrived in the City to find the same electricity the Big Apple always afforded—but on a night like tonight, with my best girl on my arm and the world at our feet, the place was nothing short of magical. We parked in a nearby garage and walked the short distance to the club.

Joanie was still unsettled. "What if we can't get in, Joey? The shows *must* be sold out," Joanie said. "What then?"

"Now, don't worry, hon," I said. "Just watch me."

There was, of course, a line leading to the club's doors, and we slid into it as though we were just any old whoevers. But I wasn't just any old whoever, and it took only seconds for someone to recognize me. Then the buzz started. It didn't take long for the grapevine to notify Jules Podell, the club's owner and manager, that Joey Dee was standing in line at his club. *Standing in line* at his club. Joey Dee!

Now, Jules Podell was no lightweight club manager. Although the Copacabana had been opened in 1940 by Monte Proser, Jules was soon put in place by Proser's partner, Mob boss Frank Costello. By 1950 Proser was out altogether and Podell was completely in charge of the club. He would continue to run the Copa until his death in 1973.

And now here was Jules Podell, the man himself, blowing through the Copa's front doors like a gale-force wind. His face was glowing like he'd just seen Betty Grable's knees. Embracing me like family, Jules spoke.

"Joey! Whaddaya doin' out here in this line?" he gushed. "We've been expecting you inside." Smiling at the crowd and raising my arm as if in triumph, he said, "Folks, this is Joey Dee and his wife Joanie. Joey Dee!" As the crowd erupted into loud applause and with Jules Podell at our side, Joanie and I jumped the entire line and slipped royally into the club.

Once inside the club Jules instructed two waiters to grab a table and two chairs and place them right on the stage. For a moment I wondered if I'd have to sing for my supper, but no. Jules was just making sure I got star treatment while I was in his club. The man accompanied us to our table, pulled the chair out for Joanie, and wished us a lovely evening, adding that we had only to call on him if we needed anything. Anything at all.

| The Show |

A show at the Copa in those days was a grand production. Every show featured a line of dancing girls to start things off. The Copacabana Girls had pink hair, blackened eyelashes that nearly hit the floor, red lips that seemed to glow in the dark, elaborate sequined costumes, mink panties, and fruit-salad turbans. They were internationally famous for being among the most beautiful women in the world, but I took slight exception to that claim. They were pretty. Okay. The fabulous females that would work in my Starliter a couple of years later were much more beautiful. Of course, in a club like the Copa, certainly there were casting requirements for the dancers that went beyond a pretty face. Now that I think of it, I carefully considered all those other qualities myself when I hired my girls.

The show usually featured an opening comedian who took the stage after the girls finished shaking their tail feathers. I don't remember who performed on this particular night, but I remember he wasn't funny. I mean, yeah, he got some laughs, but not from me. I didn't give it up that easy.

And then it was time for the headliner. The orchestra crescendoed to a magnificent fanfare to bring out the man himself. Singing his way onto the stage, Bobby Darin was a sentence with no commas. Star quality and confidence radiated from him so brightly you almost had to look away. Here was a man who knew how to sing a song—no, who knew how to *perform* a song—and he knew where he was and what he was doing every single second he was on stage. And talk about looks! I always prided myself on how classy the Starliters and I looked, and we did—but this guy, now. *This* guy was the very personification of class, carrying himself like rhythmic royalty and dressed to the floor in tuxedo, bow tie, tastefully bejeweled fingers and shirt cuffs, and shoes that splashed the stage lights like a happy toddler's feet in a puddle.

Although Bobby Darin sang every genre of music imaginable, he was on record for being less a fan of rock & roll than of standards, jazz, and pop. In fact, he once responded to a friendly challenge by saying he could make a hit rock & roll record any time he wanted. It wasn't a hollow brag. Perhaps you remember "Queen of the Hop" and "Splish Splash." Enough said.

| THE PERFECT FINISH TO A PERFECT NIGHT |

On this special evening Bobby gave us about ninety minutes of heaven. Somewhere toward the end of his performance, he was kind enough to recognize me from the stage. Happily surprised, I stood and acknowledged his kindness and the audience's applause. In that moment I felt a different kind of pride in myself than I'd ever felt before. More than that, I felt Joanie's pride in me, and *that* was among the best feelings I've ever experienced in this life.

After the show ended and we prepared to leave, I summoned the waiter to ask for the check. I was surprised by what he said to me.

"Mr. Dee," the waiter began, "Mr. Podell wishes you to know that tonight's dining and entertainment are on him, and he thanks you and your lovely wife for being at his club tonight."

After the waiter helped Joanie from her chair, I gratefully tipped him fifty bucks. As we began to leave, Jules popped seemingly from out of nowhere to embrace me like family and personally wish us a good night. I was just this side of flabbergasted, and it was the crowning moment of a night never to be forgotten. Joanie and I had experienced star treatment at its finest—a table where there wasn't supposed to be a table, no check where there should have been a check, and a personal welcome and farewell from the owner who seldom showed himself. That's as good as it gets.

Now, there's a sad—but instructive—postscript to this story.

| It Comes, It Goes |

I attended another show at the Copacabana about two years later. This time a different Joey Dee sat at a table, waiting to enjoy a performance by the great stand-up comedian and King of the One-liners, Henny Youngman. This Joey Dee had no records currently on the charts and somewhat less celebrity than the Joey Dee of two years previous. This time I sported some bimbo on my arm instead of my lovely wife. This time I had waited in line to get into the club, even after asking a waiter to please inform Mr. Podell that Joey Dee was there and would like to see him. "Mr. Podell is otherwise engaged and regrets that he cannot see you right now," was the response I got to my request. So, we waited in line with the herds, hoping to make it into the club.

We made it in, but on this night there were no special table and chairs. The rat table at which we were seated tonight stood directly behind a large support post that obstructed our view of the stage. Fortunately, Mr. Youngman's comedy was spoken—with short bursts of "Smoke Gets In Your Eyes" on his violin between jokes—and he was hilarious, so we had a few laughs even as we stared at the damn pole. But even before Henny had taken his final bow, the waiter came to our table and presented the check. This was the final insult of the evening. It was now clear to me that I was no longer eligible for star treatment at the Copa. Wait in line, shitty table, check before the end of the show, not so much as a *kiss my foot* or *have an apple* from Jules Podell. What a difference a couple of years can make.

C'est la vie, my friend. C'est la vie.

ELEVEN

MEET THE BEATLES: TOURING EUROPE

By 1963 our fame and recognition reached international proportions. Europe was now beckoning with offers of obscene amounts of money for appearances in ten countries. I signed to do a two-legged tour of Europe—three months on, six months off, and another three months on, all in 1963. Our dates included both civilian and military gigs.

| BON VOYAGE |

In January my loved ones came out to wish us bon voyage as we boarded the Queen Mary at a pier on New York's West Side. I was accompanied by my wife Joan, my manager Don Davis and his wife Kay, and the Starliters: David Brigati and Larry Vernieri on vocals, Billy Callanan on organ, Sam Taylor, Jr. on guitar, and Ronnie Davis on drums. Ronnie often substituted for Ed Shaughnessy, the regular drummer for the Johnny Carson Tonight Show Orchestra conducted by Doc Severinsen. At first Joanie didn't want to come along. The boys were only two years and three years old, and she was reluctant to leave them for so long a time. But her sister Ida, who had a two-year-old daughter herself, offered to watch the boys and promised that they would be in good hands. With that settled Joanie agreed to come along with me. Also with us were Billy's new bride Jan and Gloria Wall, a secretary I'd hired for my newly opened office in the City. Gloria would marry an American GI in Germany and remain there.

I waved farewell to Mom, my sons Joey and Nicky, many of my siblings, and a plethora of friends as the Queen pushed back and headed out to sea. Joey Dee and the Starliters were headed for new adventures in the Old World.

The Queen's interior of rich, dark, natural-wood paneling and brass polished to within an inch of its life was beautiful, but we weren't always comfortable. See, crossing the North Atlantic by ship was at times anything but calm, and this particular crossing was nearly one continuous storm. At times we encountered swells that rose to twenty feet. These watery Everests weren't friendly at all, and the drops could put your stomach right into your throat. Dinner seating often found few hungry passengers; even David, Larry, and Ronnie skipped meals, having pretty much bought the farm. Their barfing gave new meaning to the word *projectile*, and I'm pretty sure that in their faces I saw every shade of green there is. I didn't get rattled by the rough seas, and I laughed as I told my band that my father was partners with Columbus. If you're a fan of the Marx Brothers, you'll appreciate that Chico line. But when the guys missed meals, they didn't miss much. The ship's bill of fare, to be blunt, sucked. The English weren't known for their palates or their plates, and what we were served paled in comparison to the great American food we knew. "Turtle soup is what we were mostly served," Billy's bride Jan complained, and more of it than she could take.

We made it to dry land at last, and the fun started—as soon as my Starliters found their feet and their stomachs.

| Military Maneuvers in Germany |

Throughout the tour I got to see many US military installations, mostly in Germany. Playing at one such base, we split up and stayed at the homes of some of the GIs. David and I stayed with the family of a Sergeant from Philly. This good family welcomed us warmly and were proud to have us stay with them, just as we were proud of their service to our country. Larry stayed at the home of another sergeant, but this didn't turn out as it should have. We soon learned that Larry was banging the poor guy's wife. I was afraid Larry would be killed, but the offended sergeant just came over to the home where we were staying and cried like a baby. It was heartbreaking, to say the least. I was pretty bad back then, that's for sure; but Vernieri had crossed a line even I wouldn't step over. Next day we all moved off the base and into a hotel. I'm pretty sure that at least one sergeant in the US Army completely lost his taste for rock & roll.

Before each paid gig, we played an unpaid performance for members of a screening board that consisted of clergy and other relevant military personnel, ostensibly to make sure we put on a family-appropriate show. These screenings were in the contract, so we complied. But I also noticed that we were playing to around seven hundred people at each of these shows, and that people were being charged ten bucks a head for admission. That was NOT in the contract, and it pissed me off. I approached my manager Don Davis about it.

"Joey, we're here already," Don said. "Just go ahead and play the shows."

"That's not the tack I wanna take, Don," I answered. "Something's just not right here. Some kind of scam or conspiracy or something. I don't know, but I don't like it. Hell, man," I continued, "they're pulling down around seven grand for every one of these damn shows, and I'm not seeing a penny of it."

"I don't know what to tell you, Joey," Don said.

"Well, I won't do anything now," I said, "but when I get home somebody's gonna hear about it. I mean, we're talking nearly fifty grand someone's getting for these shows without paying me a dime," I continued. "That's not right."

True to my word, I didn't cause trouble there. No matter what was going on behind the scenes, we were playing for our troops and their families, and I was good with that. But later at home I lodged a complaint with the American Federation of Musicians. I lost the argument—and lots of money. Oh well.

| THE World-Famous Star-Club |

The key date of the tour was the Star-Club in Hamburg, Germany. Joanie, Don, and Kay took a later train to Hamburg to meet up with the rest of us who were there already. On that trip Joanie quickly learned it was a good thing that she'd brought along her mink coat, because she was cold all over and everywhere. The three of them weren't just cold but hungry too when they boarded the train, but the dining car wasn't near, so they headed for their compartment. There they met two Germans. One was slight and bald, while the other was a handsome ex-pug of larger stature, with hands the size of Vermont. Fortunately, the two had a large basket filled with wine, sausages, and fruit—and Joanie, Don, and Kay weren't too proud to accept an offer to share. Now, I've no idea how such a subject came up in their conversation, but the big German shared that he'd killed his wife and the man he'd found in bed with her. With no way of knowing whether this was a joke, some kind of fantastic plea for attention, or the true confession of a mass murderer, Joanie never closed her eyes, all the way to Hamburg.

In popularity the Star-Club was to Hamburg what the Pep was to New York. From 1962 to 1969, this club featured top name entertainers such as Ray Charles, Brenda Lee, Chubby Checker, Fats Domino, Gene Vincent, Bill Haley, Little Richard, Tony Sheridan, Tommy Roe, and the like. Being a port city and in many ways similar to New York, there were some pretty tough areas in Hamburg. In fact, the Star-Club was located smack in the heart of the city's red-light district. Our walk to the hotel after shows took us along Herbert Strasse, where hookers brazenly displayed their wares from storefronts and apartment windows along the street. There were old ones, young ones, skinny ones, fat ones. Some were pretty, most were . . . not. I usually kept my eyes on the ground when we walked that sex gauntlet, and I never availed myself of the offers that were shouted out to us. Now, don't misunderstand; I hadn't suddenly become a puritan. Far from it, sad to say. The truth is, I never paid for it. I wasn't about to pay for that questionable stuff when so many fans were willing to donate much higher quality stuff.

The Star-Club also showcased up-and-coming British acts, of which there was a never-ending supply in 1963. Sometimes the club churned through maybe a half-dozen in a night, future greats such as Gerry and the Pacemakers, Billy J. Kramer, the Searchers, the Dakotas, and the Undertakers. Such groups opened for us each night, playing for peanuts—about a hundred marks, or twenty-five bucks, per week. Clearly, they were playing for the exposure.

These Brits played good music and worked their asses off, but they spent nearly as much time drinking as playing and were usually pissed by the time they finished for the night. This was where manager Horst Fascher sometimes figured into the game. See, Horst was an ex-pug who had to keep order in the club as these performers—and patrons—would get pretty belligerent when they were in their cups. Horst had a special punch that he landed just below the troublemaker's heart, dropping him where he stood. Big man or little, the punch would put anyone down. I saw Horst do this several times every night. And I found it a bit funny when the tough ex-pug would land the punch and then calmly say to the collapsing drunk, "I told you not to get pissed." Horst reminded me of Tommy "One Punch" Carcone, my ex-pug bouncer friend at the Pep. Talk about a match-up! I'd have paid to see those two gladiators go at it in the ring.

Among the up-and-coming English bands that played the Star-Club was a little four-man band called the Beatles. The band didn't play the club during the week I was there, but word of mouth made it clear that this Liverpool band stood out from all the other British groups. Everybody said the same thing: "Man, you gotta see the Beatles!" Beatles, Beatles, Beatles. That's all we heard. Even though I didn't get to see them play, I began to feel as though I knew the Lads, and the day was coming when I would.

Knowing the superstars who'd appeared there, playing the Star-Club was a dream come true for me. To top it off we were a huge success there and agreed to another week-long gig when we returned to Europe in the fall.

| Ossi and Fats |

Elsewhere in Germany we played very successful gigs in Wiesbaden and Frankfurt and recorded the songs "No No" and "Immer Wieder." We were a national favorite, so the Germans were eager to record us. Two of our records, "Peppermint Twist" and "Ya Ya" had hit number one on the charts there. Radio Luxembourg presented us its prestigious Bronze Lion Award for "Peppermint Twist," and the second tune was especially popular because *Ya Ya* sounded like *ja ja*, which is German for *yes yes*.

In Frankfurt I met a club owner named Oswald "Ossi" Buettner, a famous heavyweight German boxer. I don't know why I crossed paths so often with boxers and ex-boxers, but so it seemed to be. This man loved American boxers and American music, and he drove me around in a '55 Thunderbird, probably the bitchinest American car ever—Cadillacs excepted, of course. The two of us visited a club where a group called Fats and His Cats was performing. This rotund gentleman sat at the piano and performed flawlessly like Fats Domino, the great American pianist/singer/songwriter. He sang Domino's songs in English, so when we met him after the show, I was surprised that he didn't know what the hell I was saying to him. The man didn't know a word of English but learned the words to all the songs phonetically. Coincidentally, that's exactly how I learned to sing the German "Immer Wieder." As for conversation with Fats, my good friend Ossi got me through it. And that turned out to be a very good meeting, because Fats and His Cats ended up backing me up on the recording of "Immer Wieder."

| Paris Takes a Toll |

In Paris we played the world-famous Olympia Hall. The venue seated nearly three thousand and had been around since 1888. I shared the bill with Cliff Richard and the Shadows, an incredibly popular group in the UK. Today, Cliff Richard owns the third-leading sales history of records in the UK, bested only by the Beatles and Elvis Presley. On its own the Shadows was the first backing band to emerge to stardom, producing hits with the now-classic instrumentation of lead, rhythm, and bass guitars, and drums. And the Shadows sold millions of records.

Paris was a great experience. I mean, it had the Eiffel Tower, the Left Bank, Folies Bergère, and French women—whom I found to be a bit hirsute, but . . . ooo-la-la, if you get my drift.

But the glories of Paris couldn't compensate for the calamity of the Callanans' cab ride on the way to our hotel. See, Billy and his new bride Jan were in one of the cabs that were to travel in convoy to the Hotel de Paris. This way we'd all end up there at the same time. That was the plan anyway. But the Callanans' driver had other plans. According to Jan, this lady cabbie with some unidentifiable foreign accent—not French—saw her and Billy as easy young marks, and the "hi-jacking" began. She brazenly drove them to every tourist site she could think of in two hours, with Jan protesting all the while that they needed to go elsewhere. The cabbie, of course, claimed to speak no English and pretended that she thought her fares wanted to see another attraction and then another. When it became clear to Jan that she couldn't prevail against this abductor, she searched for and found a French gendarme (policeman) at a street corner and shouted *help!* loudly enough to get his attention. Now, the officer didn't speak fluent English, but the Callanans were able to make a case for getting them to the American Consulate where everything was sorted out. The cabbie's plan, of course, had been to run up a fare of a couple hundred bucks (a LOT of money in '63) and then take Jan and Billy to the police to make them cough it up. Her plan was scuttled, and our friends made it at last to the Hotel de Paris, more than a little shaken by the ordeal.

Sadly, the hotel itself was another horror story—well, unless you liked roaches, which this hotel had, wall to wall. The quality of the hotel, the terror of the cab ride, and a serious dose of homesickness were just all Jan could take. She asked to go home. At the same time, Joanie learned during her daily phone call home that Nicky and Joey had contracted chicken pox. She decided to join Jan and return home to be with them.

A week later, Billy decided that he too had better return home and caught a flight from Germany.

Well, hell. This put me in a bind. I was smack in the middle of a tour, without a keyboard player.

"Billy's gone home, and I need an organ player," I said to Don. Why don't you give Sally a call at the Choo Choo and see if we can get that Felix kid. He's good enough. I can plug him in, and I'm sure he'll fit. Find him," I said, "and see if you can fly him here to join us."

Don reached Sal, and Sal connected him with Felix. And so it was that Felix Cavaliere, soon-to-be vocalist and organist for the Hall of Fame band the Rascals, flew out from Jersey to finish the tour with us. More on that later.

| Wrapping It Up |

Having played to sold-out audiences and standing ovations from a quarter-million fans in Germany, Austria, France, Holland, Finland, Sweden, and Denmark, we made our way back to the States. Interestingly, we never worked

Belgium, where we'd scored six number-one records in a row. Who the hell was in charge of the bookings here? Just wondering.

Nor did we play Sicily, the homeland of my mother. Mom and my Uncle Joe had decades earlier boarded a ship and traveled steerage class to America, the land of their dreams and opportunity. Dad never returned to his homeland, but I'm happy to say Mom did. While we were touring, I was grateful to have sufficient money to bring her over to visit her home of Ribera, a commune in the Sicilian province of Agrigento, where she got to visit cousins and distant relatives and once again enjoy the beautiful land she had called home. From then until she passed, my sainted mother never stopped talking about that trip, and it makes my heart glad to have been able to make it possible for her.

| Crossing the Pond Again: Welcome Back to the Star-Club |

In October we boarded the SS France to cross the pond again. This time I brought along Larry for vocals, Felix on organ, Vinnie Corrao on guitar, and Willie on drums, To manage everything and keep order, I brought along my brother Al and Fat Frankie Scinlaro, whom I usually called simply "Fat." Oh, and I brought along a couple of cute chicks to back up Larry and me. One was a Peppermint Lounge dancer named Kitty Guillepot, and the other was Elaine Mays, a cousin of Ronettes Ronnie Bennett Spector and Estelle Bennett.

On this voyage we enjoyed French cuisine morning, noon, and night, always with bottles of red and white wine on the table. This ship's bill of fare was a far cry from the gastronomical slop we endured aboard the Queen Mary. This time we crossed the Atlantic in just a little more than four days—a record at the time, I was told. I wished the Queen Mary trip had been the record-setter, and the SS France journey had taken longer. My stomach and taste buds wholeheartedly agreed.

We docked in France at Cherbourg, boarded a boat train, and traveled north to Sweden. From there we took a train to Hamburg, Germany. We were met at the Star-Club by my old pal Horst, with whom I'd become pals during our first tour. I also met a sound engineer named Adrian Barber and guitarist Chris Huston of the Undertakers. Fortuitous meetings, to be sure. I would later bring super-soundman Adrian to my Starliter in 1964 to design and manage sound for me there, and Chris would replace Jimi Hendrix as a Starliter in 1966.

At the end of the Star-Club gig, I went into the office to be paid. The manager of the club was Manfred Weisleder, a blonde, blue-eyed man standing about six feet tall who looked like he'd been put together by Hollywood to be the perfect Aryan type. My friend Horst informed me that Manfred had been an officer in the

German army during World War II. On a wall in his office hung a beautiful oil painting depicting the night life around the Star-Club. I admired the work so much that Manfred took it down, handed it to me, and said, "Please. It is a gift to you for the fabulous job you did." The man spoke better English than I did. One of the few such treasures I've kept through the years, the painting still hangs on the wall in my office, beside my "Peppermint Twist" gold record. Thank you, Manfred.

| Meet The Beatles |

Included in that tour was a gig at the Kungliga Tennishallen (Royal Tennis Hall) in Stockholm, Sweden. Seating five thousand, this venue has hosted many great events since it opened in 1943. In 1962 it was the site of the heavyweight boxing title match between Ingemar Johansson and Wim Snoek. Since 1969 the Stockholm Open tennis tournament has been played there, as well as several Davis Cup matches. In the years following our appearance, the Rolling Stones, David Bowie, Louie Armstrong, and other superstars have played to SRO crowds there. I didn't know it yet, but opening for us at this gig would be that little four-man Liverpudlian band I'd been wanting to see and meet ever since I'd played the Star-Club a few months earlier.

Arriving in Stockholm, we were greeted by hundreds of shrieking Swedish schoolgirls bearing flowers. Talk about a Swedish smorgasbord! Of course, these beauties were nearly one hundred percent blonde and blue-eyed, and I've always been a sucker for blondes. That's what initially attracted me to my beautiful wife Joan who, by the way, was much prettier than any of the women there that day. You'd think that having such a beautiful and loving wife would have been enough for me, but I was always such a glutton for sex and found it very difficult to define the limits of my appetite for it. I eventually did, but it took years too long.

We hadn't yet been told who our opening act would be. When we arrived at the Kungliga Tennishallen, I saw on the marquee "Joey Dee and the Starliters," "The Beatles," and "Jerry Williams." I thought to myself, *I'll finally get to meet those damn Beatles*. The boys had scored a hit record in Europe with "Please Please Me," but they hadn't yet crossed the pond to invade the colonies.

On October 26 I met John Lennon, Paul McCartney, George Harrison, and Ringo Starr in our dressing room. They were regular guys, and I liked them right away. Young and eager, some would say they had success written all over them. They were polite, deferential, and indeed pleased to be opening for us.

The Beatles took the stage after Williams. When they were announced, the house exploded—or it sounded like it had. Pandemonium, that's what it was.

There were John and his Rickenbacker guitar, Paul and his Höfner violin bass, George and his Gretsch six-string, Ringo and his newly acquired Ludwig drums—and all four of them sporting soup-bowl haircuts, collarless suits, and pointy-toed shoe-boots, all of which would change the face of men's fashion. The noise of the crowd hit a pitch I'd never heard before, and it never let up while the Beatles were on stage. People in this audience had obviously been exposed to the Fab Four, and they loved what they saw and heard—not that they were able to hear much over the screaming. I don't think any panties or room keys were tossed onto the stage, but more than a few young ladies swooned here, fainted there, or otherwise hit the deck. Seeing and hearing the Beatles perform and the crowd's response to them and their music, I knew I was experiencing something special. Although I questioned how they'd fare in the States, it was clear that we'd all hear more from these boys. And now here comes one of the most obvious statements you'll ever read: The Beatles turned out to be something not only special but phenomenal and legendary, taking the global stage and changing music forever—despite my skepticism.

The band was a difficult act to follow, but follow it we did. We pulled out all the stops, using our extensive experience at the Peppermint Lounge and on the road to crush the stage. The crowd loved us.

After the show I invited Lennon, McCartney, Harrison, and Starr to a smorgasbord—on me. The damn thing cost about eight hundred bucks, but what a memory it made for us all. In addition to wonderful food, there was what you might call *heavy imbibing*. It wasn't long before Paul and Kitty began to hit it off, and Ringo and Elaine also got quite cozy. Faster than you could say *bring the car around*, the four of them had split.

I enjoyed talking with John and George. We were comfortable around each other from the start. John and Larry got on especially well. Both drawn to the devil weed, at some point the two of them stepped away for a breath of fresh air. I guess in Liverpool that's how one says *let's go blow some weed, man*. Whether that's true of the Liverpudlian vernacular or not, it's what John and Larry did. Drugs not being my bag, I stayed and talked with George. He mentioned that the Beatles had released a record in the States.

"So, mate, whatcha think of our chances in the colonies?" he asked.

I was actually a bit surprised by the question. "What makes you think you have a chance in the States?" I asked. Clearly, I'd somehow forgotten the crowd response I'd witnessed in the Kungliga Tennishallen.

"Well, the crowds here seem to like us. I figure it the same for the yanks."

"Well, George, here's the way I see it," I said. "You fellas are good, no doubt.

You're gonna get better, no doubt. But all you played tonight was "Please Please Me" and a bunch of covers. Everly Brothers, Little Richard, Buddy Holly—you know, American artists. Over there we've got the real deals. So," I answered, "I think your chances in the States are slim to none."

As I was spitting out the final syllables of perhaps the worst prophecy ever uttered by man or angel, Larry and John returned to join us. Larry heard enough of what I'd said. "Joey, what are you talking about?" he said. "These boys are gonna be big. Huge. *Everywhere.*"

How I missed this one, I'll never know; but in the little game of *Guess How the Beatles Will Do in the USA* that Larry and I played that night, the score is Vernieri one, Dee zero.

Knowing we had a hard schedule ahead of us, my brother Al chased everyone out of my suite—but not before George promised me that he and the guys would visit the Peppermint Lounge when they came to the States. True to his word the Beatles showed up there one night a short time later, along with Murray "the K" Kaufman, who called himself the "Fifth Beatle." I like to think they came to the Pep to repay the hospitality I'd shown them in Sweden. Sadly, I was on tour when the lads visited, and, as it turned out, I never saw John or George again, nor has my path crossed Sir Paul's or Ringo's since Stockholm. Happily, Kitty and Elaine were able to meet with them at the Pep. I suppose that was good news for Paul and Ringo, but you'd have to ask them. Based on my own performance—and encores—with Elaine at the Henry Hudson Hotel, I'd say Ringo enjoyed a couple of nice drumrolls, rimshots, and paradiddles on his drums that night.

It's surreal to think back on that time with John, Paul, George, and Ringo, when none of us could possibly know the incredible events that would play out from there. To this day I consider it a unique honor to have had the Beatles open for Joey Dee and the Starliters and to have made their acquaintance.

| Firing Squad at the Ready |

The trip to and from our gig in Berlin was nothing short of a Hollywood script—an Oscar-winning Hollywood script.

We were to play in Berlin, which had divided into Soviet and Democratic sectors about two years earlier. To reach Berlin we had to travel through Russian-controlled East Germany. All along the Autobahn (freeway) after we left West Germany, we saw machine gun turrets manned by Russian and East German troops. Our bus was stopped at numerous roadblocks. Each time, our German agent had to explain to heavily armed soldiers who we were, showing them contracts and passports as evidence. But none of that seemed to matter to the guards. They still made us wait for hours, claiming that they couldn't allow us to proceed without approval from their superiors. Yeah, right. After they'd busted our balls enough to suit themselves, they raised the gate arm and laughed as we drove through. Thanks to their fun and games, we barely made the gig on time.

Commie pricks.

Despite the delays, we did make Berlin on time and played a great show. Afterward we had some free time on our hands. Being an extreme history buff since I was a kid, I *had* to visit "Checkpoint Charlie," a place I'd read about and seen on TV newscasts. It was the point through which everyone had to pass going into or out of East Berlin. German nationals weren't allowed to cross through, but documented American citizens were—and I wasn't going to miss this opportunity.

Charlie was manned by US, British, and French forces on our side and Russian and East German forces on their side. As we passed through, our border guards cautioned us to be very careful and attentive while we were on the other side. From time to time, they warned, visitors didn't return. But the guards knew us and were surprisingly lax in checking our credentials as they permitted us to pass. That accommodation, while appreciated at the time, would come back to bite us.

And then we found ourselves in East Berlin. What a contrast we saw! While the West was filled with lights and gaiety, East Berlin was rubble and bombed-out buildings that had never been rebuilt after the war; it was as it had been since 1944. We went into a pub for a drink, but it was drab and dreary inside. No celebration. No merriment. The patrons were gloomy, quiet. It wasn't difficult for me to read their forlorn faces. They didn't want to be where they were; if they could have done something to change that, certainly they would have done it. But there was nothing to be done. Sensing this great hopelessness, I began to understand why so many were willing to risk—and sometimes lose—their lives trying to escape to the West. And the pall that covered this bar greatly affected us. I mean, after a while in a downer bar like that, you needed a drink just to keep drinking there.

Having had all the fun we could stand at that morgue of a pub, we hailed a cab and headed back to West Berlin. Preparing to show our documentation at Checkpoint Charlie, we discovered that Vinnie had left his passport at the hotel. And now came the stern faces and the scurrying boots. It was immediately clear that we were one wrong word, one errant move, one misunderstood glance away from being at ground zero of an international incident of mammoth proportions. It was also clear that some of us would have to change our shorts when—indeed, if—we made it through Charlie and back into West Berlin.

Telephones and radios were called into service, and soon enough the

American Consulate was involved. An official representative appeared at Checkpoint Charlie to confirm that we were touring professionals, not international spies. I guess we must have looked more like the latter than the former, because it took several hours for the consul to make the case that we were who we said we were. The consul prevailed at last, and we were allowed to return through Checkpoint Charlie to breathe again the sweet, fresh air of West Berlin democracy and freedom.

Vinnie never forgot his passport again.

| Remember Where You Were When... |

As great as it was to have the Beatles open for us in Stockholm, that wasn't the only memorable—no, *unforgettable*—moment of this tour.

On November 22 at about seven-thirty p.m., we were preparing to take the stage at a German club. I felt an intangible, eerie sensation I couldn't define. The audience and the stage crew were unsettled. Something was going on, but I didn't know what. Then the stage manager approached my brother Al and said, "What kind of country do you live in?"

At once confused and surprised, Al asked, "What are you talking about?"

"They just shot your President Kennedy," the stage manager said. "In America. They shot your President Kennedy."

What an understatement it is to say we were stunned. We found a radio and tuned in to Armed Forces Radio, which broadcast in English. At first the story was that shots had been fired as President Kennedy was traveling in a motorcade in Dallas, Texas. That was shock enough, but then came follow-up word that he'd been shot, not just shot at. And then the coup de grâce: confirmation that President Kennedy had been shot and killed.

We didn't take the stage that night. The next several scheduled concerts were also canceled. US military bases went immediately on high alert. The next days were difficult. I had no contact with the States to speak of. There were of course no cell phones then, and landline connections were difficult to secure—and expensive. Media coverage was sketchy and in the wrong language for me, but I learned what I could. I remember how affected I was to see German citizens openly weeping in the face of this tragedy. President Kennedy was beloved in Germany, and he loved Germany. At the end of a public address in Berlin a mere five months earlier, he had spoken the words, "As a free man, I take pride in the words, 'Ich bin ein Berliner.'" Owning his German heritage—"I am a Berliner"—endeared him to the citizens of that wonderful country.

When an American president is assassinated, you don't just read the story, grunt and say *hmm look at that*, and then move on to the comics section. It's a horrific evil that sends shockwaves clear to your soul—and you don't forget. I suppose everyone alive now who experienced that day can tell you where (s)he was when the news broke, if (s)he was old enough to understand. Certainly I can, and I'll never ever forget that awful time.

A general sadness shrouded everything. Even music production slowed. No one felt like singing, and creativity dropped off. The number-one record for the remainder of the year was the Singing Nuns enigmatic "Dominique"—not rock & roll, but number one on the rock & roll charts anyway. Everything just seemed to come to a halt. It was a sad, difficult time for so many.

| Returning Home: High Jinks on the High Seas |

Our second tour in the books, we boarded the Queen. I was ready to be home; I missed Joanie and our boys. But this voyage would be nearly as much fun as any of the gigs we'd played in Europe. It may have been the second funniest cruise ever enjoyed by man or mermaid, topped only by the Marx Brothers cruising in the 1935 MGM film, *A Night at the Opera*.

For whatever reason other passengers seemed to look on us with disdain. They were so arrogant, aloof—frankly, just a bunch of prigs. (No, that last word is no typo, but the word you probably thought I was trying to write would work too.) In a flash of cultural inspiration, I concocted a plan to help these blokes and plonkers dislodge that stick a mite.

The Queen had elevators leading to each deck. Strategically selecting one, I had the entire band—including Elaine, Kitty, and Fat—board it, wearing nothing but underwear. When the door opened to a deck, the people waiting to board faced a passel of nearly naked yanks. Here were all these stodgy prudes who held themselves in higher esteem than Marlon Brando at the Academy Awards, choking on their Meerschaum pipes and popping their monocles as they faced these "ugly Americans." What a blast. Man, this was more fun than watching the Three Stooges repair plumbing. Still, I thought we could raise the fun bar a bit.

After a few ups-and-downs Fat, Larry, and I dropped our drawers for good measure—so to speak. Those wankers went arse-over-elbows scrambling away every time that door slid open to reveal our bare asses. There's just no telling how many had to seek therapy to delete that mental picture.

Uppity bastids.

Right: The close-knit family of Italian-born Giuseppe (Joseph) and Sicilian-born Anna Orlando DiNicola, circa 1942. Front, from left: Rose, Poppa with Joey, Jr., John, Momma with Angie, Nick (II). Back, from left: Al, Vera, Mary. Nick (I) had died as a child, and baby Joann was yet to come.

Left: Joey with Poppa at their home on Washington Place in Passaic, NJ, circa 1944. A few short years later Poppa would be taken from young Joey's life at the hands of an angry neighbor.

Right: From Washington Place came the Washington Colts—and other friends there and on Columbia Ave. What one did, all did. Pals for more than 80 years: Anthony Cuva (standing, second from right) and JD (middle row, last on right).

Left: A handsome young Jersey boy, not far from choosing between the life of an educator and the life of a musician.

JOEY DEE FAN CLUB
1639 Broadway
New York 19, N.

Even before fame hit, Joey's sister Mary and her husband Sam "Shuffs" Mistrette (pictured below with Joey and wife Joan, circa 1963) organized a fan club for the boys and served as its first presidents.

Above: This JD and the Starliters appeared live on TV in 1956. From left: Tony Seragusa, JD, Ralph Fazio, Tony "Dutch" Sciuto, John Yanick, Ernie Casini. The band would soon change. Brothers David McLean and Rogers Freeman were waiting just around the corner.

Joey already had experience performing with his Thunder Trio and even singing doo-wop by the time his "orchestra" and then his Starliters took on gigs like these. Word of mouth quickly made JD and the Starliters the hottest dance band in Jersey.

JD and the Starliters, 1958. Front, from left: Tony Sciuto, JD, Vinnie Corrao. Back, from left: Ernie Interella, Rogers Freeman, David McLean.

From left: David Brigati, JD, Vinnie Corrao. Circa 1960. (Photo courtesy Sal Bonura)

Wedding Day! August 10, 1959. From left: Anna Orlando DiNicola, Joan Wuthrick DiNicola, Joseph DiNicola, Jr., Mary DeMarco Wuthrick. (Photo courtesy Mary DiNicola Mistrette)

The band Don Davis heard at Olivieri's and offered a four-date gig at the Peppermint Lounge in 1960. Standing from left: JD, Rogers Freeman, David Brigati, Don Martin. Sitting: Carlton Lattimore. (Photo courtesy Van Joyce, Joyce Theatricals)

JOEY DEE
and THE STARLITERS

Exclusive Bookings
JOLLY JOYCE THEATRICALS

From left: Willie Davis, Sam Taylor, Jr., Bill Callanan, Rogers Freeman, David Brigati, Don Davis (manager), JD. Circa 1962. (Photo courtesy Mary DiNicola Mistrette)

A seedy, hole-in-the-wall, Mob-owned Hell's Kitchen bar in Manhattan exploded onto the scene in 1960, transformed overnight into the world's most famous night club by the music and electric stage performance of JD and the Starliters. (Photo used by license from Alamy)

Louie Lombardi (standing, center, circa 1961) was one of the two hands-on managers of the Peppermint Lounge. Ray (sitting) and Teri Noel (standing, far right) were Pep dancers. Teri would later do the interior design for JD's Starliter night club.

Standing between Ray and Teri and looking ambivalent about the mock choreography, Sam "Kon" Konwiser was the other of the two hands-on managers of the Pep. Circa 1961.

JD and the Starliters, circa 1962. From left: David Brigati, Carlton Lattimore, Willie Davis, JD, Larry Vernieri. Larry joined the Starliters after Roulette Records president Morris Levy insisted that Joey replace Rogers Freeman with a "white guy." Complying with that order was one of the greatest regrets of Joey's career.

It was always big news when JD was in Wildwood, as heralded by the best local entertainment guide of the day in 1962. "Shout!" was started by Richard Bonelli and Dennis Grant in 1962, taking its name, of course, from JD and the Starliters' hit song. The guide ran its last issue in 2005, after a very respectable 43-year run.

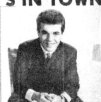

Joey invited a very young Veronica Bennett (aka Ronnie Spector), her sister Estelle, and their cousin Nedra Talley to join him on stage at the Pep one night in November, 1961. The trio then joined and toured with the Starliters through the following summer. The girls performed as Starliters here at the Riptide in the summer of '62. Shortly after that they rocked the music world as the Ronettes. (Recreated poster artwork by Thouse @ Wildwood Legends)

Hanging at Broadway, 1962. From left: David Brigati, Joey Dee, Larry Vernieri.

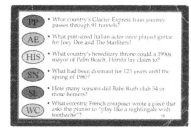

"What pint-sized Italian actor once played guitar for Joey Dee and The Starliters?" (Trivial Pursuit® board game by Hasbro)

Joey first met Dick Clark (center) when he, Tony Orlando, and Glen Campbell came to the Pep to see JD and the Starliters. A short time later Dick invited the band to appear on his *American Bandstand* TV show and then again after "Peppermint Twist" reached number one on the charts. Joey went on to appear on that show many times and became fast friends with Dick, even collaborating with him on important business projects. Pictured here with Joey (left) and "The Amazing" Jimmi Mayes (right) in Clearwater, FL, 1998.

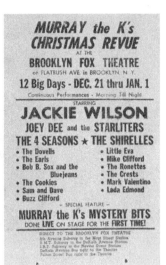

The star-studded marathon Christmas show in 1962 had DJ Murray the K's name on it, but Roulette Records president Morris Levy walked away with most of the gate. And Murray learned the hard way not to question Levy in such matters.

The best of the best played the Star-Club in Hamburg, Germany, which opened in 1962 and closed in 1969. JD and the Starliters played the world-famous venue during both tours of Europe in 1963.

Posters advertising the 1963 concert in Stockholm, Sweden, where JD caught up with the Beatles at last—when they opened for the Starliters at the Royal Tennis Hall. The Lads may have had the photo and the "The Beatles Are Coming" headline (right), but the P.S. at the bottom reads: "Joey Dee arrives at Stockholm Central tonight at 11:45 pm!!!" Another version of this poster featured a photo of JD and the headline, "Joey Dee is Coming."

Joey met the lovely and talented Lois Lee (right center back, at microphone) when she was performing at the Peppermint Lounge with Johnny Maestro's (left center back) group after JD and the Starliters had become too pricey for the Pep. Little did Joey and Lois know they'd be married just a few years later. Also pictured: Pep Lounge Dancers and band, circa 1963.

Pictured together at a Lodi, NJ, summer concert in 2002, Joey and Maestro (right) became fast friends at the Pep. They performed together many times over the years and remained close until Johnny's untimely passing in 2010. The music world lost a magnificent voice and talent, and the world lost a true gentleman on that sad Wednesday. (Photo courtesy Phil and Sue Scaglione)

"Dad used to remove his jacket and tie during the closing number and jump off whatever he could climb," says Joey's son, Ronnie. "Once, in Orlando, he hit his head on the ceiling and knocked himself out after landing on his back." On drums: Jimmi Mayes

PHONE CIRCLE 6-1566-7

JOEY DEE'S
STARLITER
"NEW YORK'S YOUNGEST NIGHT CLUB OWNER"

225 WEST 46TH STREET   NEW YORK CITY

Joey Dee's Starliter opened in 1964, making JD the youngest night club owner in NYC at the time, as his business card (left) proudly announced. Above: JD always booked the best entertainers of the day to front the best house band in the City. Below: A treasured moment for Daddy and sons inside the Starliter. Joey III sitting on the throne and little Nicky standing between JD and the kick.

In 1965 Sammy Davis, Jr. (left, with JD) invited Joey to a gala at Big Wilt's Smalls Paradise Club in Harlem and then surprised him by bringing him on stage to perform "Peppermint Twist" with full orchestra backing and Sammy himself providing the *bop-shoo-bop*s. Performing beside one of the greatest entertainers of all time was an honor that Joey has never forgotten.

JD's Starliter was short-lived, but three of its house band went on to the Rock & Roll Hall of Fame as the Rascals, pictured at left performing in 1965 at an East side club called the Phone Booth. From left: Eddie Brigati, Felix Cavaliere, Gene Cornish, Dino Danelli. All but Danelli had been in JD's Starliter house band. (Photo courtesy Joe Russo, TheRascalsArchives.com)

Lifelong friend and road manager "Fat" Frankie Scinlaro (left, photo courtesy David Brigati) was the perfect foil for JD's compulsive pranking and practical joking. But Fat often gave as good as he got, making for interesting life on the road. The two were also close as brothers with Sal Bonura (pictured above with JD in the dressing room at Sal's legendary Choo Choo Club), who launched many superstars from his Garfield NJ club, including the Rascals and Vanilla Fudge. Fat has passed, but Joey and Sal remain closest of friends. (Photo courtesy Sal Bonura)

Right: Frank "Little Frankie" Guerra, JD's valet or roadie or whatever you wanted to call him, had dwarfism—but his knack for stirring up trouble was three times his size. Pictured here with Starliter vocalist Tommy Davis (right), circa 1965. Boys will be boys.

In 1965 the Starliters' drummer, "The Amazing" Jimmi Mayes, recruited and JD hired a young Maurice James to play guitar for the Starliters. Maurice played with the band for about a year before going on his own to become the legendary Jimi Hendrix. Pictured right, at microphone: JD; far right, on guitar: Maurice James (Jimi Hendrix). (Photo courtesy Jimmi Mayes)

Left: The audience at McVan's Nite Club in Buffalo, NY, got an extra special Halloween treat in 1965, when the Starliters donned go-go dancer outfits and makeup for a unique encore. From left: David Brigati, Jimmi Mayes, Maurice James (Jimi Hendrix), Tommy Davis, JD (on drums). (Photo courtesy Jimmi Mayes)

Right: When your backup musicians are, in fact, virtuosos, you can't miss—and JD only hired the best. From left: Maurice James (Jimi Hendrix), Jimmi Mayes, Calvin Duke. Buffalo, NY, 1965. (Photo courtesy Jimmi Mayes)

In 1972 Joey organized and promoted an R&B show featuring James Brown, but even Brown's star power couldn't save the show; it went bust. The Godfather of Soul is pictured left at Herbie's Club on Long Island in 1968. Front, from left: Lonnie Youngblood, club emcee, Brown, Starliter Jimmi Mayes on drums. Back: Chris on bass, David Bay on guitar. (Photo courtesy Jimmi Mayes)

Left: Lois Lee was a hugely talented performer and an integral part of the Starliters in the later years, on and off the stage. Pictured here performing with Joey, 2000. Steve Benson on bass.

Right: Joseph DiNicola, Jr. and Lois Lee, circa 1995 .

While an amazing family is certainly Joey's greatest legacy, his life and career are greatly honored in the naming of the corner of Washington Place and Columbia Avenue as well as the auditorium at his own jr. high school, both in his NJ hometown of Passaic, for JD and the Starliters—honors that are well earned, well deserved, and very much appreciated.

And the beat goes on—with three generations of Starliters still getting it done. Above, from left: son Ronnie, grandson Jake, JD, grandson A.J., 2017. Right: JD (center), son Ronnie, and daughter Jamie, 2014. Joey's still in the running for "Best Dressed in America," an honor he already claimed once—but these days he's clearly not without competition from within his own house.

The ironies of life can sometimes bring things full circle. Joey and Joan remarried in 2007 and live happily today in Clearwater FL, enjoying their children and their children's children and their children's children's children. And Joey still rocks & rolls for audiences where love is a two-way street between them. Right: Relaxing aboard Harmony of the Seas between shows in *Rockin the Caribbean*® 2020.

Twelve

LIVE! AT THE APOLLO

The guys and I played the Apollo Theater in 1964, but we weren't the first white folks on that stage. Swing band leaders Harry James and Woody Herman, jazz greats Dave Brubeck and Stan Getz, and the great Buddy Holly had played there. And my buddy David Brigati had appeared there with the Hi-Fives ("Dorothy"), as well as my friends Jimmy Beaumont and the Skyliners ("Since I Don't Have You"). But I believe I'm the only white entertainer to claim the honor of appearing at the Apollo *and* in *Jet* magazine, when both the magazine and the venue catered primarily to Black audiences.

| The Power of Glaser |

Our booking at the Apollo was arranged by Joel "Joe" Glaser, president of the Associated Booking Corporation (ABC), the agency that represented me at the time. ABC had also booked my tours of Europe just a year earlier. In addition to myself, ABC represented a plethora of legendary talent: Louie Armstrong, Billie Holiday, Duke Ellington, Benny Goodman, Sarah Vaughan, Lionel Hampton, Dizzy Gillespie, "Sugar" Ray Robinson, Woody Herman, Dave Brubeck, Barbra Streisand, B.B. King, Allman Brothers Band, T. Rex, and many others.

Glaser was an interesting and complex man who turned out to have quite the personal history with the Mob and otherwise, about which I knew nothing at the time. But I did witness once the power Mr. Glaser wielded in the booking industry.

In 1963 I was sitting in Joe's office along with the magnificent Sarah Vaughan, and he was speaking on the phone with the entertainment director at a Las Vegas hotel. He said to the director, "I'm inking Sarah Vaughan to perform there beginning March one." He didn't ask whether the hotel wanted Miss Vaughan or not. He didn't ask what dates worked for the hotel. He didn't ask how the freakin' weather was. He simply told the man when Miss Vaughan *would* play his hotel.

I swear I could hear beads of sweat popping out on Mr. Vegas Hotel's forehead. Right through the phone and across the room I could hear it. And I know what the guy said. He said, "Uhhh, yeah, Joe, okay. That works for me." I know that's what he said, because the conversation was over. That was power, and I was terribly impressed. I mean, this man could book any entertainer, any time and at any venue, with a single phone call.

| Legendary Room, Legendary Performer |

We contracted to play six nights a week for two weeks at the Apollo along with Jackie "Moms" Mabley, a girl group called the Fascinations, and host-emcee-performer King Coleman. Moms was one of the funniest people ever to grace a stage. She was an international headliner, a world-famous veteran star of stand-up and television comedy. She'd played the Apollo many times before this, and she carried weight at the theater. The portly doorman at the club, nicknamed "Mississippi," allowed no one past him without Moms's say-so.

The thought of being on stage in this R&B cathedral was drawing down all my cerebral and spiritual energy. It was daunting to think I was about to play the Apollo. From my first step into the theater, I felt as though I were on hallowed ground. It was if I were going to church—a reverent, even sanctified feeling. I mean, every great R&B group you can name had walked that stage, and we were about to stand on those very same planks.

In the first rehearsal I watched Moms go through her paces, and she was smoother than the bottoms of James Brown's shoes. Then we set up and ran down "Peppermint Twist." Of course, there was no audience present, but a handful of day workers scurried around, preparing for the evening. As we played I became aware that the workers were dancing and enjoying themselves. When we finished the piece, these kind people gave us a standing ovation. Color me surprised. I thanked them and said I hoped this was an indication of things to come. At that moment I realized I was nervous—for the first time in my career. And rightly so. The boys and I had played some tough audiences, but I knew the one we were about to face would be the toughest of them all. Apollo audiences had seen everything imaginable, and they were known for their brutal honesty in judging talent. If you weren't liked, you didn't have to be a mind-reader to know it. You knew clearly, and you knew immediately.

Moms sensed my anxiety. I'm glad she did, because I'd hate to have felt that ill at ease and have it be just my little secret. Yep, the veteran Moms could see what I was going through emotionally and called me to her dressing room.

"Joey, you got to get a grip, hon," Moms said. "Remember—you're here for a reason. You got talent, boy, and the people will love you. Now you don't worry about a thing." Then she added, "You play gin rummy?"

"Uhhh, ma'am?" I answered, a bit taken aback by the sharp turn in conversation. "Do I play gin rummy?"

"Yeah. Gin rummy. Do you play?"

"Well, sure. I play gin rummy," I answered.

Moms retrieved a new deck of playing cards from her bag, cracked the seal, removed the cards, ferreted out the jokers and end cards, and shuffled. By the time we finished playing and talking, I felt calm as clam shells. Moms had tricked me into believing I was playing just any old regular gig. A psychiatrist or hypnotist couldn't have done it any better.

This game of gin began a two-week marathon that's probably remembered even today at the Apollo as the *Bloody Gin Duel of '64*. Every hand was a knock-down-drag-out affair with every shade of cheating known to man. Moms was good. Moms was *very* good. But the title went to yours truly. Far more important than winning, however, were the many things I learned as we spoke together, and how deeply I came to respect Miss Jackie "Moms" Mabley.

| Rubbing the Stump |

Moms hadn't only distracted me from my nerves; she'd made the time melt away. In a blink it was an hour before showtime. Then, after what seemed to be five seconds, I heard, "The half is in!"—meaning thirty minutes to curtain. As the guys and I dressed, we heard the great Apollo band warming up. It was—ahem—music to our ears, and we enjoyed that beautiful sound as the last minutes flew by: fifteen . . . ten . . . five . . . showtime!

King Coleman took the stage and did his thing. Now, King had a shiny bald head that tended to . . . how should I say . . . sweat. A lot. After only minutes he was sweating so much that he had to excuse himself to wipe his head with a white handkerchief the size of a movie theater screen. The flood averted, King introduced the Fascinations, who performed nicely.

During these opening acts we stood in the wings and wished each other bad luck. Remember: You can't wish a performer *good* luck, because that's *bad* luck—so you say things like *break a leg*. And right smack in the middle of cursing each other,

I heard King Coleman say the words I'd been fearing and dreading and looking forward to all day—and even longer than that.

"Ladies and gentlemen," King said, "I'm proud to introduce to you the world-famous group from the Peppermint Lounge on West 45th Street: Joey Dee and the Starliters!"

I was thankful that Moms had soothed my nerves, but when I heard our name, I just couldn't stop a million thoughts from ricocheting around in my head like shrapnel from an exploding grenade. Were we good enough? Had we prepared well enough? Was the audience prepared for a mixed band? The answers didn't matter. There was no turning back now.

Willie made his way to the drums; Billy, to the Hammond B-3 organ; and Sam, to the guitar. David, Larry, and I took our places at the mikes. On the way to our places we made sure to "rub the stump" for luck and a bit of hope. Yes, there's a twelve-inch shellacked log sitting atop a gold pillar in the right wings of the stage, and you just don't play that stage without rubbing the thing. It's the only remaining piece from the Tree of Hope that stood in front of another Harlem business, the Lafayette Theater, where it allegedly brought hope and luck to the community. After it was cut down in 1934, a piece of the Tree of Hope was preserved and given honorable residence on the Apollo stage. Oh! to think of the hands that rubbed that stump over the years. Humbling. And now we too had rubbed it.

| Facing the Challenge |

When we took the stage, the crowd applauded politely and then went dead quiet. We broke into "Hey Let's Twist" and played it well—no gaffes, no blunders, tight harmonies. We were good—and still, the audience was quiet when we finished. It was only a heartbeat, that pause; but in my mind, it was an eternity.

And then it came.

The crowd erupted! Applause, shouting, whistling . . . all manner of noise that told me we'd done it. Whatever fragments of nerves remained evaporated in an instant, and I was ready to rock and roll, baby. And that's what we did. We just got better and better as we went, and the crowd loved us. By the time we closed with "Shout," I was physically, emotionally, and spiritually drained. So much anticipation. So much worry. And now, so much success.

We acknowledged the standing ovation and exited stage right. There stood Moms in the wing, of course, waiting to take the stage after us, wearing her trademark raggedy stage dress, baggy sweater, frumpy hat, and cheap handbag.

"Now how am I supposed to follow that?" she said as she caught my eye to offer a smile and a wink. We both knew.

Despite her kind, encouraging words as we passed in the wing, she *did* follow that. Moms could follow the parting of the Red Sea and still stop the show—she was that good. I stayed there in the wing to watch her perform, and I was amazed to see this genius and master artist ply her craft. Even without her teeth—she always removed her dentures when she worked—she could set up and punch lines better than anyone I'd ever seen.

"The only thing an *old* man can do for Moms is bring a note to a *young* man."

The audience roared right up to her last punch line and final step into the wing. Talk about a mike drop. No one would ever want to take the stage after Moms Mabley. Nobody in his right mind anyway.

I got baptized that day, and it was an experience I'll never forget.

Sadly, Moms and I never met again after the Apollo; other than on TV, I never saw her again. Moms left us in 1975, at age eighty-one. It makes my heart happy to look back on that special time she and I enjoyed together. And, of course, I never play a hand of gin rummy without thinking of the great Jackie "Moms" Mabley.

| Amateur Night at the Apollo |

Amateur Night at the Apollo is a solid tradition with its genesis clear back in 1933. Lest you think this was some kind of cheap-ass affair, please know this: The winner of the first contest in 1934 was none other than Ella Fitzgerald. Miss Fitzgerald had come prepared to dance. But when she saw the high mark set by dancers in the act before her, she changed her mind and sang instead. Talk about the winds of fate. Well played, ma'am. Well played.

No matter who was headlining at the theater, Wednesday was reserved for Amateur Night. It was a showcase for unsung talent to compete for a shot at the crown, some cash, and a performance contract. It was an ongoing contest, concluding after several weeks of competition with a final winner being crowned—and the audience decided all winners along the way. The Apollo crowd was no pushover, and a contestant could launch a career or suffer the greatest embarrassment of a lifetime. See, if you had "it," then you got to see a standing ovation and hear lots of applause and whistling and whatnot. Plus you lived to compete again. But if the audience decided you *didn't* have "it," then a very different ending played out.

As each contestant performed, vaudeville tap dancer "Sandman" Sims, known as Porto Rico, waited in the wings, keeping an eye on the performer and an ear on the audience. If he sensed a downturn in the relationship between the two and determined that the show must not, in fact, go on, then the "executioner" shot onto the stage and charged the contestant like a bull to the cape. Carrying a starter's pistol or a broom, the executioner either swept the contestant off the stage with the broom or fired the starter's pistol at the poor soul's feet till he or she or they got off the stage. Of course, the crowd booed and hissed all the while, adding insult to insult. More than one contestant left the stage in tears. Despite the slightest twinge of shameful, sadistic smile, it was near impossible to watch this ordeal and not feel embarrassed for the banished entertainer, imagining the hopes and dreams that must surely be exiting the stage in shame. Showbiz can be the toughest, most heartless of things. You've got to really want it.

| When We Weren't on Stage |

I always loved being in Harlem. I felt safer there than I did in Times Square. When we weren't rubbing the stump, there was plenty to do. To keep ourselves looking fresh and making sure our hair was just right for our shows, we all went to "Sugar" Ray Robinson's barbershop in the Hotel Theresa. Outside the joint there was always a pink Lincoln convertible with a Continental kit installed on the trunk to make the thing look even longer than it already was. It was Ray's ride of course. I often spent time with the legendary boxer. He was a class act, I can tell you that. Now, I'm talking about the real, original Sugar Ray *Robinson*. Sugar Ray *Leonard* was still jumping rope on the school playground.

After a show at the Apollo, I'd sometimes get into my Caddy and drive to Big Wilt's Smalls Paradise Club to unwind a bit and see what's up. As soon as I entered the club, I could feel the electricity. The place was bustling with all kinds of business discussions and decisions and disagreements. Many people lived at the bar, drinking and scheming and telling stories that evoked roars of laughter. The joint was always exciting. The music, the clothes, the atmosphere, the people—everything about Big Wilt's made it rock & roll heaven. As a bonus for me, every Tuesday night was "Twist Night," so you know I had it knocked when I was there on a Tuesday. But the place was happening, every day and every night.

I was never surprised to find no parking space out front. Same story, different day. This wasn't a problem, however, because we didn't just *double*-park there; we *triple*-parked there. It was against the law of course, but people were seldom ticketed for this—at least not those who were connected. If the driver of a blocked car needed to leave, the cops would just go inside, find the owners of offending vehicles, and kindly ask them to take care of it. A great spirit of cooperation.

Wilt's had the best stages and bars but the smallest dance floor. When it was busy, it was said that all you had was a dime's worth of space to dance on. The club hosted a couple of rockin' bands upstairs, while the downstairs venue was reserved for the headlining star. Many great talents performed there, including James Brown, King Curtis, the Drifters, the Coasters—and I saw and got to know most of them. Having met him at the Peppermint Lounge many times, James Brown and I got pretty tight. He went out with Geri Miller, a dancer at the Pep who was quick to tell everyone that she was dating the Godfather of Soul. James and I would be connected again a little farther down the line when I tried my hand at promoting shows. More on that later. I also became close friends with Carl Gardner and Billy Guy of the Coasters, sax player King Curtis, and Charlie Thomas and Ben E. King of the Drifters. I remember going backstage one night after a show featuring the Coasters, the Drifters, and my old friends the Shirelles to shoot craps with King, Charlie, and Ben. It was no low-stakes game, I can tell you that. We shot hundreds at a roll. This was big time. I've forgotten how much money I lost or won, but I remember that the brothers treated me as I knew they would: as an equal in every way.

Of course, King Curtis was there because he played sax on all the hit recordings of the Coasters. He approached me there at Smalls one night.

"Joey, you got some one and one?" he asked.

Now, I'd been asked lots of questions in my life up to that point, but I just couldn't remember the last time I was asked for some *one and one*. I didn't know what the man was talking about. Fortunately, I had my man Bo at my side that night. Seeing that I was stumped as a politician asked about ethics, my friend stepped in and pulled my coat. "I'll take care of this, Joey." Turning to Curtis, Bo said, "Nah, King. We clean."

Of course King was asking if we had any cocaine, coke, blow, toot, nose candy . . . well, you may know other slang terms, but back then I didn't know even the one. I guess I wasn't as cool as I thought I was. In my defense, I couldn't have known what King was talking about. I'd never used any kind of drug. Bo had saved me from my own embarrassing naivete. Again.

Big Wilt's is no more; it exists now only in the memories of those of us who enjoyed it. But don't be distraught about that. There exists still a place where you can go to catch the real side of what's going on in the hood. Simply find a brother friend and ask him to take you to a local barbershop. The perspectives you'll be exposed to there about the real world will be profound, and the stories you'll hear will make you laugh till you cry. I believe you could put cameras in such an establishment and produce the best reality show ever.

I'll leave that gold mine for someone else.

ThiRTEEN

STARLITER PART ONE: YOUNGEST CLUB OWNER IN THE CITY

Many people thought I owned the Peppermint Lounge. Of course that wasn't true, but Joey Dee the Great had a lot of chutzpah—enough to believe that he *could* own a night club. In 1964 no one of my young age owned a night club in the City, but that didn't make any difference to me. So, after the Pep's popularity had peaked and slid and Joey Dee and the Starliters had waned a bit, I figured time was ripe for me to try my hand at this ownership thing—something I'd long wished for. But as they say—be careful what you wish for. . .

| So Long, Sweet Chariot |

Of course, you can't have a club without a place to put it, and I found what I liked just a block northwest of the Pep on 46th Street. Several factors made it a good location, one of them being that it was situated in the heart of the theater district. Across the street *A Funny Thing Happened on the Way to the Forum* was playing. Just down the street, *Oliver!* was drawing huge crowds. Up the street Richard Burton was wowing the crowds in *Camelot*. Of course, where Burton was, Elizabeth Taylor—his wife—was never far away. And when she came by the theater each day to pick up King Arthur, it was a social event. To say the least. Surrounded by such theaters and the crowds they drew, I knew I'd found the perfect location for my night club.

Previously at this location had been a concept club owned by Joe Scandore, who later became actor/comedian Don Rickles's manager. The Sweet Chariot featured the gospel music of some sanctified singers, solo or in groups, accompanied by piano and/or organ and drums. I was always impressed by the sounds and energy produced by groups such as the Sweet Chariots (house group), the Nat Lewis Singers, the Herman Stevens Singers, and the Ellison Singers. Of all the performers I saw there, my favorites were the Miller Sisters, and our paths would happily cross again later. The singers in the club were clad in angelic robes and dresses. And the club's "bunnies" were singers who doubled as waitresses, wearing shorty gowns with angel wings attached. The costuming was feminine, to be sure—but not what you'd call provocative.

Tambourines were placed on every table for use by any in the audience who "got the feeling" and wanted to participate with the performers. Being that alcohol was served, lots of people "got the feeling." Unfortunately, drunk people aren't the best at feeling rhythm or finding a beat, so what they mostly did with the tambourines was screw up the groove of the performers on stage. But this unique gimmick was effective, and word of mouth created a strong business with lots of paying spiritual customers. But word of mouth can sometimes work as strongly against a business as for it.

Cue the preachers.

A group of ministers in Harlem got word of the Sweet Chariot's format and was interested in it—interested enough, in fact, to come down from Harlem to catch a show and meet with Joe. Knowing Joe and knowing Harlem ministers generally, I imagine the meeting went something like this.

In a brief but pointed discussion the ministers asked Joe to stop the audience participation and change the clothing of the performers and the waitresses, all of which they believed were generally blasphemous and ridiculed their beliefs and worship.

"Gentlemen," Joe explained, "I've got lots of money invested in this business. Everything's working just right, and I don't believe what we do belittles your beliefs in the slightest." He continued, "We entertain, and the crowds love it."

"Are we to take it, then," a minister asked, "that you are not willing to make the changes in your club that we would like?"

"With all due respect, gentlemen," Joe said bluntly, "I won't be changing a damn thing."

"And would that be your final decision then, sir?"

"Yes sir, it would—except that I might add, get the hell out of my club."

It was clear that neither side was willing to budge. They were at an impasse, and the conflict was destined to end badly for one side or the other.

It wasn't long before the preachers showed up again at the Sweet Chariot, armed this time with dozens of parishioners who came prepared for the long haul. They picketed Joe's club night and day, for days.

Now, Joe didn't like being blackmailed or pressured or threatened, so he turned to his Mob-connected father-in-law for help. But after all was said and done, even the weight his father-in-law carried wasn't enough to dissuade the ministers and their minions. Eventually it got just a tad too uncomfortable for customers to pass through the picketers, and they simply stopped coming. No customers, no money. No money, no business. The ministers' efforts ended with a new sign out front: *Sweet Chariot* became *For Rent.*

The place went dark. It was an unfortunate and ignominious ending for a nice business enterprise, but where shit falls, roses bloom. I saw this as my opportunity to make my move. I made arrangements to rent the space and immediately applied to the SLA for a liquor license. Given that the previous club already had a liquor license in good standing, and I had nothing of record that should have been a problem, the license should have been a slam dunk. Perhaps there might be one little problem, however. See, my last name, DiNicola, ends in a vowel. Yep, that was a problem. The SLA dragged its bureaucratic feet, shining me on with every excuse in the book. I swear, these guys must have taken classes to learn all those "reasons" for foot-dragging: There were too many liquor licenses in the City already. I had no experience running a night club. Months would be needed for all the background checks and red tape. It had been two weeks since it rained and it was too freakin' dry to issue a license. I mean, these guys came up with everything you can imagine to push me back. But they weren't the only ones who knew how to push.

| Will the Mystery Guest Enter and Sign In, Please |

Dorothy Kilgallen was a highly respected and talented journalist working for the Hearst Corporation's *New York Journal-American*. Many will remember her regular gig as a panelist on the CBS game show *What's My Line*, which aired from 1952 until 1967 and can be seen even now in reruns here and there. But Miss Kilgallen's greatest skills were in reporting and writing. Her column, "Voice of Broadway," focused primarily on the entertainment business but eventually branched out to include politics and other social sectors. The column was syndicated to well over one hundred newspapers nationwide.

I'd met Miss Kilgallen when she invited me to appear on her television show on New Year's Eve, 1961. Knowing her influence, I called Dorothy and explained my dilemma. She was appalled that I'd been treated so carelessly and given the runaround by the SLA. She kindly agreed to do what she could to help. In her column she asked the unrhetorical question, "Why doesn't the SLA grant Joey Dee a liquor license?" But this journalist didn't just ask the question and then let it lie there. She was relentless, clamping down on this thing like a pit bull on the leg of a mail carrier and shaking the hell out of it. At last the SLA cried uncle. I got a call from one of its bureaucrats informing me that the club had been granted a liquor license. I would be the youngest night club owner in New York City, and I was ecstatic about it.

Without the power of Dorothy Kilgallen's pen, I might still be waiting for that license. When it was done, I called the beneficent lady to thank her for what she'd done for me. Her response to me was simply, "My pleasure, Joey."

| Building a Club |

Now it was time to put together the best club in NYC. I mean, if I were going to be the youngest club owner, my club absolutely had to be the best. I thought long and hard about my concept of the place, and I began with the name Joey Dee's Starliter. The chase was on.

My first stroke of genius was the hiring of my gay friend Teri Noel, a dancer at the Pep. Teri's task was the interior design and decoration of the Starliter. It didn't take long for him to decide that the ceiling should be black and everything else blue and green. Because of its below-ground location, there were many square support posts to be considered and treated. Teri settled on a wonderful scheme of painting them, alternating green and blue throughout the club. It looked magnificent. Floor coverings, tables, chairs, accessories throughout—all was spot-on. He also took great pain to appoint my office beautifully, adding a small desk and a very large casting couch—just, you know, in case.

Whenever you decorate a home or business, always hire a gay man to do the job for you. No one can do it better. Now, if this seems prejudiced, please check out the world's top fashion designers and interior decorators, and then tell me you'd rather have a straight truck driver do the work for you. Not likely, right? Trust me. I know what I'm talking about. I'm simply complimenting a pure gift.

Next I determined to put together the best sound system money could buy. At the Star-Club in Hamburg, Germany, I'd met a man named Adrian Barber. He'd been excellent at controlling the sound system there, and now I wanted him here. I called and asked Adrian if he'd come to America to be my soundman. He agreed to the gig, and I secured a working visa for him. Before you could say *transatlantic crossing* he was in the City and putting together a sound system at the Starliter that was second to none. I'd settle for nothing less than that. I knew I'd have top-name stars and entertainers at the Starliter, and I insisted that my sound system make them shine. Adrian created a system to do just that. The amplifiers and microphones he selected were all German-made, and the Germans have always known technology. Those pieces would be worth a great deal even now. From the Starliter, Adrian would go on to produce records for some of the best recording artists ever, including the Beatles, the Rascals, Buffalo Springfield, Vanilla Fudge, the Allman Brothers Band, Aerosmith, the Velvet Underground, Cream, Diamond Rio, and more. I'm proud to be the one who recognized his engineering skills back at the Star-Club in Hamburg and brought him to our shores. You're welcome, music.

And now, the waitresses. Ah, yes . . . the waitresses. I had a certain type in mind, and that's what I'd have. Not open to negotiation or discussion. Every girl had to be blonde and zaftig (full-bodied and sexy). Well, okay . . . There was one slight exception. If the chick weren't blonde but otherwise eligible, she could wear a blonde wig. This not only suited my personal taste; it was a gimmick, and show biz is all about gimmicks. And they had to be tall. This requirement wasn't difficult to fill, given that all the girls wore high heels and most wore beehive hairdo. This combination made shorter chicks look six feet tall and taller chicks even taller. Either way, I won. And, of course, I had to use that very large casting couch to audition some of these tall, blonde, zaftig ladies, if you know what I mean.

Continuing on, I hired a friend from Harlem, Dominick DiTomasso, to be my manager. I knew Dom from the Pep, when he would come in with the Harlem crew (every neighborhood had its own crew). The man was also very funny, but I'll get into that later. Dom then hired a kid named Buzzy, also from Harlem, to be our lead bouncer. I got a few brothers from Jersey, a guy named Mendy from Passaic, and another guy from Lodi. To round out the floor staff and give the place some class, I hired a maître d' named Bobby Greco.

David and my brother Al would handle the service bar, mixing drinks and managing the waitresses. David found plenty of time for both parts of that job description. On the other hand Al was true-blue to his wife Kathy. Now *there* was an interesting concept: being true to your wife. Al and I came from the same gene pool dammit! Why couldn't I have been more like him?! It should have been a simple thing for me—I mean, of all the girls I went out with, none was more beautiful than my Joanie. What the hell?!

In the vestibule between the outside entrance and the door to the club, I set up a Wall of Fame. I knew I'd have many celebrities coming in, and I wanted them all to "sign in please," just as the mystery guests did each week on Miss Kilgallen's program, *What's My Line?*. After all was said and done this Wall of Fame would be covered with the names of the most famous, popular, and influential people in entertainment, society, arts, politics—even the Mob.

I spent a truckload of money to make my Starliter the best club in the City. The harsh truth is, I spent a little *too* much—but onward we trudged.

| The Mob Makes a Move |

The evening before we were to open, I walked into the club. It took but a moment for me to notice that every one of my staff was silent as a mime. I looked around curiously to see what was going on. At a table sat a nefarious-looking guy, quiet and somber. One of the staff caught my eye and nodded subtly toward the strange man. I went over to him to see what was going on.

"Who are you?" I asked bluntly.

"I'm your partner," the man said, unflinching.

I said with a smirk, "I don't have a partner."

"Well," he calmly explained, "if I'm not your partner, then you don't open tomorrow, and this place will be a parking lot. My name is Sally Burns."

Burns. Yeah, right. I knew the guy wasn't Irish, no matter what he called himself. A lot of Mob guys used Irish names just to break the balls of the cops, many of whom had Irish roots. Whatever his ancestry, I didn't like at all what this guy was saying. Discretion being the better part of valor, however, I didn't want to do or say anything that would get me into hotter water than I cared to be in. I let my wannabe partner leave peacefully without argument or contest.

"Lemme think it over and get back to you," I said.

"Think it over real good," Sally told me as he left. "And real fast."

As soon as the coast was clear, I got on the phone to my Uncle John Lamela. Uncle John knew people, and I needed his help. Before I could explain the whole thing to him, he said, "Don't say anything on the phone. Drive up here now and we'll talk." I should have thought of that myself; I knew the telephone put lots of guys in the can. You could never know for sure that the line wasn't tapped. By the time you found out it was, it was too late, if you were discussing something you didn't want heard by anyone but the guy you were talking to.

I drove the ninety minutes to Marlboro, New York, where Uncle John lived with Aunt Millie and their kids. Aunt Millie—my mother's sister—greeted me and took me to Uncle John. Then she left the room. Everyone else was asleep, so Uncle John and I had privacy.

I quickly and anxiously explained about Sally Burns.

"Joey, why the hell didn't you come to me sooner?" he asked. "You should've come sooner. You would've been protected. Now I'm afraid it's too late," he said. "The guy made his move on you already."

Uncle John made frequent trips to Tampa, and I knew he was a close friend of Simone DeCavalcante, also known as Sam "the Plumber"—the man who was named as the head of the DeCavalcante crime family in the 1950 Kefauver Committee investigation into organized crime.

"No one would have stepped in on you if you were with us," Uncle John explained. "I'll talk to Sally tomorrow, but I'm sure there's nothing I can do. I'll have somebody stop by," he said, "and let you know what happened."

I thanked Uncle John, kissed him on the cheek, and returned home to Lodi. I was glad I'd reached out to him, but I had a very unsettled feeling that things weren't going to work out how I wanted them to.

Next day, a guy stopped by the club.

"Joey, your Uncle John wants me to tell you Sally's your partner," the guy said. "He also asked me to stay here and give you a hand—just to make sure you get a fair shake and all."

The guy introduced himself as Joe, and I gave him the moniker "Laine." So, Joe Laine it was. He became the manager of my club, and my friend Dom was relegated to manager in name only. That's the way it worked. Joe was an interesting type. He looked a little like the inimitable Wally Cox's television persona Mister Peepers, a shy, slightly built junior high science teacher who constantly faced problems but was never outwitted. The similarity between the two was the glasses they both wore. But there were differences. Peepers was wiry and fragile; Joe Laine wasn't. He was built like a cross between the Incredible Hulk and a Mack truck. And he was tough. *Real* tough.

That's what those two thieves learned when they were emptying Joe Laine's car as it sat parked outside the Starliter one day. He surprised the crooks in their work and beat the hell out of them. I went out with him and even helped out a bit with the beat-down. Not much, but I got a few kicks in. It was enough to prompt Joe Laine to report to my Uncle John that, "Joey's a pretty good guy." There was such irony in this meeting between Joe Laine and the robbers. I mean, those hoods were doing no more than what Joe Laine used to do, but he wouldn't allow it to be done to him. Honor among thieves and all that, I guess.

It lifted my spirits considerably to know I had somebody on my team who was personally assigned by Uncle John. I would have been too vulnerable without him. I'd seen what could happen without that kind of help. The City was full of sharks.

If you owned a club or a restaurant, chances were very good you had a silent partner just like Sally Burns. Or worse.

Uncle John brought Sam the Plumber into the Starliter one afternoon. Sam was very personable, very friendly, and we talked for a while.

"Joey, you should listen to your uncle," Sam told me. "You wouldn't have this problem with Sally Burns if you did. You should *listen* to your uncle."

It was good advice. I wished I'd gotten it a little earlier. But I hadn't gone to Uncle John in time, and I did have the problem with Sally Burns. Every week after that, I filled an envelope with cash for Sally—for doing nothing.

Shortly after we opened, a guy came in and asked to speak with me.

"My name's Earl," the man said. "I'm from Yonkers. I'm your partner."

What the hell?! I mean, was Bloomingdale's having a sale on partners?!

Again, I didn't make a scene or tempt trouble. I simply told Earl hat someone would get in touch with him. I told Joe Laine about Earl and never heard from the Yonkers man again. I'm not suggesting he was whacked. I think he just got a clear explanation of how things were and then moved on to greener pastures.

This has nothing to do with the story, but in New York the name *Earl* is pronounced *Oil*, and the word *oil* is pronounced *earl*. Go figure.

| Realizing a Dream |

In spite of all the aggravation of determining just who was and who was not my partner, opening night was a dream come true for me. I had invited some heavy hitters, such as entertainers Sammy Davis, Jr. and Lola Falana (who became regulars at the Starliter), boxing legends Rocky Marciano and Rocky Graziano, Jim Brown of the NFL Cleveland Browns, Joe Pepitone of the New York Yankees, and many others. Lois Lee—my future wife—and Teri Noel brought some of the other Pep dancers as well. My singer/songwriter pal Chuck Jackson was there and introduced me to his friend Marvin Gaye, himself a pretty fair singer/songwriter. And, of course, Miss Dorothy Kilgallen stopped by to wish me well. Everyone signed my Wall of Fame, and I was thrilled and proud. So proud.

At the very top of my guest list were those most important to me. My wife Joanie was there, glamourously dressed in a custom-designed black gown with sparkling sequins. She was so beautiful, you nearly needed sunglasses to look at her. With her were our two boys Joey and Nicky, who made only a brief appearance before being whisked away to a more serene environment. And there was, of course, my lovely mother. How proud I was to have them there with me to celebrate this, my life's dream.

The joint was filled with celebrities, and it was jumping. Teri had the place looking like a million bucks. The waitresses were hot, and the band was smokin'. I performed with my new Starliters: David and Eddie Brigati with me on vocals, Felix Cavaliere on the Hammond B-3 organ, Gene Cornish on guitar, and Ricky Chanin on drums. There were more bitchin' chicks in the joint than you could count. I had my pals from Harlem: GiGi, JoJo, Johnny Echols, Joey Gee, Frankie the Nose, and Louie Chink. I found myself surrounded by all the things that were important to me at the time. From where I stood, I had the world by the tail, and I figured I'd be hanging on to it for a long time to come. It was just the beginning—of that I was sure.

As the club became better known, I hired some of my favorite performers to appear there: King Curtis, Tommy Hunt, Ben E. King, Frankie Lymon, and my favorite performer, Jackie Wilson. And of course I had my backup band behind all these stars, the members of which would become three of the four Hall of Fame-bound Rascals in just a short time from then: Eddie, Felix, and Gene. I also had an exciting dance troupe by the name of Mama Lou Park's Parkettes. They could do the Lindy hop better than anyone I'd ever seen before. I knew about the Lindy and other dances of that era. Remember, I was around during the war years, albeit just a youngster; and my older sister Mary danced all the time and even won dance contests with her soon-to-be-husband and my godfather, Sam "Shuffs" Mistrette. (We called Sam "Shuffs," a shortened version of his nickname "Shuffles.") I used the Parkettes several times at the club, and they became very popular with the crowds. I also used a group that had performed at Joe Scandore's Sweet Chariot in its good days: the Miller Sisters. These ladies could sing standards and rock & roll in addition to gospel. They were very talented, and I loved having them at my club.

No doubt the lineup and popularity of the Starliter put a dent in the bottom line of the Peppermint Lounge, but there was no bad blood between me and my old bosses Sam and Louie. In fact, we remained quite good friends. If only I'd listened to them I'd be a wealthier man today. I could have bought brownstones in the Village for forty grand each, and all I had to do was cut the check. Now, of course, those units are worth millions. I suppose others have such what-if stories, but that doesn't make me regret any less my own failure to grab such opportunities that would have set me up for life.

Things were working great at the Starliter, and I committed myself to its success, determined to do whatever and everything required to put it on top and keep it there. I rarely went home, but—sadly—not always on account of business. See, I still managed to discover ways to keep my casting couch—and other furniture—in good working order. Joan kept waiting for me at home and looking the other way, as her mother and mine advised her to do. But I could easily see that she was running out of patience with me and with our finances. My commitment to the club left no time for paying gigs, and I lost untold thousands in income that would have been generated on the road.

What with all the sexual perks and other king-of-the-hill accommodations of being the youngest club owner in the City, once again the "little" head was in charge of the "big" head, and that seldom worked out for the better.

FOURTEEN

STARLITER PART TWO: FUN AND GAMES TO THE END

As the saying goes—I think it's a saying—everything's fine till it's not. And when the Starliter was firing on all eight, it was a grand ride. A grand ride indeed. There was money. There was fame. There were women. There was prestige, respect, networking—all that King-of-the-Mountain stuff. And I enjoyed it. It was a magnificent rush—especially at my age. But no matter how rosy things seem to be at any given time, there's always a slap of reality coming—and the one headed for me was a doozie. But the ride I was on till that slap arrived? It was a helluva thing.

| Louie Chink |

Louie Chink was a regular at the club every night, bumming a ride with Dom when he came to work. Louie would jog the length of the club ten or twenty times and then sit at a table to read the paper while everyone else prepared for the night. Sometimes Dom would sneak up on Louie and light the bottom of the newspaper afire. It was amazing—and scary—how much of the paper would be on fire sometimes before Chink noticed the problem.

Now and then Dom would use the office phone to call Chink on the club payphone. Tootsie or another waitress would take Louie to the payphone.

"Hey Chink!" Dom would say. "Joey Dee's a no-good stool pigeon rat!"

Now, Louie Chink had become a great friend and fan of mine, and he wouldn't stand for any disparaging remarks about me.

"What?!" he'd answer. "No, you fuckin' bitch!"

I guess he'd have used more—and more sophisticated—words to defend me, but the sad truth was that this was pretty much the extent of Louie's vocabulary. See, Chink was older than the rest of us, and he'd suffered a stroke. A few vulgar words were all he could manage. Was Dom cruel? Probably. But funny as hell. Dom thought so anyway.

Now, Chink was an enigma, to say the least. Here was a man who'd been a numbers runner for the Mob before his stroke. Despite having never finished elementary school, Louie could memorize hundreds of his customers' numbers and report them verbally to his boss. I found such skill to be astounding. As it turned out Louie never did any time for running numbers. See, numbers runners only went to jail if they were caught with their betting slips on them. Louie memorized everything, so he never had any betting slips. No slips, no evidence. No evidence, no crime. No crime, no time. Simple.

| A Yankee in King Joey's Court |

I've been a dyed-in-the-wool New York Yankees fan for my whole life. If you draw my blood, I'm pretty sure you'll see pinstripes. When I allow myself to think about the demolition of Yankee Stadium, I get a bad case of the blues. How could such a landmark be destroyed in favor of a few more seats and a few more bucks? Is nothing in this world to be valued more than hard, cold cash? Ruth, Gehrig, DiMaggio, Mantle, Berra, Ford, A-Rod, Jeter, Munson, Mattingly—the sod of that field had carried the feet of the greatest baseball players ever to have lived, and we scraped it up like any common backyard to be paved over. Some things simply aren't right, and the destruction of that hallowed place was one of those things.

And still it's gone. Shame on us.

Being a Yankees fan, I held it to be a great honor to get to know some of the players of my day, even becoming close friends with some. Joe Pepitone was one who became a regular at my club. This man was cool, and the ladies loved him. He always looked sharp and even blow-dried his hair—something nearly unheard of in that day. Could he party? Yep. I'd watch Joe party till four in the morning and then head to the park for a day game. Like as not he'd get a couple of hits or even a homer, without missing a beat. He was party-proof.

As I said, the ladies loved Joe. And Joe loved the ladies. He'd often come to the club with more than one beauty on his arm. At times it seemed to become too much for him though. I mean, even a guy who loves the ladies can sometimes crave a little bro time. When that need struck, Joe would sneak out to the back service bar to hang with Al and David. Sometimes David would challenge Joe to a "friendly" game of stick ice. Out came the broom handles and ice cubes. Game on, bro. Brigati gave Pepitone his best stuff but to no avail. This isn't to say David wasn't good. He was. But Joe was better. I mean, the guy could hit a BB with a straw. This competition would go on for a half-hour or longer, or until a waitress popped in to tell Joe that his dates were restless and asking for him. He'd leave the kitchen, but reluctantly.

Some of Joe's shenanigans landed him in more trouble than just a restless date or two. And so it was that a confrontation he had at the Copacabana followed him into the Starliter one night, and we both paid a price.

| In the Men's Room with Pepitone |

I'd become friends with Junior at the Pep, and I was happy to see my Brooklyn friend at my club. We greeted each other with a good word and a hug, but he seemed distracted—maybe a bit troubled. As we spoke he was looking around for something or someone.

"Junior, seems like maybe you got something on your mind," I said. "Something wrong?"

"Nah, it's nothin', Joey," Junior answered, as he continued to scan the nearly wall-to-wall crowd. "Just looking . . . for . . . there he is." His face morphed into a stern look. "I need to talk with Pepitone. Okay, Joey?" Junior was polite with me and respectful, but I had an inkling that he might not be feeling as courteous toward Pepitone. Yeah, I had a bad feeling about this whole thing, even though I didn't know what *this whole thing* was. Worrying about what might be coming next, I took preemptive action.

"Just wait here, Junior," I said. "I'll get Joe for you, okay?"

I approached Joe and asked him to come with me to talk with Junior. I had no way of knowing that a female relative of Junior's had been at the Copa a couple of nights before, and Pepitone had made some derogatory remarks about her. I don't know what he said, but it wasn't good. And it got back to Junior. And *that* wasn't good either.

Joe followed me to Junior, but what I saw on Junior's face as we approached him told me he had more on his mind than just talking.

"Not in here, Junior. Okay?" I hoped to stop this before it began.

"Okay, Joey," Junior said. "Let's go to the men's room." Then he looked at me and said, "Don't worry, Joey."

The three of us made our way without talk to the men's room.

"Junior," I said, "you know I gotta go in there with you."

"Joey, I need to talk to Joe alone, okay?" Junior said.

"No, Junior. I gotta go in with you."

Junior shrugged slightly and nodded, and the three of us went into the men's room and closed the door. Now, Pepitone was well over six feet tall. Junior was about five-seven. But it sometimes turns out that there are things more powerful than size. Tough is tough, and Junior was tough. Pepitone started the conversation, making it clear that he knew what was eating Junior.

"Man, I didn't know she was related to you," Joe began. "Hon . . ." He was going to add the word *honest*, but before he could get it out, Junior unleashed a flurry of blows and kicks accompanied by a stream of profanity and threats and promises, only pieces of which I could understand.

"Pinstripemufuratbasyankprickmuthassballsofffeeddogsonof . . ." I Can't quote Junior verbatim here, but I'll beg your understanding, considering I was dodging kicks and walls and fists and garbage cans and paper dispensers and whatnot. Made it a bit hard for me to focus on syntax and such.

I don't know how many of the kicks or punches landed on Joe, but I know I caught two of Junior's kicks very nicely on the inside of my thigh. I guess you could call me *collateral damage*, because I'm sure Junior wasn't aiming for me. That the kicks were unintentional sure didn't make my leg hurt less.

Whatever the kicks- or blows-count, I guess Junior finally landed enough to suit himself, so he just finished the whole thing off with a stiff slap and a hard two-handed push. Now, when I say *stiff slap*, it's as if I were calling a tornado a *brisk wind*. I expected more to come after the slap and the push but no. It was finished. I believe the only reason this encounter didn't end so much worse than it did was that Junior respected me. Maybe he even felt a bit sorry that I'd caught a couple of his kicks. Whatever the reason for it, Pepitone was allowed to walk away after a relatively light dusting. Even though it ended with "just" a slap, I'm sure it was difficult for Joe to take it and walk away. But when certain people slap you, you let it go, log it as *message received*, and walk away. Joe was smart enough to know that.

The whole thing ended as quickly as it had begun. Junior hugged me. "See ya, Joey. Be well."

| You're Killing Me, Brigati |

After closing the club for the day, Dom, Chink, Al, David, and I would often go up to 116th Street and First Avenue to the Delightful Diner, where we'd have breakfast and some laughs. On this day David and I were sitting in a booth, not knowing that the place was under police surveillance. From the table next to us, he heard guys speaking in an Irish brogue. Smiling, David determined to bust their balls just a little. He began to sing "Does Your Mother Come from Ireland or Some Other Dirty Place." Turned out the Irish guys were on-the-job plain-clothes cops checking out the place. Of course, they weren't pleased with David's singing, and they had in mind to do something about it. Now, these guys were big, and I mean *big*. When they stood up, it seemed like they'd never stop standing up. Big. *Big* guys.

"What are you, a smart guy?" one of them said to Brigati.

Of course, cop partners always have each other's back, so the other one joined in with, "How 'bout I break you in half, smart guy?!"

Quickly into the potential fray leaped our friend Johnny Delightful, the owner of the place. Putting himself between David and certain bruises, Johnny was a voice of reason. "Okay boys," he said. "Let's all just calm down, right? Too early for this, guys. Let's just calm down, okay?!"

I can only guess that the cops had enjoyed breakfasts that lay heavy on their stomachs, because they didn't press the issue. Mumbling threats of doing things to us that I'm pretty sure were physically impossible, they plunked some cash onto their table and rumbled out of the place, no one the worse for wear.

No thanks to Brigati. Courtesy of his poorly timed sense of humor, I'd enjoyed another thrill that could have led to the beating of a lifetime for me, just for being with him. Chalk up another narrow scrape for us.

We also enjoyed a pizza from time to time at Patsy's uptown, and we frequented lots of other after-hour joints at Mob-owned clubs. Everybody in those joints was already toasted from bouncing and drinking all night at clubs in the City, and under such circumstances nothing good could happen. And it usually didn't. What *did* happen were threats, fights, and unholstered guns—for no reason at all, other than that they were smashed. And they'd have sit-downs that would get out of hand: Your nephew said this, your brother said that, your mother . . . whatever. It was all bullshit but usually led to trouble that ended before a tribunal to straighten it all out. It just wasn't worth it, if you ask me—but that's the way things were then.

So there I was, spending fruitless time surrounded by hoods and booze, and I kept compounding the stupidity by not reining in my sexual appetites. Lois Lee came by the club every night, and before you could say *you'd better think twice* we were going out together. She had her own place in the City, even though she lived in the Morris Park section of the Bronx. I started seeing her at her place every time I had too much to drink, which was nearly every night.

I should have been home with Joanie and my sons. That was my place.

| Fickle Foul Winds of Fortune |

New York's youngest night club owner was riding high for about six months. Then, like all things New York, the club's success began to wane. Sooner or later fickle New York crowds always find That New Place, whatever it is, and abandon That Old Place, whatever it was. The crowds aren't only fickle; they're easily bored, even in circumstances that aren't actually boring. They just grow tired of sameness and move on to the next happening thing. And now we found ourselves fighting even more than the ticklish feet of the New York crowds. We were also fighting the British Invasion, which was destined to change not only clubbing habits but tastes, trends, and styles in music as well. Thinking back, I guess I must have felt like I was up against it and all washed up, what with the Brits storming our shores in '64 and my old friends John, Paul, George, and Ringo leading the charge.

It was painful. I had no hit records, no publicity, no gigs, no prospects. I still had the club, but everything was starting to feel upside down, and my bills—just like those damn Brit bands—just kept on coming. Yeah, I'd made a ton of money in the last couple of years, but I also spent like a drunken sailor. Now I found that I'd pissed it all away. In my defense I'll say I'd had some help in the spending. See, I had lots of partners besides Sally Burns: bartenders, waitresses, and everybody who touched the cash before I did. Some were honest, most were not.

I know now that I should have faced my circumstances more honestly than I did. If I had, I'd have been looking for a j-o-b instead of a b-j-o-b. I should have been touring, earning money, and going home to count that money with my family. But I had to be the great entrepreneur—not to mention having to be available at the club all the time in order to give proper attention to the business as well as to all those waitresses. But, as a very wise man once said, "The years teach much that the days never know."

It's not a fun thing to be short of money after having a lot of it. It's an amazing and harsh truth that when the money vanishes, so do most of the "friends." I found it to be so. And banks? Hell, they're no help. You try to get a loan from them, and they want to know what collateral you have. It seems they'll lend you money only after you prove you don't need it. I remember thinking to myself during conversations with bankers, *if I had collateral, I'd sell it and use the money and wouldn't be having this conversation with a prick like you.*

It seems to be true that musicians and money don't mix—but that can't stop a musician from plying his trade. Here's my applicable "Dee-ism": Good credit, bad credit, no credit—most musicians don't ever get any real money, and most die broke or close to it. But this was the life we chose, and we'd never want to do anything else.

I joined my band on stage every now and again to see whether I still had it or not. I did. And when I say I had *it*, I don't mean only that I could still play the sax and sing. I had *it*: the love for performing, the unspeakable feeling that comes from making music, the connection with the band, the connection with the audience. I had *it*. And I thanked God that it was so. I would need it.

| Auld Lang Syne |

My last hope for putting things right with my club was to hang on until the New Year's Eve party. That celebration would be the big payoff. The club seated three-hundred-fifty, and, at a hundred bucks a pop, that would come out to a nice round thirty-five large, plus more for extras like special champagne and cognac. With that much revenue I could make things right. And reservations came pouring in. We could have sold out the place twice. Things were looking as bright and shiny as a newly minted silver dollar, and I was beginning to feel some relief.

The stage was set. I arrived at the club a little early and went to the upstairs dressing room. From there I could hear the hustle and bustle of a great night club atmosphere. I felt a bit like I was hovering in heaven.

Around nine-thirty the band kicked off a dance set, and at ten I did an hour with them. At eleven-thirty the band was to go on and play up to the witching hour and lead the crowd into 1965. Things would wind down after that, checks would be paid—all in cash—and everything would be fine.

Sitting ringside for the evening's entertainment were my Harlem pals Johnny Echols and GiGi and their wives. Along came a guy from the Pep days named Jimmy Gums, who accidentally bumped into Johnny's pregnant wife. You'd think a simple *sorry* would have fixed it, but it wasn't to be that simple. Jimmy Gums said it, of course, but Johnny Echols wasn't in a forgiving mood.

The guys from Harlem started punching and kicking Jimmy Gums, and that was the catalyst. Before you could say *let the wrecking ball swing*, the entire place erupted into a melee, an all-out donnybrook, and nearly everyone in the crowd joined in. Jimmy Gums was chased into the service bar, and full bottles of booze were broken over his head. Even with that, Jimmy wouldn't go down, but his assailants weren't finished yet. Five or six of them pummeled him into a bloody mess, and he went down at last. That's when the kicking started. When you're on the floor and five or six guys are landing kicks to every part of your body, it just won't end well for you. Jimmy Gums was in trouble and would be, until the kickers tired. My brother Al, who was working the service bar that night, told me later that he'd never seen anything like the beating he watched that night.

David and I were upstairs. It took a minute for us to understand that the sounds coming from below us weren't sounds of celebration and partying. It came clear to us that something else was going on, so we dashed out to see what it was. What we saw was utterly jaw-dropping. I'd never seen a fight like this—and believe me, I saw some lulus at the Pep. This was like watching the bloodiest barroom brawl ever in a John Wayne western, staged and directed by Quintin Tarantino—except these weren't stunt actors, and the blood wasn't ketchup. We could do nothing but watch and listen to guests scream and moan as they fled the scene, not one having paid a check for the night.

David and I said nothing. There was nothing to say. We simply stared blankly into each other's eyes, knowing we were witnessing the end of Joey Dee's Starliter.

| And Now What? |

To call that New Year's Eve at the Starliter a disaster would be soft-pedaling it. Heartbreaking ruination—that's what it was. We hung on for a while longer, but I knew it was only a matter of time—for the club and for me, if I didn't do something fast. I was fresh out of Starliters—again. Felix, Eddie, and Gene left to form the Rascals and follow their path to the Rock & Roll Hall of Fame. My finances were in shambles. My marriage was in trouble. Everything was upside down. How easy it would have been for me to throw in the towel and just say to hell with it all.

But I wouldn't do that. I had to get off my ass and refigure things. At the very least that meant creating a new Joey Dee and the Starliters. It wouldn't be easy, but I just had to hunker down and get it done. After all, assembling bands was my forte, my gift—I'd done it many times before, and I could do it again. Yes, for the moment I was out of the limelight. But I had music and adventure left in me, and I wasn't ready to take up residence at the Old Musicians Home. Not just yet . . .

Fifteen

JIMI HENDRIX:
FLOPHOUSES TO STARLITER

I've never backed down from a challenge, and capitulation was never an option. I've always had confidence in my talents, abilities, and luck. Hell, I have confidence in my *confidence*. That wasn't going to change now. It was time to get that band together.

| REGROUPING |

First step, front line. Vocals. I went back to my old reliable pal David Brigati—he of the golden pipes—and asked him to give it another go. He wasn't particularly interested, but I begged him till he broke. Now I had a bona fide star back in the group—one who'd done it all before and with whom I was as close as any brothers could be. Knowing I had David up front on stage and behind me off stage, I was inspired and knew this was going to get done.

I needed still another vocalist who could work with David. At the Pep I'd met a great singer with a group called the Orchids, but I only knew him as Tommy. No last name. With a little effort I discovered that he was living in New Rochelle, New York, playing at the Country House (a.k.a. Deercrest Inn), where I'd met and befriended Billy Vera, later of Billy Vera and the Beaters ("At This Moment"). Billy gave me Tommy's number, and I wasted no time making him an offer. "You bet, Joey," Tommy said. "When do we start?"

I was thrilled to have Tommy Davis's funky voice joining with Brigati's and mine. Besides his talent, the buzz on Tommy was good: He got along well with others. This was important; I needed team players for this thing to work.

I had a great front line once again. Next step: backing musicians.

"The Amazing" Jimmi Mayes was a Mississippi-raised, Chicago-based drummer. Our first meeting came when I walked past him and Sam Taylor, Jr.—my old friend and ex-Starliter—as they stood at Jimmi's "sidewalk office": a parking meter outside a café on Broadway. Sam introduced us, and we chatted a while before I went on my way.

A band called the Freeman Brothers—formed by my friend and ex-Starliter Rogers Freeman after he left us—was using my Starliter club for rehearsals. As it turned out, that same Jimmi Mayes was playing for Rogers. I liked what I saw and heard when Jimmi was playing, and I told him so.

"Man," I said, "you can play the drums. And I need a drummer. Interested in being a Starliter?" Again, I wasn't above stealing talent when I saw what I needed. I could pay a little better than what Jimmi was making with the Freeman Brothers, and we had some nice gigs coming up in Syracuse, Buffalo, and elsewhere.

"When do we start?" Jimmi asked, and I had my drummer.

The two of us became instant running partners. I made Jimmi my band leader because of his talent, intelligence, experience, reputation, and most excellent people skills. In the coming months Jimmi and I would become best friends, and I'm proud and blessed to say we're the same today.

At my Starliter I'd met a cat named Calvin Duke, a self-taught keyboard man from Harlem who made some funky music. He was a big, handsome, black-skinned man with a great sense of humor and remarkable talent. I hired him and his Hammond B-3.

With that I had my front line. I had my drummer. I had my B-3. I was almost there. Now I had only to find the right guitar player.

| Final Piece of the Puzzle |

I put Mayes on the job. Jimmi was—and is—not only a talented artist but widely known, highly respected, and broadly networked as well. He invaded every nook and cranny of New York, all up in Harlem and everywhere, trying to get a lead on a guitar player who could fill the bill. In those days Black musicians had an exclusive and incredibly effective network. Nothing, especially talent, could stay hidden; someone would hear, someone would know, someone would tell.

But even the network wasn't paying off for Mayes this time. He was stonewalled. Everyone he talked to or heard about was already gigging or not interested or not a good fit for the Starliters. But then, walking down Broadway, he ran into Johnny Starr, who was playing guitar for Jackie "Mr. Excitement" Wilson. Mayes told Starr that the Starliters needed a guitar player and asked if he knew anyone who might be available and interested.

"Maybe," Starr said. "Share a room with a guy. He sides for the Isleys, but he don't care shit for that. They treat him this and thataway. Sometimes the van don't even wait for him at the George Washington Bridge when he even a little late to get picked up for a gig," Starr continued. "And he don't do the gig, he don't get paid. He don't get paid, he get hungry. Maybe him. You might get him."

Starr took Mayes to the Alvin Hotel on 51st between 7th and Broadway. Now, in those days there were many posh hotels in the City, but others weren't quite five-star residences. They weren't what you'd call *run-down*, but they were no longer the splendid hotels they'd been when built; time, wear, and neglect had taken a toll.

And some so-called hotels were . . . well, they weren't good. Just not good at all. Roaches, rats, no heat, no air conditioning, beds and mattresses that barely resembled beds and mattresses, clean towels that were dirty. These were the run-down places where, too often, a starving, trying-to-make-it musician was forced by sheer poverty to flop.

Jimmi Mayes was about to meet a young man who knew the flophouses and the dives. He'd come to New York from Seattle, by way of the "Chitlin' Circuit," which was a string of performance venues throughout the East, South, and upper Midwest in which Black entertainers could play their music without race-related difficulties. The man had stayed in seedy, cheap-ass hotels where rats had surrendered and retreated to the alley, which was an upgrade for them. He'd stayed in near-forgotten holes where every corner was occupied by a roach or a rat—or an addict huddling there against the fears and terrors that played out in his jumbled, confused, deluded, strung-out mind.

The Alvin Hotel wasn't ritzy, but it wasn't a dive. One man at the desk handled all guest needs. He assigned and (sometimes) cleaned rooms, collected rent, swapped clean towels for dirty ones, and threw out personae non grata. The Alvin frequently housed both up-and-coming and down-and-out entertainers.

Inside, Starr and Mayes made their way to the room where Mayes was introduced to a young, lanky, disheveled brother with long hair and worn-out clothes. In the corner stood a pair of old, worn-down, pointed-toe boots with chains over the ankles. The boots and his appearance told a story to anyone who cared to notice. He wasn't doing well—that was the obvious story.

"Maurice James, this here's Jimmi Mayes," Starr said. "Jimmi's looking for a guitar player for Joey Dee and the Starliters."

"Yeah?" Maurice reached for the electric guitar that lay on his bed—it was there because he slept with it—and broke into "Johnny B. Goode." Then he played an Isley Brothers tune. He had no amp, but that didn't seem to bother him a bit; nor could it hide the talent—no, the genius—Mayes saw and heard.

And then Maurice segued into a Curtis Mayfield piece.

"That's enough," Mayes told him. "Mayfield. That's enough for me." Mayes knew I was a freak for Curtis Mayfield, and he offered Maurice the gig.

Maurice wasn't interested. "Already been in too many groups," he said flatly. "Don't like 'em. Not a sideman. Not a backup player."

"Man, you won't be no sideman. You'll be a Starliter," Mayes said. "And Joey don't care 'bout being shown up. If you got talent, you do your thing, man. Joey's good with that."

"Yeah . . . well, shit," Maurice said. "Did my thing for Little Richard, and his brother fired my ass."

Mayes straightened him out. "Won't happen with Joey Dee. Nope, won't happen. And you gonna like the way he pays. You don't play jus' for the door. Joey pays fair—hundred twenty-five a week and rooms on the road." Mayes continued, "And you never been in a group fronted by a white man. You'll see. It's different with Joey than it was with the others. Lemme get in touch with the man," he added, "and get you an audition. Talk later."

Mayes called me. "I got the guitar player," he said.

I asked , "You sure?"

"Man YEAH I'm sure!" Mayes said. "Done checked him out. Might need a little polish, but I'm sure."

"Polish? What the hell's that—polish?!" I asked.

"Not talkin' 'bout his guitar," Mayes said. "This cat can play. What I mean, he looks a little scruffy is all."

"Long as it's not his playing," I said, "we can polish the hell out of him. Let's get together. Take care of it, man."

Mayes took care of it. I sent my young nephew Johnny "The Count" Van Bodegon, who was working as my driver, to New York to pick up Mayes and Maurice at the Alvin and bring them to my home.

| THE AUDITION |

The three men arrived at my home in Lodi. I was living there with my wife Joan and our sons Joey, five, and Nicholas, four. It was a beautiful, comfortable home on a full acre, and I loved it. The stained glass windows made it almost a cathedral, and the furniture was specially created by an Italian designer. The neighborhood was just right for us, too, with almost every name in Lodi ending with a vowel. That meant lots of good Italian neighbors.

Mayes and Johnny walked into our home with a tall, wiry, young man in tow and introduced me to Maurice James. He was dressed in a red and white shirt, ripped skintight pants, well-worn boots, and a rolled-up bandana tied around his head of raucous hair. I couldn't tell at first if this guy was a musician or a pirate. In spite of his in-your-face appearance, I could tell immediately that Maurice was shy, reticent—but with a good sense of humor. I liked him. We talked comfortably and laughed for a while, getting to know each other. He told me bits and pieces about his gigs with Little Richard as well as with the Isley Brothers. For him the Isleys were just okay, and he didn't care much for Little Richard—and, if firing Maurice was any indication, the feeling was mutual. I was particularly interested in what he had to say about the Isleys, because I was a fan. They had recorded "Shout" in 1959, the song we used as a closer. And we scored a hit with our cover of it, reaching number six on the Billboard Hot 100 in 1962—the only version of the iconic hit to make Billboard's top ten. That shared music somehow made me feel close to the them, even if they hadn't been exactly Maurice's cup of tea.

At last I got around to asking Maurice to show me what he had. Accompanying me to the garage, he pulled an electric guitar—I'm told it was a Fender Jazzmaster, but what did I know . . . I was a sax player—from a makeshift canvas gig bag that looked more like an abused gunny sack or a discarded hotel towel. He took the Jazzmaster into his hands upside-down, plugged into a battered little amp he'd brought along, and plucked a pick from between two strings. He stroked—I could say *strummed*, but that just doesn't quite describe it—the strings a couple of times with his left hand for a quick-and-dirty sound check, and then the man morphed into someone else, right before my eyes. The guitar melted into his hands and seemed to become a part of his very being. He rolled his eyes upward, as though he were seeing or hearing or feeling something no one else could—then he slowly closed them.

And then he played.

As if they were connected to one another in some magical, mystical way, Maurice's hands began to make love to those strings in a way I'd never seen or even imagined. He slid seamlessly from arpeggios into a Curtis Mayfield tune, and under Maurice's fingers it became its own special thing. I'd never seen one man and a guitar love each other so much.

Thirty seconds. That's all it took.

"You got the gig," was all I could manage to say.

After he freed himself from the embrace of his guitar, I shook the man's hand. "Incredible, Maurice. Just incredible," I said.

"Thanks, man," Maurice said. "And you can call me Maurice or Jimmy, either one. Don't matter to me. Real name's Jimmy."

In less than two years from then, Jimmy would be managed and produced by Chas Chandler, who had recently left the group the Animals to pursue production and artist management. In addition to producing Jimmy's first hit UK recordings, Chandler would persuade James Marshall Hendrix from Seattle to change the spelling of his name from *Jimmy* to the more exotic *Jimi*.

Jimi. Hendrix. Jimi *Hendrix*. The same Jimi Hendrix who some years later would be named by *Rolling Stone* magazine as the greatest guitarist of all time and the sixth greatest rock & roll artist. The same Jimi Hendrix who would change the face of music forever and who, despite enjoying only a few short years of playing, creating, and innovating, would be enshrined in the Rock & Roll Hall of Fame here and in the UK Music Hall of Fame. The same Jimi Hendrix who would achieve the rare, enviable status of Legend.

That's who I'd just auditioned and hired. Our paths had now crossed; from there neither of our lives would be the same again.

| Just a Small Tokin' of Friendship |

We were excited, Jimi and I, to have found each other. I write *Jimi*, but he still spelled his name Jimmy and mostly went by Maurice during the time he was a Starliter. Over the course of his life and career, Hendrix had more aliases than a Jersey mobster: James, Jimmy, Buster, Jimmy James, Maurice James, James Maurice, and Jimi. For clarity, I mostly use his most famous moniker.

Whatever his name or the spelling of it, one thing was certain: Jimi needed me, and I needed him. We discussed a business arrangement in more detail and came to terms. I reassured him that I had no problem with the stage antics for which he'd been fired by Little Richard. I explained that anything that made the show better also made *me* better, so his impulsive stage behavior was not just okay with me; it's what I wanted and even required. I gave him some records to listen to, so he could become familiar with the songs we played. He'd start next week and join Joey Dee and the Starliters for the upcoming Syracuse gig.

Jimi thought this new partnership was worth a little celebration. Heaven knows I was never one to thumbs-down a party, but I was about to learn that each of us had his own idea of celebrating. I thought we might just dip our beaks a bit, but

Hendrix had another notion.

"How 'bout we smoke the peace pipe on this?" he said, reaching into the hip pocket of his worn-thin pants to retrieve a small plastic bag. I recognized the bag's contents immediately.

"Uhhh, no," I said. "I don't use. Never have. How 'bout a drink?"

Jimi was unfazed and undeterred. As he opened the bag, I thought to myself, *You fire that damn thing in here and you're gonna catch the hot hell of an Italian-American Catholic Jersey mother's righteous*—that word may be slightly misplaced here—*indignation.* Maurice's only hope was that Joanie hadn't yet returned from getting her hair done. But she had. She had returned and was hovering somewhere out of sight, quiet and watchful.

Maurice lit the devil weed. Now, I don't hold myself to be anything of a prophet, but . . . yep, here she came. The man had barely filled his lungs with that contraband smoke when my wife rushed into the room like a lioness that had set herself between her cubs and the threat of danger. And now, seeing the danger become real, she sprang, baring words like fangs and claws against the attacker.

"Now you, Mr. Whatever-your-name-is, you just take that fuckin' thing outta here already, and you just haul your ass right out with it."

She was just getting started.

"I mean, what?!" Joanie continued. "You're gonna come into my house? Into MY HOUSE with two small children in it, and do dope?! They're right upstairs, my little boys. Right upstairs! MY. LITTLE. BOYS! You should be ashamed. Shame, SHAME on you. Now you just get out. Go on now . . . OUT! Before I snatch that shit out of your bony hand and shove . . ."

Before Joanie could finish her last screeched threat, Maurice was on the move, half running, half stumbling toward the front door, barely able to hang on to his sacred Jazzmaster guitar and raggedy little amp as he went. All he left behind was an errant whiff of outlawed smoke and an enduring snapshot in my mind of a future Hall of Fame rock & roll legend being chased from my house like an unwelcome drunk from a tavern.

And where was I during the uproar? Well, at first I didn't know whether to spit or go bowling, but then I made a simple defensive maneuver. As she was ramping up her tirade, I calmly said to Joanie, "But hon . . ." When she snapped back at me, "But hon HELL!" I just shut up, glad I wasn't the one in her cross-hairs and wanting it to stay that way. Now, Joanie and I were usually equal in household authority, but she was insisting on leading this dance. So, as I dumbly watched the grandest outpouring of rage I'd ever seen, I reached a decision that was equal parts confusion, fear, caution, reason, and smarts: NO WAY was I gonna get between Joanie and my new guitar player, no matter what his name was or how he played that guitar. I sneaked and slithered around the claws and the fangs to disappear relatively unscathed through the door, right on the heels of the exiled Hendrix et al.

Johnny and Mayes were on the lam too. Mayes seemed embarrassed about the whole thing, but he also didn't want to step into the line of fire. Behind the protection of their silence, the two of them had been mercifully spared the full force of Joanie's fury. Still, they must have sustained injury or damage to some degree. I mean, a hand grenade exploding in one man's shorts may take him out altogether, but anyone standing nearby won't feel too well either.

As the James boys climbed into the van with Johnny, I called after them. "You got the gig, man," I said. "Sorry about all this. My wife's just a little protective. It's all right. I'll call you tomorrow to set up rehearsal."

The three of them drove away. There may or may not have been some tire-squealing as they fled. And I don't know what Hendrix did with the joint. For all I know he swallowed the damn thing.

| New Family Ties |

And so it happened that the legendary Jimi Hendrix was thrown out of my house. The good news is, Joanie later found it in her heart to forgive and forget, eventually welcoming Jimi—sans joint, of course—back into the house. We had him and the rest of the band over for dinner often. There were other family get-togethers as well with my sisters Mary and Rosie and my brother Al. My siblings considered everyone in the band to be family and loved us and what we did. While all the boys loved those family dinners, I have to think Hendrix must have especially appreciated them. He had little connection to family. I knew his mother had died, and he occasionally sent a postcard to his father while we were on the road. And I had met one of his sisters. That was about it.

On one particular occasion Rosie served up spaghetti and meatballs to a table surrounded by Jimmi, David, Jimi, Calvin, Tommy, myself, and other family. Everyone ate so much at that meatball-fest, we thought we might have to cancel rehearsals for a time. I mean, we ate so much that, if there'd been a 9-1-1 service in those days, we'd have called it. Hendrix later remarked to me that those had been the best meatballs he'd ever eaten. I couldn't argue.

And how happy was I that Jimi hadn't felt the need for an after-dinner doobie.

SixTEEN

HENDRIX ON BOARD

What I call confidence, some may call ego. Be that as it may. Whatever it is I've got, it's served me well when I've needed it. I knew I'd find a way to put together another primo band, and I'd done just that. Again. It had taken a lot of blood, sweat, and tears and a double dose of that confidence or ego or whatever you'd like to call it. But it was done. David, Jimmi, Maurice, Tommy, Calvin—we were strong at every post, and I could hardly wait to hear these boys make music together.

| Solid Sound, Solid System, Solid Style |

I picked up the James boys at Big Wilt's and drove to my home for our first full rehearsal. We got squared away and played. From the first notes, the sound was good—even powerful. Yep, it was a *powerful* sound we had to sell. Not only that, but—and nearly as important—it was clear to me right from the get-go that the boys meshed like the fingers of hands playing *here's-the-church-here's-the-steeple*. There was no friction, no competition, no tension, no argument—and it would stay that way with this group.

I wasn't a taskmaster. I'd never had to be. But I did have a system, and I expected everyone to respect it. I told the guys, "You wouldn't be with me if you weren't a professional. I shouldn't have to chase you around, and I don't believe in fining. I expect two things from you: Be on time, and be a gentleman." See, I figured if you were on time, that was good business. If you were a gentleman, then you were contributing to a class act that would be remembered. These things were important to me; I believed they were integral parts of a good band, good music, and good performance that would please an audience and keep us relevant.

One aspect of being a gentleman was the way we dressed on stage. I'd taken my appearance seriously from the beginning and dressed in a suit and tie whenever I was on stage—and I insisted that the boys follow suit. As a matter of fact, one might say I was tyrannical when it came to stage dress. I insisted that we dress for class. Just as I'd done with other Starliters, I often reminded this group that the audience would see us before it heard us. If we had a clean, appealing look, the audience would be free to focus on our music.

Of course, I did commit that *one* fashion faux pas, but I just couldn't pass up a deal like that. I mean, brand new suits for twenty-five bucks each! But I had a hard time getting the boys to wear them. Even the brothers, who had much more liberal tastes in fashion than we boring white guys had, said they wouldn't be caught dead in those *pink* suits. "We ain't wearing that shit," is, I believe, precisely how they put it. The pink suits went away.

When you see me perform today, you'll find my notion of proper attire hasn't changed. On stage I'm in a suit and tie. Even if I'm playing outdoors in triple-digit weather, I'll be wearing a suit and tie. Such apparel may seem odd for an outdoor performance in Florida, but that's the way I dress. It's proper. It's civil. It's class. It's gentlemanly. It's Joey Dee.

Now, when Hendrix came on board, he didn't have a suit. He barely had any clothes. I took him to the place where I always bought suits: F & F Tailors in New York City. My friend there, Dave Alter—good last name for a tailor—fitted Jimi for a couple of suits, one of which was a silver sharkskin number. Hendrix rocked it. He looked every bit as good in a suit and tie as he did in the trademark psychedelic garb he wore after leaving the Starliters and finding his own unique place in the sun.

| Don't Sing, Maurice |

I liked to feature members of the band in every set. I don't mean everyone in every set, but I always featured someone. Whatever the names of my Starliters at any given time, I liked to show them off. When this particular group performed, Tommy might do his Elvis stylings. David might front a Johnny Mathis tune. Calvin would take a solo on the keys, Mayes would show his amazing stuff with the sticks, and Hendrix would step up to the front with his six-string. Everyone had a special thing to offer, and it was my pleasure to feature each of them and give each the spotlight. They loved it. I loved it. Crowds loved it.

As for vocals, I counted on everyone to back up the lead sometimes, so I tried Hendrix backing up David and Tommy on "Peppermint Twist." Please note that *tried* would be the operative word in that sentence. See, what that man did to a guitar was beyond marvelous, but when it came to vocals, it was immediately clear that Hendrix was a lost soul. He wasn't good. As a matter of fact, he sucked. And I had to tell him so, because what his voice did to our biggest hit song just plain couldn't happen on stage. To be accurate, Jimi didn't really *sing* per se. He mostly just *talked*. It's been my experience that it's quite hard to harmonize with actual music chords when you're just talking.

It fell to me, of course, to break the unhappy news to Jimi, but I had to make sure to let my man down gently. I didn't want to do damage. I had to be subtle. I had to be kind. I had to be tactful. Yep, *tactful* is what I had to be.

"Maurice, don't sing."

Damn. I forgot the *tactful* part. But at least I was clear. "You just stick to the guitar, okay?" I said. "We need your guitar. You're a guitar player. We'll take care of the vocals. Don't worry about it."

If you listen to the music of the Jimi Hendrix Experience, you know his singing style was not so much singing as it was talking—much like Dylan, whom Jimi studied diligently. As good a way as any to disguise a weak singing voice, I guess, and it certainly didn't limit his success. It only limited my options for backup from time to time.

Now I return for a moment to my *system*. Most of the time, the band respected my request to be gentlemen and on time. But once in awhile . . . not.

| Hendrix Goes Missing |

Our next rehearsals were held at my Starliter club. It was conveniently located for all the guys, especially for Hendrix; he could walk there from his room at the Alvin. We also were to meet at the club to leave for our two-week gig at Lorenzo's in Syracuse. But when we all joined up at the Starliter to leave for Syracuse, we didn't ALL join up at the Starliter to leave for Syracuse. Our newest member and only guitar player, Mr. Hendrix, was neither present nor accounted for. This was a bit unsettling. We were pressed for time and had to leave soon in order to make the gig on time.

Not good. Not good at all.

"Where the hell's Maurice?!" I said. "What the fu. . . I mean, what the hell's going on around here?"

Crickets. Maybe the guys thought my question was rhetorical; it wasn't. Still, I got no answer, no explanation. No one knew any more than I knew.

"Well, we gotta find our guitar player, I think," I said. "And fast."

After a quick thought I said to Mayes, "Man, you're the one who found him. Now you gotta go find him again. And all four of your feet better be with mine on that stage when the man calls our name."

Mayes seemed more than a little flustered by this random turn of events and with his assignment, but he didn't argue or complain. In just a minute or two, he was disappearing into the early morning dark, in a cab headed for wherever Maurice James was.

Mayes checked in with me a couple of times during his search. First, he told me he'd gone to the Alvin, but no Hendrix. A bit later he reported that he'd checked with Johnny Starr, but no Hendrix; however, Starr had given him a lead on a party at Fat Jack Keller's place. Otis Redding had just closed at the Apollo Theater, and a bunch had gone from there to Fat Jack's. "I'm headin' there now," Mayes told me.

Mayes arrived at Fat Jack's place and, after finally getting someone to answer the door, stepped into a scene that would have made guests at an ancient Roman orgy blush. The clothing he saw wasn't enough to dress a one-armed manikin. And smack in the middle of it all was our prodigal guitarist. Mayes told me later that Hendrix hadn't wanted to leave the party, even after his (Mayes's) loveliest invitation, if you know what I mean. See, Jimi was protecting his girlfriend Lithofayne "Fayne" Pridgon from the advances of Mr. Redding, and he couldn't afford to leave his post just then. He thought Fayne and Otis might get too friendly if he left. He was right; still, Fayne was able to persuade him to join Mayes and honor his commitment to the band. The two jumped into the waiting cab and headed to the Starliter.

Our departure already three hours delayed, we left the Starliter almost the very moment the James boys arrived. I didn't chew anyone out, nor was I even all that upset. I can't say I was *happy* with what had happened, but the band was together and ready to leave for Syracuse. That's what mattered. I pointed my Caddy down the highway, and the guys followed in the band's van, along with the equipment.

Better late than never.

SEVENTEEN

HAVING SEX WITH JIMI HENDRIX

W
e made it to Syracuse timely enough and dropped off our equipment at Lorenzo's, where we would be playing. From there we drove on to the Hilton Hotel, our accommodations for the next two weeks. Now, despite its name, the Syracuse Hilton wasn't exactly a classy hotel. To be blunt, if you spit on the floor, your mouth would hurt. Apparently, it hadn't been remodeled since the turn of a century—and I'm not sure which one. The furniture was ancient, the carpet worn and blotchy, and the paint stained and peeling. The elevator was just a cut above camel-drawn, with an accordion gate instead of doors—and a rickety ride that was more Disneyland than a hotel amenity. And the odds of a guest's safe arrival up or down were always long, in the house's favor.

The good news about the hotel—and the news was REALLY good—was that every go-go girl working at every joint in the area was staying there. You couldn't launch a lasso without snagging an off-duty dancer. At certain times of the day, you literally had to step over girls who were sitting or lying on the floor. The hotel was a smorgasbord of female beauty, experience, and favorable disposition. This was an unexpected windfall for us, and we would certainly do our best to capitalize on it; however, we'd never really needed any kind of head-start with the ladies when we were on the road. It was a rock & roll thing.

| Rock & Roll & Sex |

Since time immemorial—okay, I can't really back that up, but it's my contention—chicks have been attracted to musicians. And, in my heyday, the

180

musicians always got the best-looking women. That's part of why I became one. Chicks first, money second—those were my mixed-up priorities. Money first, you knucklehead! It should have been money first! The lesson here—which I learned too late—yielded another of my "Deeisms": Life is a money chase, and you've gotta keep up.

It was no surprise, then, that when Joey Dee and the Starliters played a gig, girls were there for the taking. It was like diving into a sea of waving arms, and ours was but to clutch any one of those arms and disappear into the nearest room. But as eager as they were, the girls knew they had to be careful. They wanted to be with us, but they didn't want to take away a permanent souvenir of the tryst—a souvenir they'd have t christen and raise and send to college. "The Pill" didn't hit the market till 1960 and wasn't widely available right away, so road sex in the early sixties was mostly oral. By the mid-sixties women were better protected against pregnancy and more likely to want traditional sex.

And they became bolder. Mid-decade girls weren't shy to make the first move, and they flaunted their intentions. They dressed for exposure, attention, and sex. In a formal venue, we could count on low-cut, curve-clinging gowns. In a casual venue, we got tight-fit clothing made of Spandex and other form-hugging materials that were the rage du jour. When a girl was rocking Spandex pants, little was left to the imagination—and we had very good imaginations. And, of course, their low-cut, skin-sucking tops—sans bra—could draw the gaze and swell the tongues of even the most virtuous and monogamous of men.

And here we had this little extra bonus, compliments of the Hilton. I mean, it being lousy with off-shift dancing girls as it was, the first days and nights in Syracuse just about hospitalized David, Tommy, the James boys, and me. Calvin didn't participate in our extracurricular activities. He did his own thing in his own way, and I respected his privacy. But the rest of us embraced the challenge before us and trudged on. I remember switching with three or four different dancers and female customers in one night. If nonstop sex were an Olympic event, then we'd all have gold medals hanging on our office walls. Maybe I should send that idea to the IOC. Talk about Nielsen ratings . . .

| Maurice Code |

What can I tell you—the girls liked us, and we liked them. We could choose from groupies, club dancers, random chicks; it didn't matter much to us which talent pool we recruited from, as long as the pick led to sex. Being Joey Dee, I usually got pick of the litter, so to speak, and I was rarely rejected.

We recruited from the audience as well. A woman there might catch our attention with a come-on look or a smile whenever we looked her way. Perhaps she licked her lips sensually and at just the right moment. Or maybe she had a body that just couldn't be ignored. When we were eyeing the house for possibilities, Hendrix and I had a system of onstage communication that helped us stay—ahem—abreast of the potential talent in the audience. He would brush casually past me, place his left hand over his mouth and say something like, "Blonde number, front right. Titties!" I'd smile or wink acknowledgment—or stifle an outright guffaw, depending on what he said to me and how he said it.

This was rock & roll fun on the inside. In a way it was essential to survival, and I'm not talking now about the sex. I mean, no matter how talented you were or how dedicated you were to the music or how much you enjoyed performing, the work and travel and repetition and hotels could grind you into the floorboards. Without such little inside games to keep us smiling and sharp, our onstage presence would eventually show the strain. Our performance depended in large measure on how well we got along with each other and how close we felt as a group, as a family. Onstage antics like this Jimi-to-Joey code, invisible to all but us, helped keep us alive and agile and fresh and together.

I scoped out my share of bitchin' babes too. And sometimes Hendrix and I eyed the same woman. When that happened, it wasn't necessarily a case of winner–loser. The two of us were close enough to share. The same was true for all the band. We all were flexible and cooperative in this thing.

| A Woman for All Reasons |

After the show one night Tommy hooked up with a girl—a "special" girl who was known for being . . . well, how should I put this . . . *freaky*. This chick was game for anything. She didn't really care what you had or where you put it. And a man's color? That was the furthest thing from her mind—black, white, green, blue, it was all the same to her.

Now, when it came to entertaining ladies, none of us was exactly what you'd call shy. Most of the time, we didn't even bother to lock our hotel room doors or knock before crashing in on each other. And so it was on this particular occasion, when Mayes, Hendrix, Brigati, and I walked in on Tommy and Miss Freaky, right in the middle of their carnal conversation. No one thought anything of what was going on atop the sheets, but I guess Hendrix figured he and Tommy were a tag team, and it was time to tag Tommy out. Now, Tommy seemed pretty much worn to a frazzle anyway, so he didn't mind the intrusion. In fact, in the deep recesses of my memory, I seem to hear him mumbling something like *help* or *save me* or *please somebody just shoot me*, or some other such sniveling. No problem; Hendrix was always eager to help a friend in need, and he didn't hesitate or miss a beat. He began shedding boots, shirt, pants, all the while talking to the girl as though nothing out of the ordinary were happening. When Hendrix was ready, Tommy moved over and [ahem] let Jimi take over with a fresh energy Miss Freaky appreciated. Sounded like she did anyway. Jimi was good at what he did on stage, to be sure; he was also good at what he was doing now. But when it came to giving head and satisfying ladies, he had to concede the title to "The Amazing" Jimmi Mayes. The master. I knew that to be true, because the girls were always ready—even eager—to tell me all about their experiences with Mayes.

And there stood the rest of us, watching a triple-X movie in living color.

| ENOUGH LEFT TO ROCK THE STAGE |

Despite our extracurricular shenanigans, we did our job in Syracuse. Lorenzo's was a good venue with sold-out houses of appreciative fans, and we gave everything we had. In our first set on the first night, I let Hendrix fly alone. He was a bit tentative, but in subsequent sets he warmed up and showed his stuff. He mesmerized the audience by playing his Jazzmaster with his teeth and behind his back. He played it while on his knees. He played it while on his back. He didn't set his six-string on fire—that wouldn't happen till the Jimi Hendrix Experience played a European tour and then again at the Monterey International Pop Music Festival in 1967. But if Maurice didn't literally light anything on fire in Syracuse, he was still smokin'. It was easy to see that he loved performing, and he absolutely absorbed the spotlight and owned the stage. He loved the crowd, and the crowd loved him right back. If Maurice didn't yet play quite like the guitarist he would become, he was still good. Damn good. And I let him play till he was good and ready to stop.

Eighteen

SHUFFLING OFF TO BUFFALO
WITH HENDRIX

W e finished up at Lorenzo's—and with the girls at the Hilton—and shuffled off to Buffalo for two weeks at McVan's Nite Club on Niagara Street—a nice venue with a roomy stage in a large ballroom, and a good restaurant. The master of ceremonies was a veteran of vaudeville whose look hadn't changed much with the times. Tony Otti (or Odei) could have been cast in any movie or stage production as the typical vaudevillian emcee.

McVan's featured an all-girl dancing revue to open the show, à la the Copacabana. I found this to be a charming touch of class. I've always been a sucker for old things: movies, music, cars, coins, stamps, even hotels, if they were nicely kept—just about anything old, I guess, except women. I liked young women in those days. So shoot me. But I seem to have a wide strand of nostalgia spiraling through my DNA, even through my soul. I was that way then; I'm that way now.

Every show was SRO, and every audience treated us to a standing ovation. We returned that generosity by blessing McVan's with one of the most surprising and unique—if not widely known—impromptu moments in rock & roll history.

| CRUSHING THE ROCKETTES |

At the finish of the show one night, we went back to the dressing room to change. Posing for snapshots for one of the showgirls and knowing it was

Halloween and that many in the crowd were in costume, Hendrix got an idea.

"Let's go back out," he suggested.

Of course, no one knew what he was talking about, but Jimi explained.

"It's Halloween, man! Let's be showgirls and bury the show."

Regardless of Jimi's enthusiasm, the suggestion earned mixed reactions. Calvin was very clear about it: He wasn't about to put on a dress. I didn't want to either. Mayes was a bit hesitant but caved after Tommy and David agreed to the stunt. After all was said and done Calvin and I compromised with the guys: Calvin would play the organ, and I'd play the drums—but not in dresses.

Let the costuming begin. The girls were thrilled to play *Dress Up the Starliters*. They found one black and three white dresses that *nearly* fit Jimmi, Jimi, Tommy, and David and somehow managed to wriggle and shoehorn the boys into them. Today, that show alone would go mega-viral, had it been recorded. Next came the lipstick and eye shadow. Mayes was okay with the lipstick, but he drew the line at eye shadow. And then there was all that beautiful, male hair just begging to be adorned. Bows should do the trick, and they were placed lovingly, if not neatly, onto the guys' heads.

Showtime.

Mr. Otti (Odei) helped out with a stage intro but not for Joey Dee and the Starliters. No, he introduced "The Pride of Buffalo" or "The Buffalo Herd" or some such ironic description. I found my way to the drums, and Calvin sat at the organ. I can only imagine the crowd's confusion at that point. Calvin and I laid down an improvised provocative little bump-and-grind rhythm—*ba-BOOM-ba-ba-BOOM*—to bring out this odd version of Starliters boasting varying degrees of sex appeal. Tommy, Jimi, Jimmi, and David entered stage right, locked together arms to waists, high-kicking the beat like Rockettes and rocking those go-go dress fringes like Ann-Margret shaking herself dry. Hilarious. Outrageous. And gorgeous, simply gorgeous. At the risk of showing favoritism, I have to say Hendrix and Mayes had the best legs—but black socks and oxfords on all the boys leveled the playing field.

The crowd went insane. Crazy. Nuts. They loved what they saw, even if they didn't have the slightest notion of what they were seeing. If only they'd known just who was in dresses on stage that night! One thing's for sure: The patrons got their money's worth. And it was as fun a thing as I'd ever done or have done since. But if we'd performed this number on the televised Ted Mack Amateur Hour back in '56, we'd have ended up selling Fuller brushes door-to-door or pushing tweed jackets and unmentionables in the garment district.

| McVan's Part Two |

We were so nicely received at McVan's and treated so well by management that we played a return gig there in November. In the time between the two gigs, we were in the City playing at my Starliter and getting in some good rehearsal time. We also played a few nearby commuter gigs on what was called the "Borscht Belt," including one at the Raleigh Hotel in South Fallsburg, New York. The emcee at the Raleigh—which was the prototype for the resort in Emile Ardolino's 1987 film *Dirty Dancing*—was Bruce "Cousin Brucie" Morrow, the top syndicated disc jockey in New York at the time. He also appeared in the movie and served as the period-music consultant. In addition to his radio show and other concerns, Cousin Brucie hosted a live show at New Jersey's Palisades Park every Sunday. Because he was THE best-known DJ, Cousin Brucie always got the most popular entertainers for those shows. Joey Dee and the Starliters had the good fortune of joining the Cuz several times there. Impressive and dedicated as ever to rock & roll, Cousin Brucie remains active today. At this writing, the Cuz has recently left SiriusXM Satellite Radio after fifteen years there, to return to the station where he worked in the sixties: WABC 77 Music Radio. No matter where his microphone and turntable are, you can be sure Cousin Brucie will be promoting and preserving the incredible sounds of yesteryear in his own inimitable way.

Soon we were on the road again to McVan's. A blinding snowstorm made it difficult for us to get to Buffalo, but traveling through inclement weather wasn't new to us. It was part and parcel of a musician's life. With all the traveling we did, we saw it all. We survived it all, too, even without four-wheel drive, snow tires, or sometimes even heaters or windshield wipers. And those were just our winter problems. Forget about summer with no air conditioner.

Slipping and sliding and cursing and praying, we managed to make it to Buffalo timely enough, but we didn't stop at McVan's to drop off our equipment as we'd ordinarily do. Figuring the storm would force cancellation of the show that night, we drove straight to the Buffalo Hotel—where we'd stayed before—checked in, and got comfortable. We were just hanging out in our rooms when the phone rang, and I found myself speaking with Joe Tearose, the owner of McVan's.

"Hell, Joey, we got this lovely stage down here," Joe said, "but there ain't nobody settin' up nothin' on it. What the hell?!"

"Man, I didn't figure on a show tonight," I said, "so we just came straight to the hotel. I mean, who the hell's gonna come out on a night like this to see a show? Unless they've all got snowplows, I can't see how they'd get here."

"Joey, this is *Buffalo*," Tearose said. "We're used to this fluffy white stuff. And anyway I know for a fact *somebody's* willing to brave the storm, 'cause we're sold out. Is that enough people for you?" Joe added, "Now will you please get your ass over here and set up?!"

We set up, and the show went on.

Again we played to SRO houses and standing ovations, enjoying the warmth and appreciation of the crowds at McVan's. To help put butts in the seats, the boys and I visited a local radio station. In addition to being interviewed, we played some numbers. The interview and songs were recorded, but I failed to get a copy of the tape. Now it's lost to the ages, I suppose. As a side plea, if you're reading this and know anything of that tape, please find a way to let me know. It would be a treasure for fans of Joey Dee and the Starliters, a gift to students of rock & roll history, and a special treat for Jimi Hendrix fans.

| Laying Off the Ladies |

The first night of the gig, Tearose introduced me to a lovely lady of advancing years. She was Lillian McVan Bain, the original owner of the club. Miss Lillian was a dignified lady who showcased fine talent and left a legacy of service to our industry. It was a privilege to make her acquaintance.

I met other intriguing people at McVan's. Interestingly, we didn't spend as much time with the ladies as was our wont. Now, don't get me wrong. We didn't go hungry, if you know what I mean. But the dancers, for whatever reasons, didn't seem to want much to do with us. But when all was said and done, somehow it didn't seem to matter that we were getting more cold shoulder than usual (any cold shoulder at all was more than usual). In an ironic turn of events, we got along well with many of the gentlemen who attended our shows there. This was unusual, because guys who went to rock & roll shows typically didn't want to get friendly with the performers, imagining that they'd steal their girlfriends if left unattended for even a minute. In many cases they were absolutely right about that. Still, during these six nights at McVan's, we got to know and like many of the men we met. We hung out, played poker, and had a grand old time with them.

This chain of events was set in motion when we played "Hot Pastrami With Mashed Potatoes." Brigati was our resident master of the "mashed potato" dance and always rocked it during the number. On this particular night, he was challenged by "Muzzy" Di Fulvi to a friendly dance-off. Make no mistake: Muzzy was good. But nobody put Davey in the corner when it came to this dance. He could cut a rug.

Or a floor. Or a stage. The man could flat move. The challenge was great fun, and topping Muzzy did nothing but put us in good stead with him.

In good stead with Muzzy meant we got to know lots of new friends. See, Muzzy was the "unofficial mayor" of Buffalo—and if you're familiar with the way things were in those days, you'll know what that meant. Large and in charge, that's what it meant. Muzzy introduced us around to lots of his many friends—people with aliases like Joe Car Wash, Joe Pizza, Joe Whatever. They all had aliases. Good guys, but no last names. It was an Italian thing; no one could pronounce their last names correctly anyway, and the nicknames solved that problem. Unfortunately, such use of aliases created a unique problem, as Mimi's daughter discovered when the Jersey man had a heart attack. Mimi survived the ailment, but his daughter pointed up a problem that he hadn't considered. "Dad," she said, "you'd better give me your friends' right names, or else how will I send notices to them if something happens to you and you don't recover? The mailman," she continued, "won't understand Nicky the Nose, Joey Blue Eyes, or Frankie the Fly."

Since the dancing girls and other females had mercifully given us a little time off, we took the opportunity to bond with these guys. We went to their favorite places, ate their favorite foods, drank their favorite wines, and played their favorite card games. That would be poker of course. It was a surprisingly relaxing change of pace from the nonstop sexcapades that typically occupied our offstage time.

We also used some of the time to channel our inner child.

| Gunfight at the Buffalo Hotel |

Boys will be boys.

At the start it was all innocent enough—just the purchase of a bunch of water pistols. Or possibly a *gaggle* of water pistols. Maybe a *bloat* of water pistols. Whatever the correct group name, the plastic toys just lay around for some time, harmless. Who knows now who first thought to pick one up, fill it, and fire the shot heard 'round the hotel. But someone did. And then a second pistol, then a third, a fourth, and fifth were loaded and brought into the fray. It was dog-shoot-dog, first in this room, then in that room. No place in the territory was safe, and no one could avoid the wet, the noogies, the half-nelsons, the tripping. Soon we were no longer satisfied with the pistols' tiny streams. We'd grab a handful of water and chuck it willy-nilly toward the melee. And then came the drinking glasses. The pitchers. The shoes. We'd have used a frickin' chamber pot if there'd been one there. Anything that could hold water. To paraphrase Coleridge: Water, water everywhere, nor any place to hide. Furniture wasn't safe from the falls, the dives, the tackles. Beds looked like they'd been hosed down and tossed about by a silly elephant. Don't even talk about the TVs or the lamps. It pains me even now to think of them. Needless to say, no one had to shower that night, and we had more fun than the Marx Brothers on vacation with the Three Stooges. Hell, screw the analogies. I can tell you *exactly* how much fun we had. Two hundred twenty-seven dollars' worth, that's how much. I know, because that's what I had to pay for damages.

Accuse the boys and me of maturity. I dare you.

NINETEEN

JIMI HENDRIX:
STARLITER TO LEGEND

Maurice James hung with me through 1965 before moving on. I hated losing him; it put a great hole in our band and our sound, and I missed my friend. But I'd known from the start that it would be just a matter of time, and I was almost always right about such things. This time I was especially sorry to be right, but right I was. Maurice's talent couldn't be kept from its destiny.

| Settling Old Debts |

People often came to the Starliter to see if what they'd heard about our guitar player could be true. Included among such visitors were Eric Burdon and Chas Chandler of the Hall of Fame group, the Animals. After Maurice left us he played around town one way or another. Performing at the Café Wha? night club in Greenwich Village as Jimmy James and the Blue Flames, Hendrix met Linda Keith, the girlfriend of Rolling Stones guitarist Keith Richards. That led to Jimi's connection with Chas Chandler, who by then had left the Animals to pursue artist management and production. Chandler ended up whisking our man away to Europe to record hits like "Hey Joe," "Purple Haze," and "The Wind Cries Mary."

It makes me happy to know that the band and I helped launch our friend toward legendary success. Jimi never forgot his time with us and spoke of often of it in later years. I'd needed him, and he'd needed me—just as we both knew, the day I auditioned and hired Maurice James, the great Jimi Hendrix.

Jimi owed me a hundred bucks that I'd spotted him once when he came up short. Before leaving for Europe, he came to my home to settle up with me. He still didn't have the money, so he offered to give me his Fender Jazzmaster guitar instead. His offer seemed excessive and unnecessary, so I refused it.

"I can't do that, man," I told him. "The guitar's worth more than you owe me, and I think you might need it where you're going."

"Man, Chas gon' get me all I need, brand new. Take the guitar," Jimi said.

I argued. "Keep it anyway, man."

"Take it, Joey. I won't feel right if I leave owin' you. Take the damn thing or I just won't feel right."

That's the kind of honorable man Hendrix was. He wore me down, and I took the Jazzmaster. Jimi left.

The rest, as they say, is rock & roll history.

| One Man's Treasure, Another Man's Trash |

As I said, losing Jimi's guitar left a hole in the Starliters. Fortunately, a British guitar player I'd met at the Star-Club in Hamburg, Germany, and whom I'd run into again at Revere Beach, was looking for a gig. Chris Huston had been with the Undertakers, but things with that gig were iffy. I asked Chris to meet me at a gig in mid-town New York. We talked, and he was interested. But he had a problem.

"I haven't got a good six-string," Huston told me in a heavy British accent.

"Well, I've got a Jazzmaster in a closet at home. You can use that," I said.

"Yeah, mate. 'at's fab," Huston said. He agreed to meet us at our next gig. I retrieved the Jazzmaster from my closet and took it with me to the gig.

"Chris, the guy who gave me this guitar owed me a hundred bucks," I said. "You can have it for that."

" 'at's wicked, mate, but I'm a tad skint at the mo," Huston said.

"No sweat, man," I said. "Pay me twenty-five a week." He agreed.

Chris opened the guitar case. Besides the guitar, it contained a number of items Jimi hadn't thought—or bothered—to remove, including an afro pick-comb, myriad guitar picks, and a little black book containing notes, names, addresses, phone numbers, and who knows what else, in Jimi's handwriting. I watched as Huston removed the guitar from the case and dumped the remaining contents into a round, brown, metal garbage can in the dressing room of the venue we were playing in Middletown, New York.

I didn't tell Huston who the guitar's previous owner had been, but it wouldn't have mattered. I mean, Maurice wasn't yet HENDRIX, so the contents of the case wouldn't have meant anything to Chris. Nor did it mean anything to me, I guess, or else I'd have taken the trouble to save those contents. At least I should have thought to return the black book to Jimi, but I didn't. And now how I wish I could rewind to that day of my life! No doubt I'd take the trouble to rescue the little black book and the other items from that case. I can only imagine what those things would be worth today in dollars—but, more important, what they'd be worth in the telling of Hendrix's personal story. Now they all lie buried deep in a landfill somewhere near Middletown, New York. Shame on me.

In some later year, I called Chris in Nashville, where he had become a successful and respected recording engineer. After a little chit-chat I asked him about the guitar and whether he still had it.

"Well," Chris said, in the British accent he hadn't lost, "it was all a bit dodgy. We were doing a recording session in New York. Can't remember the studio, but we left the gear there overnight, 'cause we were going back next day to re-record. But when we came back, we found everything had been nicked. Turned out," he continued, "the bloke who owned the joint owed a bit of dosh to the Mob, so they just cleaned everything out. All the instruments, all the equipment—everything that could be moved. Gone."

I guess only heaven knows what happened to the guitar after that. But someone out there may own the Fender Jazzmaster guitar that launched the legendary career of Jimi Hendrix, not knowing what treasure (s)he has.

| The Last Time I Saw Maurice |

I saw Jimi once more after he gave me the guitar. In February 1968, I was playing a Milwaukee club called the Attic. Jimi was also in Milwaukee, playing the Scene, a venue that from 1965 to 1971 featured the likes of Hendrix, Chuck Berry, Miles Davis, the Temptations, the Four Tops, Cream, Little Richard, John Mayall, and Sly and the Family Stone. I sent word to Jimi to stop by after his show and say hello to the old gang, if he could.

We were on stage at eleven p.m. when the genius strolled out from the wings. He wasn't wearing the suit and tie he'd worn as a Starliter; he was no longer Maurice James. He was Jimi Hendrix, sporting the psychedelic fashion that had become his trademark look: hip-hugging crushed velvet pants, vest, wide-brimmed hat, and—of course—boots. But I could see through all the "image" that this was my friend

Maurice. His hair was still impeccable, and he still had the same infectious smile. As you might have guessed, the show stopped when he walked onto the stage, and David, Tommy, and I shared hugs with our old friend while the audience made it clear that they recognized this welcome intruder.

It came as no surprise that Jimi's guitar was nearby and accessible. I'd have been disappointed had it not been, because it would have been a rare thing for me to see him without it. He asked if he could sit in. I told him, "Hell no you can't sit in. We're doing a damn show here." Jimi hung his head and left the stage, and I never saw him again.

Not really. Just making sure you're paying attention.

"Hell yes you can sit in!" I said.

But he didn't really *sit in*. Jimi would never again just *sit in*. Since he'd left us, he'd become The Show—and tonight we happily watched him steal ours, just as he'd done so many times as a Starliter. Playing with his teeth, behind his back, between his legs, on his knees, on his back. This was Hendrix at his best. The audience went insane. This time they knew who it was they were watching, and it was a privilege most of them would never have again.

Including me.

Jimi joined us in the dressing room after the show. It was great to visit with him and get caught up. Lots of water had passed beneath his bridge since we parted. At last I got around to asking what I owed him for his guest performance.

Jimi smiled. "You don't owe me nothin', brother," he said.

"Whaddaya talkin'?!" I said. "Sure I do. You closed the show. How much?"

Jimi said, "Look man. I got paid twenty-five large for my show tonight. Don't need no more. Great just sittin' in with my brothers."

Twenty-five *thousand* for a *night*?! I was only getting twenty-five *hundred* for a *week* at the Attic—for the whole damn band. It was suddenly clear to me that I should've stowed away in Hendrix's baggage when he went to Europe.

In less than two years' time from then, Jimi would make his historic appearance at the Woodstock Music Festival at Max Yasgur's farm in Bethel, New York. Way too soon after that, in September, 1970, the great Jimi Hendrix—my friend Maurice—left us. His passing affected me deeply, and it was a blow to the world of music that leaves us all wondering even now what music would be like today had he been granted more time to innovate, create, imagine. Some questions in this life can never be answered, only pondered.

Jimi joined the Starliters when he was only twenty-two years old. Now he was gone, at twenty-seven years old. About two weeks after Jimi's death, rock star Janis Joplin left us, at age twenty-seven years. About nine months later, the great Jimmy Morrison left us, at age twenty-seven years. These legendary shooting stars of rock shone only briefly but so very brightly. Each in his or her own way changed the world. Sadly, their lives and deaths also supported one of my "Dee-isms": Sometimes, success is tougher to handle than failure.

I miss you, Maurice. I miss your smile, your humor, your music, your genius. Knowing you as a friend and as a colleague made my world a better place; and me, a better person. I hope you're still sleeping with your guitar and killing your solos.

TWENTY

JOE PESCI:
STARLITER TO OSCAR

I'm proud to say that Joey Dee and the Starliters was a smooth surface off which the light of stars other than just Jimi Hendrix reflected. Those reflected lights reached varying magnitudes, but each made a difference in the world—and in my world. Every success these friends and colleagues enjoyed after their time with us I consider a personal success. At times I've felt a pride in their doing that's akin to that of a brother or father who watches his sibling or child succeed. In the next four chapters, you'll learn of some very special successes and meet nine very special friends whom I've been privileged to know in this life.

| Friendly Rivals |

I met Joseph Frank Pesci in 1958, in Nutley, New Jersey. The occasion was a competition to select the best local band. Pesci played guitar in a group with Billy Callanan on the Hammond B-3 organ, along with some other guys I didn't get to know. At the time this was the best group Jersey had to offer—but my guys and I were there to announce that there was a new sheriff in town. Both groups were good, but when Rogers Freeman unleashed his golden voice and crushed Ed Townsend's "For Your Love," it was all over but the shouting.

And speaking of *the shouting*, contestants were judged by the volume of clapping, screaming, floor-stomping, and whistling the audience could muster in favor of a group. The group that drew the loudest noise won the contest. When I see the 1996

Tom Hanks film, *That Thing You Do*, I'm reminded of this contest. There was no cool chick serving as the dial of a big "applause-o-meter" like in the movie, but the idea was the same.

Now, the competition was tight. To be honest and factual, Pesci's group got plenty of action during the audience judging. Probably at least one girl suffered a temporary loss of hearing when the guy behind her finger-whistled at the decibel level of a Ted Nugent concert. In the final analysis, however, we prevailed. Simply, no one could top the mellow voice of Mr. Freeman. There aren't enough "o"s in *smooth* to describe his sound.

The winner/loser thing didn't affect the most important outcome of the contest though: I became fast friends with Pesci and Callanan. We talked a lot that night and agreed to stay in touch with each other. Just a couple of short years later, both men would be Starliters.

| Pesci at the Pep |

Joe put together a band that included a fantastic drummer named Frankie Vincent, who became and remained a very close friend of mine until his death. Right to the end he and my original drummer and best friend, Judge Anthony "Dutchie" Sciuto, constantly duked it out over which of them was the better drummer, and the "fight" always ended in a draw. When Pesci's movie career heated up, he got parts for Frankie in all of the big Mob movies: *Raging Bull*, *Goodfellas*, and *Casino*. Now, *that's* what friends do. In *Raging Bull* and *Goodfellas*, Pesci's character beat the piss out of Frankie's character. In *Goodfellas*, Billy Batts (Vincent) got hurt when he told Tommy DeVito (Pesci) to go home and get his shine box. But in *Casino*, Frankie's character turned the tables on Joe's and gave him the beating of a lifetime with a baseball bat—and a dirt overcoat for good measure. Sadly, our good friend Frankie Vincent passed away in 2017. A loss for me and all of entertainment. Ciao, Frankie. Riposare in pace.

Back in Joe's band days I'd go to see him perform in clubs in Newark and down the Shore. True to the movie persona for which he later became famous, Pesci commanded the stage when he performed. The man played a mean guitar and was a talented singer as well. His performance of "My Mother's Eyes" was a particular favorite of mine. Joe was a great admirer of James Victor "Little" Jimmy Scott, a uniquely talented jazz singer from Cleveland who inspired Joe and many other singers. Joe closed every set with the Warner Brothers Merrie Melodies cartoon theme and his impersonation of Porky Pig stammering, "Ba-dee-ba-dee-ba-dee . . . That's all folks!"

Joe knew we played at the Peppermint Lounge and often went there to see us. When the Pep began to be very popular and exclusive, a thousand or more people were turned away some nights, including such notables as Shirley MacLaine and the Aga Kahn. But not Pesci. He always got in. The bouncers thought he was a good kid with a quick wit and a wise mouth—in a good way. We liked him too. One thing led to another, and we soon found ourselves joined on stage by Mr. Pesci and his guitar. Before you could say *and the Oscar goes to,* Joe became a regular with us at the Pep.

One night Joe brought his friend Larry Vernieri to the Pep. Larry liked us, we liked him, and we quickly became friends. He and David got real close. Not long after that, Larry would replace Bo Freeman as our lead singer—a move for which I've never forgiven myself. I don't mean the hiring of Larry; I mean the firing of Bo. I did it for the wrong reasons, and even now I'm heartsick about it. I confessed this earlier, but it bears repeating.

| THE START OF SOMETHING BIG |

When something becomes as wildly popular as the Peppermint Lounge had become, I suppose it's perfectly reasonable to figure Hollywood into the fray somehow. And sure enough, Hollywood came knocking. We began to hear talk of the making of a feature motion picture that would involve the Pep, its regular crowd, and, of course, Joey Dee and the Starliters.

Production began on *Hey Let's Twist!* Harry Romm produced the movie and put up the cash for Paramount Pictures to release it. The film was directed by Greg Garrison from a screenplay written by Hal Hackady, and the all-star cast included Joey Dee and the Starliters, Teddy Randazzo (my idol), Kay Armen, Zohra Lampert, Dino Di Luca—and Jo Ann Campbell as my love interest in the story.

When extras were selected for dance shots, the casters focused on kids who actually frequented the Pep. Girls were chosen in the way you might imagine: The good looking ones who could shake their asses about a hundred miles per hour got the nod. Then the costumers put fringed go-go dresses on these chicks, which seemed to double their ass speed. Oddly, some of the best dancers didn't make the cut. Go figure. Guys were selected using different criteria. The best-looking guys were chosen, of course, but also—at my urging and insistence—some of my friends and Pep originals who'd been there for us when we needed them, also joined the cast. These included Chucky Daniels, Mickey Burns, and a guy they just couldn't leave out: Joe Pesci.

This was Joe's big-screen debut, and he made the most of it. During my singing of "Peppermint Twist" in the movie, you can see Pesci in a cutaway, Twistin' right square in the frame, with an energy and vitality that hinted of future superstardom. He knew exactly what he was doing and what he wanted, even then. Still, no one could possibly have imagined that his well-timed hogging of a shot as an extra would lead him to three Golden Globe nominations, an Oscar nomination for the 1981 film *Raging Bull*, and an Oscar win for his performance in the 1991 *Goodfellas*. Not many people—if any—can boast of having had an Academy Award winner playing guitar for them.

As for the movie . . . well, it was released on the last day of 1961 to awful reviews. Despite that, Hal Hackady would be nominated by the Writers Guild of America (WGA) for Best Written American Musical of 1962. And the critics did like the music and the way the movie captured the vibe of the City. And the soundtrack contained killer songs, most of which were written by myself or by Henry Glover and me, and performed by Joey Dee and the Starliters. And one couldn't ignore the terrific singing by Teddy and Kay. Still, no Academy Award for *Hey Let's Twist!*

But Joe Pesci, now. What a guy. We've remained close after all these years. We even share a question card in the Hasbro game of *Trivial Pursuit*: "What pint-sized Italian actor once played guitar for Joey Dee and the Starliters?" With all his fame and accolades, Joey's never forgotten his friends, and he's never forgotten where he came from. I try to see him at least every summer, when he goes to his Jersey home. Until his recent death during the writing of this book, my dear friend Tommy DeVito, the founding member of the Four Seasons, usually set up a meet at Goodfellas in Garfield, a restaurant owned by my doctor friends Dan and Ken Conte. At one of those get-togethers, Pesci got to prove his real-life toughness.

| Tough Enough, On and Off the Screen |

Dinner was going pleasantly. Joey, Tommy, David, Dr. Dan, Dr. Ken, and I were having a nice meal and getting all caught up on each other's comings and goings. And then the uninvited guest showed up: a drunken man who recognized Pesci and decided to introduce himself.

"Hey!" the man blurted, pointing to Joey. "Hey! I know you!"

"Yeah, how ya doin'?" Joey said politely.

"Man, you don't look like much to me," the man said.

Joey was calm. "Yeah, man, how ya doin'? Everything's okay. Okay?"

The drunk wasn't going away. "Stand up, Mr. Goodfellas Casino. Let's see whatchyou got. I can take you. You ain't so tough."

The last thing Joey or any of us wanted was a scene at our friends' restaurant. It was a very upscale place that catered to doctors, lawyers, politicians—not to mention Academy Award winners and Hall of Fame musicians. And tonight, as always, the place was packed with people. That in mind, Joey tried to calm the guy.

"Yeah, man," he said, "that's right. That's right. Everything's cool. You could take me. Now let's just calm down and get back to our dinner, okay?"

But this guy wouldn't be denied. No matter what Joey said, the drunk kept coming. And I guess he said the right thing at last, because Joey got riled.

Now, Joey's not a fighter. He's a *scrapper*. There's a big difference between the two. Being small in stature—as I also am—Joe's learned from experience that he has to get the first punch or kick or head-butt in, or else things could go sideways. Scrappers may not look as pretty as fighters when they're in combat, but they usually win.

Joey was sitting at the table with his back to the main windows, and the guy was coming toward him from the bar. Pesci stood up from his chair, walked around the table and met the guy head-on. One punch, and the drunk was down. And this was no small man—six-two, maybe six-three. But you know the old saying: The bigger they are . . .

The bartenders rushed over, took the guy into custody, and escorted him to the door and out. When they came back, the bartenders apologized. The guy was actually a regular at the bar, they explained, and had even done some work for the place as a handyman. But on this particular night he was already ossified when he bellied up to the bar. They were very sorry.

We returned to dinner and conversation. All was quiet. All was peaceful.

And the rock crashed through the window. We thought we were under attack. Not so; it was the work of the exiled Mr. Belligerent. Dr. Dan and Dr. Ken stood up in unison, exclaiming, "What the hell?!" Dr. Dan rushed over to the maître d'–slash–bouncer and gave him instructions. The bartenders joined the maître d', and together they went outside in search of the offender. The rock-chucker was located, and a brief chase ensued. It wasn't much of a chase; the guy could barely walk, let alone run. When the boys caught him, they gave him a taste of Jersey justice before sending him on his way with the clear instruction that he was never to cast a shadow on Goodfellas again. Even drunk, I'm pretty sure he understood that—and the lesson that preceded it.

We returned *again* to our dinner and conversation. Ten minutes later it was as if nothing had ever happened. No one mentioned the ruckus again.

At one of these get-togethers, Joey was wearing a baseball cap imprinted boldly with the words *Phuc Luzin*. I first thought the words had something to do with Viet Nam, but then I thought to sound them out phonetically.

That's Pesci.

Twenty-One

THE RONETTES: STARLITERS TO HALL OF FAME

In 1962 I was living the good life. The Starliters and I were famous as the house band at the Peppermint Lounge. We had a recording contract and a number-one record with Roulette Records. I had starred in a feature motion picture and would soon star in a second. We were fielding offers of five thousand, ten thousand per night, amounts that were practically unheard of in 1962. But I felt an allegiance to the Pep; it had, after all, made the Starliters and me famous. So, I did what I considered to be the right thing by continuing on as the house band—despite the lucrative offers—for a time before hitting the road and doing more of my own thing.

That summer I toured Shore joints with three new Starliters who hadn't replaced anyone in the band but only just added to the mix. Well . . . let me take a tiny step backward and give you the full story.

| Surprise Guests at the Pep |

On a night in November 1961, as the Pep was beginning its ascent, the place was absolutely on fire. The guys and I were hitting on all eight cylinders, and the crowd was along for the ride. Outside, three young colored girls stood in line, hoping to get in. They were dressed like they meant business—tight skirts, generous makeup, cigarettes hanging from the lips—but accompanied by a woman who appeared to be a chaperone. Despite their femme fatale look, these were young ladies. When I say *young*, I mean you could practically smell the Stri-Dex pimple pads. As it turned out, two of them were, in fact, underage. But they made it into the Pep because Sam mistook them for stage dancers he'd recently hired and brought them to the stage. I saw the girls in the wings and approached them. "We're singers, not dancers," one of them said. "Can we sing with you?"

Hmm. Three young ladies whom I'd never met before this exceptional moment, asking me if they could sing with us. For some this situation might have been a head-scratcher. Not for me. I thought it would be fun to have them join us, and I made up my mind immediately.

I had no way of knowing that the girls had some experience under their belts. They'd begun to sing together in 1959 under the name the Darling Sisters. Using the name Ronnie and the Relatives, they'd released a single on the Colpix label: "I Want A Boy" b/w "Sweet Sixteen." The record hadn't exactly set the music industry on its ear. In fact, it hadn't charted. The girls were still looking for That Big Break, and now here they were—on stage with Joey Dee and the Starliters. If I didn't know about the girls' experience, I certainly knew what they looked like. *Anyway they're cute*, I thought to myself, *so if they can't sing, we'll still be okay.*

I asked, "Do you girls know 'What'd I Say'?" Yes, they knew the Ray Charles tune.

David handed her a mike. "Sing."

"You don't have to ask me twice," she said.

And they joined us. And they sang. And they . . . Wow.

These gals blew the room away. The audience just about came apart. There was no getting around it—these girls could flat-out sing. Strong voices, seamless harmonies, and just as comfortable on stage as anyone I'd ever seen. And they were kids! But, to my thinking, talent trumps age every time. So the three of them spent the rest of the night with us, singing and grooving.

I've always had the ear and the eye to see and hear talent when I'm near it. Okay, so I missed the call on the Beatles, but let's call that the exception that proves the rule. I didn't miss this one. In the moment when I heard these gals sing, I knew I was seeing and hearing something special. And I wasn't about to let them get away. I was afraid that, if I did, I'd someday be listening to them on the radio, wondering why I hadn't brought them on board when I had the chance.

| Gigging with the Girls |

Night after night, the girls danced and sang along with Joey Dee and the Starliters to the always-sold-out crowds and standing ovations at the Pep. These girls were terrific. They were humble, they were hungry, and they were talented. *So* talented. We became good friends, and it was clear to me that they were on the same mission I was on. I asked them if they'd like to gig with us. Of course they would, they said. I visited their family in the Harlem projects, hoping to get permission for the girls tour with us over the summer. The family was huge—lots of uncles, aunts, and cousins. But the crowd didn't make me uncomfortable at all. It reminded me of my own family.

Their folks liked and trusted the guys and me and consented to the trip. Even though they trusted us, Aunt Helen would, of course, accompany them as chaperone. Yes, they trusted us, but they weren't dumb. So, in the summer I took the girls and Aunt Helen with us to Atlantic City; then to Wildwood, New Jersey, for a three-week gig at the Riptide; then on to Virginia and Maryland. David started dating Ronnie, and I dated her cousin Elaine Mays. Figure this one out: Each of these girls was prettier than the other.

Before touring with us, Ronnie and the Relatives recorded "I'm Gonna Quit While I'm Ahead" b/w "Guiding Angel" on the May label. Again, the record didn't splash or even make much of a ripple. But the girls were just getting warmed up, and we were introducing them to the crowds. The girls—Veronica (Ronnie) Bennett, older sister Estelle Bennett, and cousin Nedra Talley were now Starliters.

Our Virginia and Maryland dates had been secured for us by an old friend who worked at a cafeteria on 45th Street in the City. Scottie was a huge fan of Joey Dee and the Starliters—so huge, in fact, that when he returned to Virginia, he made phone calls and got us these gigs. And they were all great—except for one unfortunate little snag in Virginia Beach.

We tried to get rooms for the girls at the Virginia Beach hotel where we were playing. "The rooms are all taken," the man said. They were sorry about that, of course, but happy to have the girls stay there if they didn't mind the minor inconvenience of sleeping upstairs. An interesting proposition, given that there were no beds upstairs to sleep on. Upstairs wasn't really an *upstairs*. It was a common attic. But we were in a bit of a tight now; it was too late to find other accommodations for them, and we were committed to the gig.

Creative heads tackled the task. My brother Al went to the nearby Army Navy Surplus Store and bought cots for the girls. No sheets and only rolled up clothing for pillows, but they made it through the night.

Now, I'm not absolutely certain about this, but I'd risk a pretty nice wager that this was the only time during their careers when these young ladies had to sleep on army cots.

| And Then…History |

We finished the tour, and the girls and I went our own ways. Some time later I was listening to the radio and heard the song, "Be My Baby," by the Ronettes. They could have called themselves anything they wanted; I knew my girls when I heard them. And there it was: the day I knew would come, back when I hired Ronnie, Estelle, and Nedra. The Ronettes. The future Hall of Fame "girl group," the Ronettes. That's who had joined us on stage at the Pep, and that's who I'd hired to tour with us. But I was surprised—pleasantly, but surprised—to hear the girls on the radio. I hadn't known that the ill-fated genius record producer Phil Spector had heard them when we played the Riptide in Wildwood and signed them to a contract faster than you could say *wall of sound*. He wasted no time recording them, and what a recording it was! "Be My Baby," written by the legendary songwriting team of Jeff Barry and Ellie Greenwich (with Spector) and backed by the also legendary Wrecking Crew, made its way to number four on the charts. Our girls had found the success they'd been chasing and were on their way to superstardom. They went on to record other iconic hits such as "Baby I Love You," "Walking in the Rain," "(The Best Part of) Breaking Up," and others. I'm proud to say they also sang backup for me on my 1963 album, *Dance, Dance, Dance*, and a 45 recording of the Bell/Watkins tune "Getting Nearer," produced for Roulette by my friend and co-writer of "Peppermint Twist," Henry Glover.

Sadly, personal success for Ronnie would be another matter. She hooked up with Spector and ended up marrying him, soon learning that she was entangled in a dark web. Spector was a bona fide genius at making records, but his interpersonal skills left a bit to be desired. He treated our little Ronnie heinously and kept her a prisoner in her own home. Spector made her life insufferable, but even he couldn't destroy Ronnie's talent. The master of the "Wall of Sound" died during the writing of this book.

After wonderful times and many outstanding performances with us, the girls found their own very special way. I feel so privileged and pleased to have been in a position to give Ronnie, Estelle, and Nedra a leg up. I felt extremely proud of them, and I was, and am still, so happy for their success. And what success it turned out to be for them!

The Ronettes were inducted into the Grammy Hall of Fame in 1999 for the song, "Be My Baby." In 2004 they were inducted into the Vocal Group Hall of Fame. In 2007 they were inducted into the Rock & Roll Hall of Fame and into the People's Hall of Fame of Rock & Roll Legends in 2010.

Through the years the girls and I remained fast friends. Sadly, Estelle left us in 2009. I'm very close to Ronnie and her husband Jonathan Greenfield. She's a wonderful, talented, gracious lady who has blessed my professional life and graced my personal life in so very many ways. When I was inducted into the East Coast Musicians Hall of Fame on June 5, 2019, Ronnie came down from her home in Connecticut to present the award to me. After the presentation I performed "Peppermint Twist," backed by Ronnie, David Brigati, and Eddie Brigati. Talk about the symmetry of life . . .

Now here's a fun little postscript to my wonderful experience with Ronnie, Estelle, and Nedra. When I opened Joey Dee's Starliter in 1964, I hired Ronnie's Aunt Helen—who had chaperoned the girls all those times—to be the head cook. She was such a lovely lady. We became dear friends and stayed in touch for many years.

TwENTY-Two

THE RASCALS:
STARLITERS TO SUPERSTARS

Putting together a house band for my Starliter club in 1964 was a matter of the most intricate timing and coincidence and networking and . . . No. It wasn't any of that. I mean, well . . . yes, it was. It was sort of *all* of that. See, what it was, was the same old magic I always managed to find when I needed to put together a special group. Except, this time, I partnered with my old friend Sal Bonura and the Choo Choo Club to produce more than just a house band. *Way* more than just a house band. I think you'll see what I mean.

| Eddie Brigati |

In 1963 we filmed our second motion picture. *Two Tickets to Paris* was written, directed, and produced by the same personnel responsible for our first movie: Hal Hackady, Greg Garrison, and Harry Romm. Its cast was a great one that included Kay Medford, star of screen and legit stage (she must have had some extra time between movies and stage productions to agree to this project); Gary Crosby, actor/singer and son of legendary crooner Bing; Jeri Lynn Frazer, a kid discovered by Harry Romm and cast to play my love interest; and an absolutely amazing Charles Nelson Reilly, whose scene as a wedding dress salesman stole the movie.

Charles was an astonishing personality and a groundbreaker in the motion picture and television industry. I only knew him casually around the set, but I liked him very much. He was unpretentious and always kind to us roughnecks—and he hated the early morning calls as much as the guys and I did.

The movie had a great soundtrack. When it came time to record "What Kind of Love is This," I found we needed another voice to create the kind of harmony we wanted. David and I discussed options and ideas.

"How 'bout Eddie?" David suggested.

David has a younger brother named Eddie. Whenever I picked David up for rehearsal or a gig, I'd hear Eddie singing around the house. To my ear the young man seemed a natural-born singer. Pure as raindrops on a tin roof, his voice was—but he was young.

"Eddie? Well . . . yeah, he can sing. I'm just not sure he's right for this," I said. "He's a boy. He's got no experience."

"Maybe. But the boy's got pipes. And an ear," David said.

"Yeah, I've heard him around the house. He's got a major league voice," I said. "But he's fifteen years old man. *Fifteen!* And he's never been in a studio."

"I know all that, man, but I say he can cut it."

End of conversation. David was a musician's musician. When it came to music, if he said something was so, it was so. And he had reminded me that talent always trumps age.

We took Eddie along with us to the session, and . . . well, what can I tell you? He was fabulous. He took to the singing and to the business of recording like Tarzan took to the trees. In just a few takes, we had it.

Having a fifteen-year-old singing behind me wasn't the only impressive part of the recording session for "What Kind of Love is This." The song was written by Johnny Nash, a recording star ("I Can See Clearly Now") who also created the Joda (also written as JoDa and JODA) record label and signed artists such as Bob Marley and the Wailers, and the Cowsills. The session was produced for Roulette Records by Henry Glover, and Henry always fought for the very best musicians to create the very best sound on any record he produced. The arrangement was done by Martin "Marty" Manning, an eventual four-time Grammy winner who was the most in-demand arranger on the New York studio scene. His credits include Tony Bennett's "I Left My Heart in San Francisco," as well as hits by Vic Damone, Buddy Greco,

Andy Williams, Barbra Streisand, Dinah Washington, and many others. In the background was a unique instrumentation that included ten strings and four trombones. Of the four, I remember only three names, but those three names are pretty much a who's who of bone players: Tyree Glenn, J.J. Johnson, and Kai Winding. If you know *anything* about music history or musicians, your jaw should be bouncing off the floor.

Now that little brother Eddie Brigati had popped his cherry in the recording studio, I knew as well as Daniel Henry Ford knew cars that this was his first step toward a very bright career in rock & roll.

| Felix Cavaliere |

Sal Bonura, my friend since our teen years, had a nice club in Garfield, New Jersey, called the Choo Choo Club. It had evolved from an establishment called Jimmy's Bar and Grill, which Sal bought when he got out of the army in 1961. Sally owned and ran the club until he sold it to his bartender, John Ferrara (and partners), who sold it to another party. With that new ownership the name of the club was also changed to Club Anthony. Giving up the equity in the name Choo Choo Club, which was so widely known and respected, was not a wise move. Business fell off and, not long after the name change, the joint burned to the ground. Someone called Sal to tell him the place was on fire. Shocked, he drove to the site, parked two blocks away, and ran down the hill. He got there just in time to watch his pride and joy melt into a smoldering heap, right before his tear-filled eyes.

But, while he owned the Choo Choo, Sal showcased fine talent. The Reasons and the Female Beatles, both girl groups, got very well known there, as a well as a rock group called the Pigeons. You know the Pigeons better by the name of Vanilla Fudge, a band with a unique sound that led to numerous hits and albums as well as induction into the Long Island Music Hall of Fame. And I remember going there one night to hear a group called Felix and the Escorts. Felix played a Hammond B-3 organ—always my keyboard of choice.

Felix had a great voice styling that I'd call "blue-eyed soul," even though he had brown eyes. No matter what color the eyes, Felix turned out a great sound. As a bonus, the man did a great impersonation of Marvin Gaye, one of my faves. I tucked Felix's name away in my mental file. One never knew when one might need blue-eyed soul vocals or a good B-3 player.

Touring Europe with me in 1963 was my keyboard player Bill Callanan. His lovely new bride Jan was there with him, and the two of them had a bad experience in Paris. After that Jan decided she'd had enough of Europe and asked to be flown home. A week later Billy also decided to call it quits, and off he flew. We needed a keyboard player—and fast! I remembered a brown-eyed blue-eyed soul singer organ player at Sal's Choo Choo Club named Felix Cavaliere and asked my manager Don Davis to call Sal and get hooked up with the guy. It worked out, and we flew Felix to Germany to finish out our tour. He (Felix) returned to Europe with us again in the fall for a second tour.

| Gene Cornish, and There We Were |

In 1964 I was still performing occasionally at the Peppermint Lounge but not too often—we'd become a little too pricey for them. But they showcased a lot of good bands. A Rochester group called the Unbeatables was playing there, and I got to know the guitarist, Gene Cornish. He confided in me that the group was going to disband, and he didn't want to leave the City. I liked Cornish right away. He had the instincts to play whatever I was thinking. It ain't just anybody—you should pardon the vernacular—what can do that. I wanted Gene in my house band, and I asked him to sit tight and see what developed. He wanted that too, he said, and he'd hang on as long as he could.

I hoped I'd found a piece of my band in Gene, but I needed to find the rest of it before he got tired of waiting and moved on.

And now, the magic.

I hired drummer Ricky Chanin from Brooklyn, whom I'd known at the Pep.

I found Eddie Brigati again and got him for vocals.

I found Felix Cavaliere again and hired him and his Hammond B-3.

Gene was able to hang around long enough and I signed him and his guitar.

I had my house band, and it was a helluva group. At the Starliter they backed up the best acts in the industry. Or maybe I should say, acts fronted the best backing band in the industry. Either way, the boys got tight musically and personally. Really *fast*, they got tight. The writing was on the wall. Felix, Eddie, and Gene soon started gigging together on the side. Along with drummer Dino Danelli, who'd played with Ronnie Speeks and His Elrods, they formed an incredible new group: the Rascals.

JOEY DEE

| Rascals to Young Rascals to Rascals |

When the boys left me and went it alone, they returned to Sal at the Choo Choo on February 15, 1965, and played six nights a week through Memorial Day. At that time they were a cover band, not yet composing their own tunes; but Sal remembers how quickly they grew: "They just got better and better and better—every night was Friday and Saturday night. The word spread; they were coming from all over. Limousines from New York, Soupy Sales—all kinds of people. It was just unbelievable. They started off with twenty-five songs in their repertoire, and every night it got better and tighter and tighter."

Atlantic Records soon came knocking, and the boys were on the way to success. But there was a problem with the group's name. Another very talented group called Borrah Minnevitch and His Harmonica Rascals often went by the shorter name "Rascals." To avoid a clash, Atlantic decided to go with the *Young* Rascals. As years passed they of course became known again as simply the Rascals. I suppose Borrah and the boys had hung up their harmonicas by then.

With the new name, costuming became the Young Rascals' gimmick. At the suggestion of our very own Larry Vernieri, they donned Little Lord Fauntleroy shirts, knickers (short pants), knee-high stockings, and tams (hats). They were cute as the dickens. But no gimmick could upstage their talent. What a group this was. What a sound it made.

The (Young) Rascals turned out hit record after hit record for Atlantic, including "Good Lovin'," "Groovin'," "How Can I Be Sure," "People Got to Be Free," and so many more. David Brigati did some of the arranging and regularly sang backup for the guys. He even took the lead on the title cut of the album *Once Upon a Dream*. This all earned David the title of the "Fifth Rascal." The group was inducted into the Rock & Roll Hall of Fame in 1997, the Musicians Hall of Fame in 2009, the Songwriters Hall of Fame in 2009 (Eddie and Felix), the Hit Parade Hall of Fame in 2010, and the Hammond Hall of Fame in 2014 (Felix).

It was my great pleasure to work with Felix, Eddie, and Gene. Once again Joey Dee and the Starliters had helped launch superstars. And it was true of these boys just as it was true of Hendrix, Pesci, the Ronettes, and others whose paths timely intersected mine:

I needed them, and they needed me.

Twenty-Three

CHARLES NEVILLE:
STARLITER & NEW ORLEANS ICON

Meeting with some musician friends at a hotel in the City in 1968, Lois Lee heard some sweet sax sounds seeping from an adjacent room. Lois always had her antennae out for a potential Starliter, and whoever was playing that sax was exactly that. She had to find out who was making that sound.

Understated, Lois had chutzpah. Without hesitation she went into the hall, homed in on that sound that drew her like moth to flame, and knocked on the door that separated her from it. A man answered.

"I'm sorry to bother you," Lois said, "but was that your sax I heard?"

"Yes ma'am, it was," the man said. "Was I bothering you?"

Lois was quick to answer. "No, no! You weren't bothering me," she said. "You weren't bothering me at all. Quite the opposite, actually. I'm Lois Lee. Could I ask your name?"

"Neville," the man said. "Charles Neville."

"Glad to meet you, Mr. Neville," Lois said. "Are you interested in a gig?"

"Well, I reckon I'm always looking for a good one of those," Neville said.

"I've got a good one for you," Lois said. "Maybe you've heard of Joey Dee and the Starliters. You're just what we need."

"Joey Dee? Sure I heard of Joey Dee," Charles said. "Love to back him."

"Good," Lois said. "We'll consider this your audition. You're hired."

Now, Lois and I generally consulted one another in any business dealing; but she knew this man was special and didn't want him to get away. And anyway, her ear for music was so similar to mine that when one of us heard something, both of us heard it.

A Musician's Musician

Lois hired Charles on Wednesday, and the gig in Pennsylvania was on Friday. We drove from Lodi to the City and picked up Charles. The conversation during the trip was light, polite, and superficial. We talked very little about music, but that was par for my course. To me that would have been a bit like rehearsing, which I learned to dislike while at the Pep. Nor did I like sound checks. Still today I dislike rehearsals and sound checks, and I rarely show up for them.

We arrived at the venue and set up. I confess a bit of anxiety as I wondered how Charles would do. I knew he could blow, but I didn't yet know how he'd do in performance. I was in for a terrific surprise, and I'd never again feel that anxiety.

On stage I called out the tunes to the guys. The keyboardist then used hand signals to let Charles know what key he was to play. One finger up, key of G. Two fingers down, key of B-flat. That was all Charles needed. He was a natural and never missed a note or a change. The man was a musician.

I should say Charles was the *quintessential* musician. His technique was flawless and his sound smooth as polished granite; but more than that, he was soft-spoken, polite, teachable, likable, and a team player—the real Simon Pure. These are the qualities every band leader hopes for but too rarely gets. I found that *talent* and *teamwork* sometimes refused to coexist in a musician. Such was certainly not true of Charles. I say to any musician reading this: Take heed of Charles's example.

The City That Care Forgot

The roots of the Neville family are in New Orleans. If I hadn't been born in Passaic, New Orleans would have been an acceptable substitute. I like everything about the place: the people, the food, the music—especially the music. It's magical, and it's a living, breathing part of that world. And funerals? Well, let's just say, if you're feeling like you might not make it another day, hustle down to New Orleans to die. The send-off you'll get there will make it worth your travel and trouble. You'll get paraded to the cemetery with a band and a passel of second-line dancers, singers, and self-invited guests celebrating you. The music may seem mournful at first, but by the time you get to the grave you'll have been properly celebrated.

I was tremendously influenced by New Orleans singers and musicians. Fats Domino, Hughie "Piano" Smith, Frankie Ford, Lee Allen—they all put their stamp on me. And there was the Meters, a funky New Orleans R&B group founded in 1965 by Charles's older brother Art who also, of course, was one of the four Neville brothers: Art, Charles, Aaron, and Cyril. If you haven't heard of the Neville Brothers, close this book and slap yourself. As a group or individually, the talent of these men is more than should have been allotted to one family. You may remember Aaron's smooth tones on "Tell It Like It Is" and "Don't Know Much" (with Linda Ronstadt). And if I could trade my voice for any other and Johnny Maestro wouldn't let me have his, I'd be happy with Cyril's funky, get-out-of-my-way-I'm-coming-through kind of voice.

Charles played with the Starliters many times, and he was among the best that ever joined us. But he was fighting personal demons. I choose not to dwell on those; he was too good a man and too good a friend for me to encourage any memory of him that doesn't represent the kind, generous, and respectable man he truly was.

But I will mention that one incident.

| Hot Sax and So Long |

Charles announced to me one day that he'd lost his horn. "No problem," I told him. "You can play my Selmer."

I got the horn to Charles, and he took it to his hotel to keep till the next gig. I tried to contact him one day soon after that, only to be told he didn't live there anymore. Now, this was unsettling; I needed the sax player, and I needed the sax. I knew we'd get the player back, but I wasn't as sure about the saxophone. Knowing Charles's struggles at the time, I was afraid it may have been sold or pawned. I called Detective John Ryan, my old friend from the Pep days, to see if he could help me track it down. See, this wasn't just any old run-of-the-mill horn; it was a very valuable top-of-the-heap Selmer Mark VI. It was very important to me to get it back. I gave John a written description of the sax, and he said he'd check pawn shops to see what turned up.

I don't know how many shops John visited before he called me with good news. "Joey, I think I found your horn," he said. He directed me to meet him at a pawn shop on 8th Avenue.

I drove into the City and met John as agreed. As I approached the shop, I saw my horn hanging in the display window. Even though I'd hoped to find it, I was surprised at my success. If anyone had recognized that Mark VI for what it was, it would have been gone minutes after Charles hocked it. Clearly, even the owner didn't know what was hanging in his window; he'd paid Charles a hundred bucks for a sax worth many times that, and his asking price for resale wasn't much more than he'd paid Charles for it. No matter. I wouldn't have to pay even *that* sticker price. I was about the catch a break.

"Seeing as how you know John," the owner said, "I'll only charge you the hundred bucks I paid your man for it." I was thrilled. I handed him the C-note and took possession of my prodigal treasure. After thanking my good friend John, who had saved my bacon this time and would do so again, I headed back to Jersey.

There was never any bad blood between Charles and me on account of this incident. He sincerely apologized later, and I forgave him immediately. I knew he was deeply entrenched in his battle with drugs. No man is in full control of himself who is following that cloud. Dope tried to steal the true Charles and bully me into mistrusting him. But I knew Charles, and that shit couldn't convince me that he was anything less than the good and honorable person I knew him to be. He was the kind of guy anyone would love to have for a father, brother, son, or friend. Charles was family to me, and I loved him.

Charles and I played many gigs together, and I figured more lay in store. But it wasn't to be. I never again had the honor of sharing the stage with him after he left us. Now it's too late. Charles passed in 2018, just a year before his older brother Art. When these two men were called home, New Orleans grieved them en masse. The city's grand world of music had been personified by the Nevilles for so long, and now two of them were gone.

But we all were blessed by their long and creative lives, and they bequeathed us their music, which will live on. How fortunate are we who knew them, loved them, and remember them.

Twenty-Four

THE CRAZY WORLD OF
DAVID BRIGATI

The Brigati family lived on Monroe Street, which runs from David's hometown of Garfield to my hometown of Passaic and is a block from where I lived as a youngster. Although we grew up near one another, we never met till we hooked up professionally.

As I wrote earlier, David fronted a doo-wop group called the Hi-Fives that recorded "Dorothy." When the buzz began, Dick Clark invited the Hi-Fives to perform on *American Bandstand*, but it never happened. Apparently, Mr. Clark required some type of agreement that Junie Dee, the Hi-Fives's agent, wasn't willing to make. "We don't need him," she said. How different things might have been, had the Hi-Fives appeared on *Bandstand*. Soon after that, David and I met at the gig in Garfield, and he became a Starliter.

Simply said, David and I are best friends. We've spent most of our lives performing and hanging out together. Of course, I've written much about David already, but here I offer a few highlights. See, we became the metaphorical poster boys for chicanery, mischief, disaster, and silliness. These things followed the two of us like thunder follows lightning. Especially the chicanery. I like that word. Haven't used it in years, but it certainly applies to David and me.

| Battle of the Bumpers |

It was 1960. On one of our nights off, David called me.

"Joey," he said. "My car won't start."

"What's wrong with that pile this time?" I asked.

"Damn battery's dead," he said. "Need a push."

"Yeah. Be there in a few minutes."

Now, David and I both drove junkers. Clunkers. Jalopies. He had an old rat, circa 1950, with one of those newfangled automatic transmissions, and I had a 1947 Dodge, for which I'd paid the premium price of fifty smackers. We would never take these pigs to the City—we couldn't trust the motors as far as we could throw them. But talk about construction! Back then cars were tanks with steel bumpers. And when I say *bumpers*, I mean B.U.M.P.E.R.S. Our cars—I use the term loosely—could withstand the attack of a rogue locomotive and suffer nary a dent on those bumpers. It was the locomotive that had to worry about damage.

John Pinto, David's grandfather, owned a pool room. John's Pool Room, it was called, and David's family lived in an apartment in the back. At the end of the block stood a chemical factory that abutted Passaic and Garfield. To enable delivery of chemicals there, a railroad track led to its loading bay from main tracks that ran parallel to Monroe Street. The road was very uneven where the delivery rail met the main rail.

Now, push-starting a car that had a *standard* transmission was a piece of cake. You simply depressed the clutch pedal, shifted into second gear, got pushed by another car or people for a few feet, popped the clutch, and vroom! You were running. Not so with an *automatic* transmission. Push-starting one of those beasts was a different dealaltogether, as I soon learned from David when I arrived at his house.

"Okay, Joey, you gotta get the thing up to thirty, thirty-five miles an hour," David explained. "Then my car will start and keep going."

"No problem," I said.

As he climbed into his disabled car, David reminded me. "Remember! Thirty, thirty-five."

"No problem," I repeated.

The intersection of railroad tracks I described was several yards from David's car, which sat in the middle of Monroe Street. I backed my car to the uneven tracks and well beyond; I wanted to be sure I'd have enough room to do what I needed to do. Leaning over the steering wheel and with a devilish smile on my lips, I floored my bumpered tank in order to get up a proper head of steam. That's when it dawned on Brigati what I was up to.

The light of day was starting to fade to dusk, and my headlights illuminated David's car and his face inside—and through the rear window I could see him looking back at me. As I came closer to his very stationary car, my headlights shaped the form of a panicked man shouting *No! No!* and frantically waving his arms—clearly a signal for me to stop.

Now, there was another interesting thing about the massive cars of that day. See, they had shock absorbers—more or less—but their effect was nearly entirely defeated by the weight of the car, which was probably in the neighborhood of fourteen tons. Unlike the cars of today, when one of those monsters hit a bump, the wheels and suspension wouldn't budge, but the car's body would start to bounce. When I hit those uneven tracks at the speed I was traveling, my car began bouncing up and down, up and down, up and down—and it just kept bouncing. When I reached David's car, mine was just hitting the downstroke of the latest bounce, giving me even greater momentum.

David was still waving me off, but to no avail. I kept coming. He was beyond panicked; from the anguished look on his face and the color of it, I guessed he was entering the first stages of apoplexy. But even that wasn't gonna save him.

I plowed into the back of his car at the suggested speed of thirty-five miles per hour. David's car fairly leapt from the middle of Monroe Street and onto the sidewalk. It didn't start; it only changed locations. And mine had careened off his and was now standing still not far from his. From David's point of view there was nothing funny about what I'd just done. From my point of view, it was funny as hell. After both cars settled I sat in mine, laughing just about as hard as a human can laugh and not die from it.

Hearing the hellacious crash, Brigatis came rushing from inside to see what had happened. David's little brother Eddie ran to him, I guess to see if he was alive. He was. But when he saw me in my car, laughing like Red Skelton at his own jokes, he quickly put two and two together. The next thing I saw through my tears of laughter was David and Eddie jumping onto the hood of my car and tap dancing over it to the roof, then over the roof to the trunk. And then a return trip to the hood.

A good time was had by all.

A few days later David drove to my house and backed his car into mine about fifty times.

Spiteful. Just spiteful.

| Spit It Out! |

When David, Bo, and I traveled together, I was usually the designated driver. In the early days before we found fame and a few dollars at the Pep, I shuttled us in my clunker du jour—that is, whenever we were brave enough to put the beast to the test. Of course, we prayed hard to make it from A to B and back to A without calling a tow truck or ambulance. Coming back from the City I routinely dropped David off in Garfield first and then Rogers in Lodi next. Because he was the first one out, David sat in the back seat, and Rogers rode shotgun.

My relationship with Bo was by and large pacific. Not much mischief raised its head between the two of us. I saved most of my shenanigans, gotchas, and paybacks for David and Fat Frankie. But David and Bo now—man, *there* was a nice rivalry. Something was always up between those two. And out of that rivalry grew an interesting little recurring competition, and I had a front-row seat to enjoy it every time I dropped David off.

See, as we approached Brigati's home, David and Bo would become quiet. I knew what they were doing: Each gladiator was steeling himself for the battle that was to play out.

No sooner did my brakes squeal us to an eventual stop in front of David's house than he and Rogers would crash through the doors and face off. Then came the battle, each man spitting at the other and cursing at the sound level of a jet lifting itself from a Newark runway. And when I say cursing, I mean *cursing*. Every obscenity, vulgarity, curse word, expletive, oath, profanity, foul-mouthed dirty word you've ever heard, read, or even imagined. In their zeal and temporary psychosis, the boys may even have coined a new phrase or two. It was downright magical. And educational, from a certain perverse point of view.

And *spitting*. Man, I never knew the human mouth could generate such moisture. And they'd spit till their wells ran dry and their shirts were soaked. Speaking for myself, I've never been a great fan of shirts that dripped saliva, but my boys didn't seem to worry about it. There was victory at stake in this contest after all, and each wanted it badly.

I don't know whether or not the guys kept a running tally of wins and losses or even how the scrimmages were judged—but I can tell you this: The contests came to a screeching halt on the day when I bought my first Cadillac. That was a no-spitting zone.

| A Funny Thing Happened on the Way to the Pep |

Mr. Brigati drove buses for Manhattan Bus Lines, and he often bused David and me to the Port Authority. He never charged us for the ride. He could do that. So, we got a free ride all the way into the City and had to walk only a couple of blocks from the depot to the Pep. Before we became famous and our budgets a bit more flush, this was a blessing for our bank accounts.

Sometimes we'd stay at the Pep and rehearse after we got done at four in the morning. When we did that, taking the bus back to Jersey wasn't an issue. But sometimes we went home after we finished. That's when taking the bus back to Jersey *was* an issue.

We had only shoe leather to get to the Port Authority to catch a bus home. And walking that couple of blocks in New York at four in the morning wasn't without a risk or two. Or three. At this time of morning, yelling, fighting, and sirens were the norm. And it seemed that every kook, nut case, and crazy in the City came out from wherever they came out from and took the streets. And the Port Authority seemed to be their conference center.

We needed a defense strategy.

I told David, "Man, the only way to deal with a crazy is to act crazier than he does. Crazy people," I continued, "won't mess with you if they think you're crazier than they are."

And that became our strategy. We'd hit each other. We'd yell and scream and spit at each other. We'd do just about anything that looked and sounded loony, short of drawing actual blood or causing death. The stratagem worked every time, clearing a crazy-free zone around us with a radius of ten feet.

A particularly kooky guy approached us one night. He wore on his face a look that could've won any international competition for the title of "Craziest Look Ever." David and I had taken a short break from our psycho routine, so this nut ball felt comfortable approaching us.

"I wish I had a machine gun," the guy said, staring into my eyes like Bela Lugosi on a lunch break.

I hope I didn't gulp too loudly. "Why do you need a machine gun?"

"Cause I'd like to shoot every son of a bitch here."

Imagine what would happen today if someone said that out loud in a public venue. But this was 1960; such horrific acts of insanity hadn't yet become terrifyingly commonplace.

David looked at me. I looked at him. We knew we didn't want to develop any meaningful relationship with this wacko. We knew what to do. He spat on me, I screamed in his face. He punched me. We both yelled at nothing. Wide-eyed, the man ran away—and with a nice high step to his get-along. In fact, if there'd been an Olympics for lunatics, this guy would have a medal, by gum.

Some things between the Pep and Port Authority weren't so dangerous as they were interesting. Or unusual. Or weird. It's multiple choice. Take the Viking for instance. Somewhere on Broadway at the 40s, we met a guy dressed like a Viking. Not a Minnesota football player. A Viking, as in conquering, raping, pillaging, and such. Wearing a helmet, breastplate, and heeled leather-strap sandals and holding a menacingly pointed spear, this six-and-a-half-foot giant was striking. At first we were in awe, but soon we simply wanted to make him smile, or talk, or do *some*thing. You know, break his balls a little. But like the Buckingham Palace guards, he wasn't gonna give it up so easy. Try as we might, we got nothing. Never did. At some pint we learned that his theatrical name was "Moon Dog," a real Damon Runyon New York City character. And when you get right down to it, he was what makes New York New York.

Oh, the sights we saw, the sounds we heard, and the crazies we met during those to-and-froms between the Port Authority and the Pep. Sirens. Gunfire. Winos. Assholes. Nut jobs. But perhaps crazier than all that was this: After a while we became inured to it all. It seems we were making the transition from Jersey boys to New Yorkers.

| Two Caddys to Go, Please |

In 1962 we were making money like we were the Philadelphia Mint. Now, there's only one thing to do with money. I mean, it doesn't taste good, and it looks crappy hanging on the wall—so, you spend it. And what's the first thing a couple of Jersey kids would think to spend a fat check on?

A car. *Of course* a car. David and I had finally torn the bumpers off our jalopies. We could buy pretty much whatever we wanted. But not a hot rod. Not a fancy foreign job. No, for us there was only one choice.

A Caddy. Had to be a Caddy.

I had my eye on a convertible on the showroom floor of a Cadillac dealership on Broadway and 57th. One day after rehearsal David and I walked to that dealership and swept in like we owned the joint and were there to fire someone. I was happy to see that "my" convertible was still on the floor, and I checked it out while David was falling hopelessly in love with the Coupe de Ville sitting next to it. Both cars were way out. The convertible was lime-green with ostrich-leather seats, whitewall tires, and every available extra. The Coupe was a white number with white leather seats and all the bells and whistles as well. Our choices were firm. These were the cars we'd have.

Apparently, we weren't the only ones who had bread to spend that day. The place was crawling with customers, and the salesmen were busier than James Brown on stage. We weren't attracting anyone's attention. Understandable, I guess, since we were only in our twenties and our faces said we were teenagers. It being a Cadillac dealership, none of the salesmen wanted to waste time on a couple of kids dreaming about what they wanted to buy when they grew up. But we were cool. For about ten minutes. That was all the patient we could be.

"Excuse me, sir," I said to a passing salesman. He glanced at me and made a rolling stop, like a student driver at a four-way. "We'd like to make a purchase." The guy didn't actually mouth the famous W.C. Fields line, "Go away kid, you bother me," but he might as well have. His eyes and his body language said it just as clearly as his mouth could have. He also said it with his feet, as he resumed speed and walked away chuckling.

"I don't think he took you seriously," David said. He too was chuckling a bit. I guess I was the only one who failed to see the humor in being ignored.

"I'll teach the bastid," I said, as I walked toward the offices at the back of the showroom in search of the head honcho. Seeing a door with the word *Manager* on it, I knocked. It was open, but I knocked anyway.

A middle-aged man with balding head and ugly tie looked up, peeled off his eyeglasses with his right hand, and said, "Yes, young man. Is there something I can do for you?"

I had some suggestions for him, but I was taught to respect my elders.

"Yes sir. Yes, there is," I said. The man straightened attentively in his chair, and I said, "My friend and I would like to make a purchase."

"You'd like to make . . . uh, yes, I see," he said, smiling. "Young man, we're quite busy here today. I'm sure you can appreciate that." He replaced his glasses and returned to his work at the desk. This knucklehead didn't believe me any more than the stupid salesman had. I thought to myself, *Doesn't anyone around here wanna make a buck?*

I returned to David. He was still smiling. "Get it all straightened out?" he asked. He could tell I was still pissed and not in the mood for his antics, so he added, "Did you happen to mention that we wanna pay cash?"

I thought for a moment. "Son of a . . ." I said. "I didn't." And back I went, bracing myself for round two. I knocked on the door, and the guy looked up. This time he didn't bother to remove his glasses. "Son," he said sternly, "I told you I don't have ti . . ."

"We'd both like to pay cash," I said.

And off came the glasses again. "Beg pardon?" he said.

"We've got cash. We wanna pay cash," I repeated.

"I see," he said. "And just which vehicles were you looking at?"

"The two on the showroom floor," I said. "David wants the white de Ville, and I want the green convertible."

"I see," the man said, standing and emerging from the protection of his desk. "Yes indeed. Let me see if I can get some numbers for you on those units. Please make yourself comfortable, and I'll be back momentarily."

At last. A breakthrough.

Within five minutes Mr. Manager had returned. "I believe we can put you in the convertible for $6610, and your friend in the de Ville for $5385." Removing his glasses, he added, "Now how does that sound?"

I'm sure he was expecting something in the way of a counteroffer, but I surprised him. "That sounds fine," I said. I sat down and wrote a check for the total amount. You could have blown this guy away with a good burp. His eyes were saucers, and his chin would surely reach the floor at any moment.

"Well," he said. "Well, my goodness. That's fine. Just fine. Now, would you gentlemen please excuse me for just one more quick moment?" He disappeared for fifteen minutes or so—to call the bank and verify funds, I'm sure. Of course, he got good news; and, when he returned, he was all smiles and fawning over us like we came with green stamps. Extending his hand he said, "Gentlemen, I'm so sorry my salesmen didn't understand that you were serious," he said, "and I apologize for having been less than receptive to you."

"It's okay," I said. Minutes ago we'd been two snot-nosed kids wasting the valuable time of his salesmen and aggravating him at his desk. Now, I guess he figured we'd blown our noses. I thought to myself, *money talks and we all know what walks*. And then, the big question.

"When can we have the cars?" I asked.

"Well now, Mr. DiNicola," he said, "there's the good news. We can have these cars delivered to you gentlemen in only three or four weeks."

Maybe he thought that was good news. I didn't.

"Why would we have to wait so long," I asked, "when the two cars we want are sitting right here on the floor?"

"Oh sir. I'm sure you understand that these floor models are for display only. But the cars we'll deliver to you will be precisely the same as these."

"Then it should be okay if we take these, right?"

The manager seemed perplexed. He certainly didn't want us to wrench that nice fat check from his hand, but the owner had his policies, you know.

"Let me just make a quick call, please," he said. "I'll be back momentarily."

And he was. Heading toward us at a near-trot pace and with a toothy smile on his face, Mr. Manager began talking before he reached us. "More good news, gentlemen!" he said. "The owner has agreed to let you take these two units right off the floor!" He looked quite pleased with himself. And why not? He'd just sold two top-of-the-line Caddys for cash. "Of course, we'll just need to give them a good cleaning first," he added.

"That's perfect," I said. "We'll wait."

Again, just the slightest hint of concern on the manager's face, but he agreed. A couple of men came to the showroom floor, opened a wall to allow access to the cars, and drove them around to the service department. After a short while the Caddys were parked directly outside the showroom, clean as the Board of Health.

How about that, as famed Yankees announcer Mel Allen used to say.

I have to confess. The showroom looked empty without our cars there. But we didn't care. This was a great day for David and me. We'd worked long and hard, and we'd put everything we had into our music. Now it was time to enjoy the fruits of those labors. We'd driven our share of junkers, and it was time for this. We were Caddy owners at last.

As the manager handed us the keys to our new chariots, David and I looked at each other and smiled. Another of our dreams had come true. We climbed into our Cadillacs, gave a wink and a nod to each other, and headed to Jersey to do some serious showing off.

| Hand-to-Floor Combat |

In 1965 we played a gig in Newport, Kentucky. Cincinnati being just across the river from Newport and having better accommodations, we stayed in a hotel there. David and Tommy met a couple of Marine Corps chicks there who were stationed nearby, and who had a little time on their hands. After the show the guys invited the leathernecks up to their room. I went along to investigate and to instigate. Emphasis on *instigate.* While we were casually chatting and getting to know each other, I said to the girls, "Did the Corps teach you to defend yourself?"

"Of course," one of them said. "Sure it did."

"Watch out, David," I said. "You might be in big trouble here."

David laughed. "Hell," he said, "no girl could ever take me down."

Right on cue, David. Right on cue.

"Well," I said, "why don't you just get up? See what she's got."

Everyone was laughing, and David hemmed and hawed and pshawed around for a moment or two, but we weren't letting him off the hook. He finally gave in and stood—then walked toward the Marine, mumbling, "See what *she's* got?! She'll see what *I've* got!"

As he approached the warrior, she wrapped her arm around his neck and shoulder and flipped him over her hip like a rag doll. He was all elbows and kneecaps as he flopped to the floor, landing with a thud. Springing back to his feet as if to say *that didn't hurt,* he said, "Hey, I wasn't ready." He dusted himself off and gingerly rubbed a knee. "Let's go again," he said.

Well, it was just like an instant replay of a great tackle on Monday Night Football. David hit the deck with a thud. My man was clearly embarrassed, but I didn't care. I was laughing so hard, I thought my ribs were separating.

It was time for me to head for my next-door room. I'd done my job.

Are female Marines still called BAMs? I don't know. Things have changed a lot for women in the military over the years. But whether they're called Broad-Axle Marines, leathernecks, or just plain Marines, these two stayed the night with the guys. I guess they must have been preparing for maneuvers or something, because I heard a lot of close-order drilling through the night.

| Birds of a Feather |

David and I were inseparable. We were together all the time. We double-dated too many times to count. We never dated the same girls, but we dated many different girls, together.

Sadly, I use the term *dating* loosely. To our shame much of our *dating* came after marriage—or, more accurately, *during* marriage. We were quite literally partners in girly crime. I'm sure the Osmond family couldn't count on their collective fingers the number of women that came through the doors of the Pep and into our beds.

David isn't what you'd call a Tarzan type. His five-foot-six frame was nothing for girls to write home about, but it just didn't matter. The man had gifts—or weapons, if you will—that trumped any need for a tall, musclebound frame. David had the gift of gab. He didn't know any strangers, because after ten minutes strangers were friends. Bundled with that gift of gab was a sense of humor. Bizarre, at times, to be sure—but he could make the girls laugh. From there it was a sure bet that he'd get into their pants. Night follows day.

And David could sing. Let me say that again. David could sing. I said, David could *sing*. I had to do all kinds of wacky things on stage to get my point across, but all David had to do was stand there and sing. As is true with all great vocalists—think Johnny Maestro, Perry Como, Johnny Mathis, Nat King Cole, Frank Sinatra—he made it look effortless. And when the vibes of his velvet voice floated over the audience, it sparked a mystical attraction that no one with an XX chromosome could resist. Every girl in the audience was steel to his magnet. When he sang, they fell out of the balcony—and the Pep didn't even *have* a balcony. The man had a strong following and even his own fan club. David could sing.

| All Good Things... |

In 2011 I was preparing for an appearance at the Mohegan Sun in Connecticut. I called David to make sure everything was copacetic.

"Man, we got the Mohegan Sun next month," I said. "Ready?"

"No Joey," he said. "I'm done."

My first thought was that this was a setup line. But I sensed a seriousness that stopped me from punching his setup. "Whaddaya mean, you're done?"

"I mean I'm done," he said. "That's all."

"You can't be done," I argued. "You're done when I'm done. We started this together, we end this together."

But I was battling unseen powers. David's girlfriend at the time was pressing him to leave the band. She knew what a chick magnet David was, and that he'd always be surrounded and confronted by girls on the road. She'd rather have him out of the business than in the business, doing what he loved doing and what he was great at doing.

"No, Joey, I've had enough," he said. "That's it."

And so it was. The end of an era. The end of a lifetime, in a manner of speaking. But not the end of a friendship. Girlfriends, wives, careers, age, troubles—nothing drives a wedge between two men who've been friends through hard times, through good times, through fame, through fortune, through . . . well, friends through life. And even after that, David Brigati and Joseph DiNicola will still be friends, happily hunting for one more gig and one more piece of mischief to enjoy together.

Thank you, my friend.

TWENTY-FIVE

FUN WITH
FAT FRANKIE SCINLARO

What can I say about Fat Frankie Scinlaro?! He was crude, rude, obnoxious, and spiteful—and those were his *good* qualities. He was a bona fide, genuine, one-of-a-kind ball breaker. And I loved him—probably because we had so much in common. Yep, he was my kind of guy. We'd been friends since forever, it seemed. As a young boy Fat started coming to my gigs at the Passaic Armory and elsewhere, and I eventually took him and his friend Joe Joe Capizzi on some tours with us. I guess you might say Fat was our first-ever "roadie." I enjoyed bringing him along. The guys and I liked him. He was funny, and we could abuse him without suffering pangs of conscience or feelings of guilt. But don't worry. He gave as good as he got.

| German Toasts and Flying Phones |

Fat accompanied us on our second tour of Europe in 1963. After one of our gigs in Germany, I sent Larry and him to get us something to eat. There were no fast food places, and it was after ten o'clock at night, so I knew it would take a minute or two for them to find something and bring it back. But I didn't think it would take *hours*. Eleven o'clock, twelve o'clock, one, two, three o'clock—and no

Fat or Larry. By this time I was starving to death and getting more and more impatient. Nah, forget *impatient*. Make that more and more *irate*. I was considering methods I could use to torture and kill that fat bastid when he returned.

Right on cue, in walked the fat bastid and Larry, empty-handed and wobbly from drink. I was certain of the *empty-handed* and *wobbly*. The *drink* I presumed.

I greeted them—with a lamp. While they ducked that, I threw the phone.

"What the hell man?!" Fat said. "Lemme explain dammit!"

So then I just rapid-fire threw whatever I could lay my hands on. They were ducking, diving, dodging, and dipping to avoid the missiles.

"Seriously man!" Larry said. "Take it easy!"

"I just wanna know one thing," I said. "Did you eat?"

"Well . . ." Fat stammered, and threw a glance toward Larry. "Yeah. Now that you mention it, we had a nice meal and drank for a while." I didn't care for the smirk on his face as he confessed the sin.

And there went the phone book. And coat hanger. And shoe.

"Now Joey stop throwing shit!" Fat said. "Lemme tell you what happened."

I didn't answer him, but neither did I throw anything, which he took as a sign of peace. But he wasn't out of the woods yet. Seeing a small suitcase in my hand and my arm cocked at the ready, Fat knew he'd better talk fast.

"Okay," he began. "Here it is. We went into this bar where nobody spoke any English. We sat down and had a drink, and then after eating a nice meal—*he had to rub it in again, the fat bastid*—we thought we'd have some fun. So, I raised a beer to toast the fellas in the bar."

I had no idea where he was going with this, but I re-cocked my arm when I heard him say, "after eating a nice meal." *He'd better hit me with a damn good finish to this story*, I thought to myself, *or he's one dead fat man.*

"Okay," Fat continued, snickering. "When they toasted me back, they said, 'Prost! Prost!' I explained to them that, in America, we say, 'Blow job!' when we toast. So they all did it just like we taught them. It was funny as hell!"

I felt my grip on the suitcase relax a bit as I began to imagine a saloon full of German barflies hoisting their beers and toasting, "Blow job!" Now, *that* must have been funny.

As Fat told the story, he and Larry started drunk-laughing, even with the threat

228

of flying luggage staring them in the face. They laughed more and more, and I began to imagine those Germans saluting each other with steins and American obscenities. I just couldn't hold it in. We all ended up rolling on the floor, laughing our asses off.

But I was still pissed. And I was still hungry.

| Jersey Weiners |

We were in the mood for hot dogs, Fat and I. A sangwich—or "sannawich," both Jersey for "sandwich"—just didn't sound good, so hot dogs it would be. We made our way to Olivieri's, the club where Don Davis discovered Joey Dee and the Starliters. Olivieri's was right there on Route 46, on the circle that no longer exists—as a circle anyway. We got our dogs.

Back in the car Fat went on a tear. He was *really* on one, and his joking quickly got out of hand, escalating from funny to silly to annoying.

"Joey, my hot dog tastes like feet," he said. "Does yours taste like feet? Lemme have a bite." He grabbed for my dog, and toppings flew. Aside from the aggravation of the mess, it wasn't fun to have his finger in my food. I knew where that thing had been.

"What the hell, Fat?!" I said. "Keep your hands off my food dammit."

"No kidding, Joey," he said. "Don't your dog taste like feet? What the hell did they do to these things when they cooked 'em? They taste like feet."

"Awww, man, they're fine. Mine's fine. Yours is fine," I said. "Knock it off and eat."

So he took off a shoe and a sock and tried to stick his foot in my face. "Smell this, Joey," he said. "No kiddin', don't your hot dog taste like this?"

"What the f . . ." I stammered as I did my best to fend off a stinkin' foot and his assault on my food, all while trying to stay on the road. "Get your damn hoof offa me, man."

"Okay, but just one bite of yours," he said, shoving his grimy fingers into my dog again.

That was it. I'd had enough, and on that particular day, enough was enough. I stopped the car in the middle of the road.

"Get out," I said.

"Get out?!" he said. "What the hell, Joey!? Whaddaya mean get out? I ain't gettin' out in the middle of the damn road."

"Yes, you are, you son of a bitch," I said. "I'm sick of it already, so get out." He refused again. "Fine," I said. "You want feet, I'll give you feet."

A "normal" car in those days had a full bench seat in the front and the same in the back. No bucket seats. No consoles in the middle of the seats. One straight bench seat, from door to door. Now, a special car like a Corvette or some hoity-toity foreign sports car might have buckets, but not your average American-made car. Mine didn't even qualify as "average" American, but it had bench seats. I just turned around, pulled my legs up onto the seat, and started kicking in Fat's direction as hard as I could. Despite his protests, resistance, and cursing, he finally gave up and opened the door, spilling out of the car onto the highway. I closed the door and drove away, eating what was left of my dog.

It was about a mile to Fat's house in Lodi, and I let him walk every inch of it. It was good for him. Maybe he dropped a pound.

That was Fat. He loved to aggravate. That's what he was put on earth for. It was his misfortune that I was put here to take care of people like that.

| The Sidecar |

Fat came by my house one day, but he wasn't in a car. He was riding a motorcycle. Not just any run-of-the-mill bike, mind you. This thing had a passenger sidecar attached to it. Motorcycles with sidecars played an important role in the military during the World Wars, but we didn't see them much in our day. They were more likely to be found at a Smithsonian museum in Washington. But today, with a grand resurgence in the popularity of decked-out motorcycles, you're likely to pass one on the highway on your way to the market today.

I was intrigued by Fat's new toy. "Can I ride it?" I asked.

"Yeah okay," he said, "but I gotta go along in the sidecar."

I wouldn't have had it any other way.

I threw my leg over the seat, and Fat climbed into the sidecar. We took off. Still young, Fat hadn't yet earned his nickname. Still, he was maybe fifty-ish pounds heavier than I, so I worried that I wouldn't be able to balance the rig with him on board. But the laws of physics and motion kicked in, and I drove with no problem.

We didn't leave the neighborhood, so we found ourselves passing many parked cars. When Fat expressed some concern about how close I was coming to those steel roadside boulders, my mischievous brain was immediately inspired.

You shouldn't have said anything, man.

As we approached the next parked car I aimed the sidecar and its occupant to veer even closer to it than the last. If Fat's hands or fingers had been draped over the outside wall of the basket, he'd have needed a Band-Aid.

"What the hell, man," he said. "I nearly hit that damn car!"

I said nothing. When we approached the next parked vehicle, I aimed directly at it and sped up. We brushed even closer to disaster.

"Joey! Hey Joey!" he cried. "What the hell, man?!"

Fat decided he'd have a greater chance of survival outside the sidecar than inside it. Intending to leap from the moving vehicle, he started to stand. But I saw what he was doing and twisted the throttle; the bike lurched forward just abruptly enough to send my buddy back to the seat.

And here came the next car.

Seeing what was coming, Fat covered his eyes. For two reasons, he did this: He didn't want to be an eyewitness to his own demise, and he didn't want me to see him cry.

"Joey, don't you da . . ."

Too late. I dragged him so close to the parked car this time that, to this day, I don't understand how we didn't scrape the paint.

The moment we'd cleared the car, my captive tried to stand again. I twisted the throttle again. The bike lurched again. Fat sat back down again.

Now my passenger wasn't even trying to conceal anything. His male pride had taken a licking at the hands of pure terror. He was outright scream-crying, beating his hands against the sidecar, pleading with me to let him out, and saying words you'd never read in the Bible.

My heart was softened with mercy toward this pitiful man. Well, not really. I had to go home. I made the block without further ado and stopped the bike in front of my house.

I don't know whether or not Mr. Guinness's book lists the fastest dismounts of a motorcycle sidecar. If so, certainly Frankie Scinlaro's name resides atop said list. Yelling and screaming like a banshee, he was out and running before my feet hit the ground. I would write the names he called me, but there were no commas separating them, so it was one big long obscenity. Emotional trauma can do that to one's vocabulary. Still crying and blurting, Fat climbed aboard, screeched one final vulgar insult at me, and sped down the road, carefully avoiding anything parked on the roadside.

I don't know how long Fat owned that rig, but I do know he never rode it to my house ever again.

| Baby Powder Olympics |

We were playing a gig in Atlantic City. Brigati and I returned to the hotel after being out and about, doing who-knows-what to who-knows-who. Hearing odd noises from Fat's room, we opened the door to find out what in the name of Aunt Fannie's girdle was going on.

Pwooof! From the bed arose a thick, white "smoke" so dense we couldn't see anything in it or around it. But we heard laughing. *Raucous* laughing, we heard. As the cloud of whiteness settled about, we saw him. There was Fat, all three-hundred-plus pounds of him, lying spread-eagle on the bed and covered with the baby powder he'd poured liberally onto the bed. Standing near him, Carl and Willie were laughing their asses off.

"What the . . ." I said. "What the hell?!"

I got no response. None. In fact, I couldn't remember a time when I'd felt so totally ignored. Without a word of explanation, the big guy rolled off the bed, the three of them laughing harder than is legal in some states. And before you could say *that was a lovely dive Keith let's see what's coming up next,* Willie climbed up onto the bedside bureau, counted down from three, and sprang to the bed, arms and legs spread wide.

"OOOOOH!!" screamed the audience—Fat and Carl—as a massive cloud of powder erupted once again into the air.

"That's a six! For sure a six!" Fat said.

"Nope," Carl said. "Yours was better. I give it a five."

I was incredulous. "Are you guys serious? Are you nuts? What the hell?!"

Crickets. I was starting to believe I was invisible. But the laughter continued as the powder settled. Carl climbed up onto the bureau, stood spread-eagle, counted down from three, and did a lovely layout onto the bed.

"OOOOOH!" Fat and Willie gushed, as the powder puffed.

"Now, *that's* an *eight,*" Willie said. "Biggest puff yet. Eight!"

Fat agreed it was the biggest puff and best dive yet, and he awarded Carl an eight as well.

Short time out for a fresh coat of powder on the bed. When it was properly covered again, Fat asked, "Okay, who's up next?"

I looked at David. David looked at me.

"Outta my way," David said, tearing his jacket off. "Get outta my way!"

As Brigati was climbing onto the bureau, I was removing my jacket. "I got next!" I said as David left the bureau and splashed onto the bed.

"OOOOOH!!" A massive puff of powder erupted from the bed.

"Now, *that's* a *nine,*" Carl said. "A pure *nine!*"

"Well, now, that's not fair," Fat said. "I just poured new powder down."

"Fair schmair," I said. "Shut up and get outta the way." I climbed onto the bureau and launched myself with all the intensity of my onstage Twistin'.

"OOOOOH!!!" There was no denying it. This was a ten, and I was proud.

When the games had ended, we looked like a herd of Pillsbury Doughboys. Now, David, Fat, and I looked awfully funny covered with the white powder, but we were nothing compared to Willie and Carl. Perhaps you can imagine the visual effect of that white baby powder contrasted with their handsome black faces. I hope you can imagine it, because I can't describe it properly. You had to be there.

| Bullseye |

As I mentioned earlier, we used two drummers in our recording of "Peppermint Twist": Willie Davis and Sammy "Sticks" Evans. Sticks had an apartment in the City, decorated very cool with African art and percussion instruments. About a week before we recorded the hit, Willie was there with him. They were calling out drum parts and making sure they had it all together for the upcoming recording session. David, Fat, and I—the triumvirate—strolled in with Bo, just to hang while the boys worked out their magic on the drums. Soon enough the *hanging* got a bit tiresome, and we found ourselves in need of stimulation. What a surprise.

Fat was the first to notice the dartboard and darts on the wall. He walked toward it. But I saw him and knew where he was headed. Even before *he* knew what he was going to do, I knew. Running to reach the dartboard before he did, I pulled two darts from the board and waited.

Fat grabbed a couple of darts, turned toward me, and said, "Okay, wise guy, let's have a dart fi . . ."

Before he could finish the word *fight*, I launched a dart and got him right in the heart. Well, okay . . . I didn't actually stab him in the heart, but the dart pierced his shirt and his chest. Seeping blood told me I'd hit bullseye.

"Bastid!" Fat said. "You stuck me in the heart, you crazy son of a bitch!"

"Yeah, that's right, you fat bastid," I said. "I'm crazy. And you're slow."

"Well, hell. I wasn't gonna . . ."

"The hell you weren't!" I said. "But I just beat you to it, didn't I? And now you're bleeding instead of me. Touche, you son of a bitch."

I'm pretty sure David and Bo would have loved to throw a game or two of darts, but they didn't dare enter the war zone. No dart fights for them. No way. They got the point without getting the point.

| Moving On |

Perhaps it wouldn't be too out of line for me to include Frankie Scinlaro in the list of superstars I helped launch. In the years he traveled with us, Fat learned a great deal about managing entertainers on the road and promoting them. And so it came as no surprise that he should leave us to follow that star.

I knew a guy from Brooklyn named Larry Martieri who was connected with a girl group called the Shangri-Las ("Leader of the Pack," "Walking in the Sand"). Larry needed someone to go on the road with sisters Mary Weiss and Elizabeth "Betty" Weiss, and identical twins Marguerite "Margie" Ganser and Mary Ann Ganser to take care of things. He respectfully asked me if it would be okay to take Fat to work as their road manager. Despite knowing how the band would miss having Fat around, I certainly couldn't stand in his way. I gave my blessing, and he signed on with the Shangri-Las organization as the girls' road manager.

Little bit of humor about the Shangri-Las. When Fat was their manager, my Starliter was up and running. One night he brought the girls to meet me. They had an enjoyable evening at my club, and I got to know them a little. When they left, I accompanied them out of the club, as any gentleman should. But that's where my gentility ended. See, while we were standing on the corner and chatting, there was some flirting and general fooling around going on. You know how boys and girls can be. Playfully, I grabbed the hair of one of the girls. I was surprised as hell when the hair came off in my hand. No, I hadn't "snatched her bald-headed," as some in the Deep South might say. The unfortunate victim was wearing a wig. I'm not sure which of us was more embarrassed by my faux pas, but I do know I never walked the Shangri-Las to the curb ever again.

Fat also managed a rock group called Mountain, which had evolved from a group called the Vagrants. Mountain included Leslie West on guitar and vocals, Corky Laing on drums, and Felix Pappalardi on bass and vocals. The band's signature song was the 1970 release, "Mississippi Queen," featuring an unforgettable cowbell intro. I met West several times, but he wasn't what I'd call a close friend. The man could play the six-string though. Very talented.

Fat was also connected with the legendary group KISS. He invited me one day to have lunch with him and the guys. I had a great time with Ace Frehley, Peter Criss, Gene Simmons, and Paul Stanley. Criss was once at Trude Heller's in Greenwich Village when we played it in 1968 or 1969, and he sat in on drums. Yep, for one night Peter Criss was a Starliter. Great player. And Gene Simmons was a helluva marketer. With his help KISS sold more merchandise than Roy Rogers, I think.

Fat's career as road manager and promoter extended to groups such as NRBQ, Alice Cooper, and Blondie. To New York City he became "Mr. Monday Night" at Heartbreak, China Club, Supper Club, Au Bar, and private parties at the Puck Building. Gordon F. Sander, in his 1996 New York Times article, "Who Owns the Night? Promoters," wrote this about my friend Fat:

"The acknowledged godfather of the trade, Frank Scinlaro, a jovial former rock-and-roll manager-turned-promoter who is the host of a regular Monday night party for an older well-heeled crowd at Au Bar, has been at it for 15 years.

"'There wasn't a name for what I did when I started,' said Mr. Scinlaro, 54, who still employs the relatively gentlemanly modus operandi he used when he began at Heartbreak in 1981: he makes his own phone calls, and he refuses to use fliers.

"'I don't want to see my name on the floor,' he explained.

"Bruce Willis, the actor, offered his own description of Mr. Scinlaro during a

235

recent stop at one of his parties.

"'Frankie has something very special and very elusive,' Mr. Willis said. 'He has heart.'"

Our mutual pal Sal Bonura, founder and owner of the world-famous Choo Choo Club, said this about Fat Frankie Scinlaro:

"[Fat] was about three hundred pounds, and he was the biggest ball buster you've ever met in your life. He got under everybody's skin, but he traveled, and he knew everything. Fat Frankie had a way with words, and he just, he could walk into a conversation with fifteen unknown people—within ten minutes, Frankie [would] have the floor with those very same people. That's the kind of guy he was. But he could bust balls. He broke everyone's chops to no end. Always, always, always with a joke. Some good, some bad. He had tendencies to overdo it sometimes, but he was a funny, funny guy. And Joey and I, still today, we might be talking . . . and something'll come up and I'll say, 'Joe, is that Fat Frankie or what?' And we'll laugh like hell."

Frank "Fat Frankie" Scinlaro left us on November 6, 2002, at age sixty years. When he passed, a part of my own history disappeared in the rear-view mirror. For all the aggravation we shared, for all the mischief we created together, for all the paybacks we inflicted on each other, for all the memories that paint an indelible mural of our friendship—for all this I can say only thank you, Fat. You were a good friend, and I miss you . . . you fat bastid!

TWENTY-SIX

SNAPSHOTS

S ometimes memories link together, one following the next in sequence to create a greater story, like the frames of old-school 35mm film spinning off projection reels at a movie theater. Other memories are snapshots, each standing alone with no need for anything before or after to give it meaning. What follows is an album of snapshots, each a moment or event that I remember as its own thing, independent of what came before or after.

| I Spy Sammy Davis, Jr. |

I was never really out of the loop, even when things weren't popping for me professionally. Even now I'm never really out of the loop. I've always had connections with people. And so it was that, in 1965, I got a call from Sammy Davis, Jr.—one of the finest entertainers and gentlemen of our time.

"Joey, my man!" Sammy said, with his trademark enthusiasm. "I'm gonna need you at Big Wilt's up in Harlem. Robert Culp and Bill Cosby just hit the air with a new TV series, *I Spy*," he continued. "We gotta show 'em some love, man! You gotta make the scene, man. It's gonna be a gas!"

Now, at this particular time, I was on the balls of my ass. The guys and I were gigging, but things were slower than I'd have liked. I didn't even own a suit that was up to my standards. But that wouldn't stop me from showing my gratitude to

Sammy for thinking of me and extending his personal invitation.

"Sure, Sammy," I said. "I'll be there."

"Groovy, baby," Sammy said. "I'll get the whats and whens to you ASAP. Catch ya later, man!"

I managed to put together a decent wardrobe and made the date. When I arrived at Big Wilt's Smalls Paradise Club, I walked into the equivalent of a Hollywood movie premiere, complete with red carpet, beacon spotlights, and Beautiful People. I went inside. Sammy was on the dais when he spotted me, and he rushed to greet me with a hug. Taking me by the arm, he swept me along with him to the microphone, where he introduced me to the audience.

"This here's my man Joey Dee," he said, with the kind of energy only Sammy could generate. "I'm talkin' 'bout THE Joey Dee, man!"

I got a nice round of applause from the crowd. I've always been a sucker for applause, and it was especially enjoyable now. I acknowledged the generous ovation and thanked the audience. I turned to go to my table, but Sammy got up in my ear and said, "Man, you KNOW you gotta do 'Peppermint Twist.' Man, I mean *bop-shoo-bop*, dig?"

Sammy had an orchestra behind us there, and I guess he'd gotten the sheets for everyone, because the guys broke right into the introduction for "Peppermint Twist." When I heard my intro, I instinctively started singing: "Well, they got a new dance, and it goes like this"—and guess who gave me my *bop-shoo-bops*. Yep, Mr. Sammy Davis, Jr. himself. Of course, the song isn't really The Song if you don't Twist while you sing it. So, Sammy and I Twisted—round and round, up and down—and the audience stood and joined in with the same energy Sammy had shown them.

Singing and Twistin' on stage with the world's greatest showman. If things could get better than this, I'll need someone to tell me how.

Being recognized by such a good friend and spectacular entertainer as Sammy was a very important thing to me at that moment in my career. It sparked in my mind and in my heart the realization that it wasn't over for me. That inspiration lifted me and enabled me to go forward with faith—faith in myself, faith in my music, faith in my future.

Thank you for that, Sammy. You were a good friend.

| Someone's in the Pimp Bar with Dinah |

In April, 1962, I was in Henry Glover's office at Roulette Records. As we discussed whatever we were discussing, in walked Dinah Washington, larger than life. I recognized the singer immediately; she was a living legend in the world in which I worked.

"Henry, introduce me to this cute boy," Dinah said.

Henry said, "Dinah Washington, Joey Dee."

"Joey Dee," Dinah said thoughtfully. "You're the one causing all the buzz and those nasty traffic jams at the Peppermint Lounge."

"Pleased to meet you, Miss Washington," I said.

"Miss nothing," she said. "Call me Dinah."

"It's a pleasure, Dinah."

"What are you doing tonight, Joey?"

"Nothing important."

"Well, then," she said. "That being the case, I'd like you to come see me at Birdland. Be there around nine."

I gave a nod and a smile, and Dinah left the room.

"Think you can handle that?" Henry asked with a smirk.

"We'll see," I said.

Named for Charlie Bird, the greatest sax player who ever lived, Birdland was the heart and soul of jazz in the City. Ironically, it was owned by Morris Levy, whose long arm seemed to reach everywhere.

I arrived at Birdland a few minutes before nine and copped a seat at the bar, giving me a great view of the stage positioned behind the bar. Just after nine the men of the backing band entered the stage. Guitarists slung straps over their shoulders, the keyboardist found his place, the drummer took his throne, and all waited at the ready for a few moments before starting their intro. And here she came, swooping onto the stage with the confidence and poise that came with having one of the greatest singing voices ever to have rocked an audience. Without fanfare Dinah got right to the music, belting out standards and blowing me away.

Now, a few brothers next to me were having a conversation, and I guess it was the demon rum that deceived them into thinking they were speaking in low tones. They weren't. Dinah abruptly stopped singing, halted the band, and started reading the riot act to what appeared to be New York's baddest.

"Can't you brothas see there's a lady singing here? Be quiet or get the hell out." And for good measure she added, "And take off your damn hats when there's a lady present."

The hats came off. The mouths went shut. The show went on. Now, had anyone but Dinah talked to those guys that way, the poor fool wouldn't have made it out of the bar alive. To say the least, these brothers were hard-nosed. But they'd been put in their place by Dinah Washington, and that was different. That was okay. Such was the respect she commanded.

After an absolutely amazing show Dinah descended from the stage like a queen from her throne and greeted me.

"So glad you could make it, Joey," she said. "Hope you enjoyed the show. Sorry about the interruption. That kind of thing happens from time to time."

"Oh, I get that too," I said. "Didn't bother me. Loved your show, Dinah."

"How'd you like to meet me at the studio tomorrow night?" Dinah asked. "I'm working with Henry on a record. Why don't you join us about nine?"

"Try and stop me," I said. Dinah excused herself and went backstage to change. I left to go home.

Next night I arrived at the Bell Sound Recording Studio just off Broadway at eight; I knew this was going to be special, and I didn't want to miss a thing. I sat next to Maestro Henry Glover in the control room, comfortable amid the knobs and switches and lights. Outside the booth a dozen or so musicians were warming up. Nine o'clock came and went; no Dinah. Henry took advantage of the extra time by going over some rough spots with the orchestra. Now it was ten o'clock. Still, no Dinah. Eleven o'clock, twelve. No Dinah. It was frustrating for Henry but good for the guys and gals in the orchestra, I guess, all of whom were getting paid for doing nothing. Good work, if you can get it.

Just after midnight, in strolled the diva.

"Dinah, you're three hours late," Henry said. I could tell his patience was stretched, but I understood the situation a bit better then he. See, being a singer myself, I knew that most of us prefer to sing at night. The later, the better. Singers are accustomed to performing gigs late into the night and then sleeping in late into the day. Our rooster always crows much later than the normal rooster.

"Don't worry, Henry," Dinah said with an easy smile. "Let's make music."

Henry placed some charts on Dinah's music stand and kicked off the orchestra. I watched in awe as Miss Washington sight-read—that means she'd never seen the charts before that moment—about a dozen songs, not once missing a note or a beat. By three a.m. the session was over. After an applause from everyone in the studio, Henry and the musicians took turns congratulating Dinah on a successful session. They were pros, and they knew *special* when they saw and heard it.

I congratulated her as well. "That was amazing, Dinah," I said. "I've never seen anything like it before."

"Thanks, Joey," she said. With a smile she added, "How'd you like to join me for a drink? I need to unwind."

I agreed. Of course.

Dinah's driver took us to a bar on West 57th across from the Henry Hudson Hotel. Outside the bar were dozens of pimpmobiles. These "shorts" (cars) and "hogs" (Caddys) were all personalized to identify the pimps that owned them. Zebra stripes, llama upholstery, ultra-wide whitewall tires. And it seemed that everything on their exteriors was chrome—except, perhaps, the door handles, which were sometimes solid gold. And they all had extra space in the back, with bright lighting that showcased the pimps' bitches as they cruised, and allowed their competitors to see them counting their massive piles and rolls of cash.

Yes, these cars were rolling whorehouses. The pimps cruised the City in them, keeping a close eye on their girls who were working the streets. Whenever those cars rounded a corner, the girls shook in their knee-high faux-leather boots. See, they knew their pimps would stomp them into the asphalt if they didn't turn enough tricks or got shorted by their johns or did anything else to upset Daddy. They were terribly abused, those working girls.

Inside the bar pimps entertained themselves with contests. They'd vie for the "titles" of largest stable, prettiest girls, most outrageous cars, most money, coolest fur coats, funkiest hats. While the pimps entertained themselves in this way, the hoes knew to speak only when spoken to. It was the unwritten order of things. If one of a pimp's stable got drunk and loud, the rest of the girls kicked her ass for embarrassing Daddy. A rough life the girls had chosen.

When Dinah and I walked into the joint, she was recognized and greeted by everyone who saw her. For her there were no strangers here. As for me . . . yes, I was recognized too, and yes, once again I was the only whitey in the place except the bartender and some of the hoes. But I was cool as Como crooning a classic. See,

I was with Dinah Washington, and she was known by everyone. Hell, she was royalty here, even dressed for the part in furs and jewelry. Never mind that the pimps wore more of it than she did.

We sat at a table and ordered cocktails. As we chatted I couldn't help noticing Dinah's clothing. She was a peacock, clad in green from head to foot. Green dress, green hat, green stockings, green shoes—she even had a green pillbox for her *medication*. And everything was the same shade of green.

Dinah noticed me noticing her. "In case you're wondering," she said with an impish smile, "my drawers are green too."

"I'll have to take your word for that," I said, returning the smile.

I'd been enjoying the company, the conversation, and the cocktails for a couple of hours, when Dinah looked me in the eye and changed the subject. I don't recall what the subject was, but she changed it. She changed it good.

"Joey," she said, "do you feel like getting it on?"

Well. She just put it right out there.

I thought for a moment about the proposition and drew a fairly quick conclusion. *She's way over your head, man,* I thought to myself—and I was right. Also, I knew there was bound to be *medication* involved, and I'd made up my mind long before that I wasn't into that. All things considered I could see it was time for me to split. I reached across the table to take her hand.

"Dinah," I said, "I'll never forget my time with you. You've taught me a lot, but now I gotta split." I gave her a kiss, pressed her hand lightly, and walked away. I didn't look back, and I never saw Dinah Washington again. Eighteen months later, she was dead.

"But [her] musical gifts were offset by a wild and extravagant personal life. Married seven times, Washington battled weight problems and raced through her profits buying shoes, furs and cars in an effort to lift her spirits.

"Washington also tried numerous prescription medications, primarily for dieting and insomnia. A mix of the pills she was taking in 1963 caused her death, which was ruled an accident. Her gift lives on through her rich musical legacy." [NPR's Liane Hansen, based on an interview with Nadine Cahodos, author of *Queen: The Life and Music of Dinah Washington*]

Too soon, Dinah. Too soon. Thanks for the memories. And the music.

| You Mess with the Bull, You Get...the FBI |

In 1962 a group called Tony Farrar and his Band of Gold was playing around. Tony (a.k.a. Tony Dafarlo), John Gazzola, Billy Helkin, and Artie were all friends of mine—and Eddie Barbato, who played drums, later became my brother-in-law when I married his sister, Lois Lee. Tony was the band's lead singer with a terrific voice, and the boys could really play. That alone was enough to pull in gigs, but Tony liked gimmicks—and he chose a good one for the band: They dyed their hair green. I don't know whether or not the green was a subtle reference to what happens to skin when gold isn't real gold, but that schtick got the band lots of gigs.

Tony had interests beyond singing. He had seriously dated Blaze Starr who'd found notoriety through her relationship with Huey Long, controversial governor of Louisiana and member of the US Senate until his assassination in 1935. Miss Starr was smitten with Tony. I visited her at her house in Maryland a couple of times. She and her sister worked as strippers there.

Tony was also a hustler on the side. Tony was a *hustler's* hustler. And friendship didn't usually get in the way of a good hustle. He'd hustle anyone. And so it was that Tony brought to the Pep a guy who had a Cadillac for sale. "It's a sweetheart," Tony told me. "And it's a helluva deal."

Okay . . . well, I love Cadillacs, and I like good deals. It was an easy call. I agreed to meet Tony and his friend next day at the Pep. Sure enough, the guy had a black Coupe de Ville, all sparkly and shiny and groovy. Right up my alley.

"What model year is this?" I asked. I knew; I was just bustin' his balls.

"What model year?! What model ye . . . Man, this is a brand new 1961 Coupe, straight off the showroom floor," the man told me. "That's what model year it is!"

"So . . . how much?" I asked while I took a quick tour around the car, touching it here and there and closing my mouth to contain the drooling.

"Now, there's the good news, Joey," the man said. "Only need five Cs for this baby. Just five hundred! How ya gonna beat it?"

"Five hundred?!" I said. "What the hell?! Is it hot?"

"Is it hot. Is it hot. He wants to know is it hot," the man said to Tony. Then turning to me, "Hell, yes! The damn thing's hotter than the devil's ass. But you don't gotta worry about any of that shit. I got your bill of sale. I got your papers. I got your tags. I got every fuckin' thing. You'll be clean."

I couldn't pass this up. No way. I shelled out the cash, in return for which I received an ersatz bill of sale, tags, and all necessary papers.

I'd been driving this sweet Caddy with fake plates for about a week when the black-suited man walked into the Pep.

"Mr. DiNicola?" the man asked as he approached, not extending a hand.

"Joey Dee, at your service," I replied.

"Sir, could you step outside for a moment?" He looked serious enough to maybe be someone's practical joke, so I wasn't sweating—just curious.

The two of us stepped outside to find another man, also dressed in a black suit and boring tie, waiting by my Cadillac.

"Sir, is this your vehicle?" the first man asked.

"Yeah, that's my Caddy. Why?"

"Can you tell us how you acquired this vehicle?" the second man asked.

"How I *acquired* . . . ?" I said. "Who are you guys?"

Flashing identification, the first man said, "Sir, we're special agents for the Federal Bureau of Investigation, and we need to know how you came into possession of this vehicle."

Gulp. I knew I was in trouble, and I didn't have the slightest notion of what I should say. "Well, hell," I said. "I got it . . . I mean, I acquired it . . . well, I mean, how the hell do you think I . . . ." Even for a man who at one time aspired to make his living teaching English to college students, sentences can sometimes be elusive.

As I stammered and sputtered, the men didn't interrupt, or clarify, or correct. They stood there unflinching, watching me tap dance through a frickin' minefield. Clearly, this wasn't their first rodeo. I decided I'd better make some kind of defensive maneuver before I stepped right smack dab on top of one of those Bouncing Betties I was tiptoeing around.

"Okay. Hold on just a minute, gentlemen," I said, throwing my hands up in front of me. "I'd like to make a call, if it's all right. Okay? Quick call?"

The first man nodded, and I walked to the nearby pay phone. As I picked up the receiver and took a dime from my pocket, I saw that the man had followed me. I guess he thought I might be taking a runout powder, and he wanted to be within arm's reach if I bolted. But for whatever reason, he stood quietly by as I dropped the dime, dialed the local precinct, and asked for Detective John Ryan. I explained the situation briefly to my friend, and he said he'd come right over to see if he could help.

After several minutes of awkward waiting with guys I'd just as soon not be waiting with, John showed up. Presenting his shield and identification to the agents, Detective Ryan asked if he could speak with the two of them in private. The three stepped just out of earshot for a little tête-à-tête. After a short time John left the agents and approached me. The look on his face was sterner than I wanted it to be, so I was sweating just a tad. This thing was turning out to be more than just a little unsettling.

Screw you, Tony. And the horse you rode in on.

As John approached me I couldn't contain myself. "What the hell, John?! What's this all about?" Like I didn't know. I knew. What I *didn't* know was what the boys at Rikers Island were having for dinner that night, and I hoped I wouldn't find out.

"Joey, give me the keys to the car," John said bluntly.

"Give you the . . . What?" I said. I acted perplexed for effect, but I wasn't. I knew I'd bought a hot car—I just didn't want to believe my ass was about to be in this particular sling.

"Joey, no dicking around now," my detective friend told me. "Just gimme the keys." I pulled the keys from my pocket and handed them to John. He in turn gave them to one of the Blues Brothers, and the three of them took off—one of them in my once-upon-a-time Cadillac.

Just like that, it was over. I've no idea what lay in store for me had I not gotten that help from John. Clearly, this had been a situation that proved the old saw, "It's not *what* you know—it's *who* you know."

I was way too big a sucker for too-good-to-be-true deals back then. Glad nobody tried to sell me property in the Okefenokee. Or a bridge.

| Making Bubbles and Stopping Traffic |

Located at 1638 Broadway, above the famed Winter Garden Theatre, was a magnificent Polynesian-cuisine restaurant called the Hawaii Kai. Its street-level entry was appointed with lush greenery, waterfalls, fountain—even capuchin monkeys. Everything about this place was lavish and spectacularly beautiful—especially the waterfalls and fountain.

Now, when the boys and I finished our work at the Pep, it was rare that we went right to our rooms to sleep. It was far more likely that we'd have a few drinks with friends and fans, get sloshed, and look for adventure. And so it was on this night in November, 1961, when we followed that pattern precisely and found the adventure we sought.

After enough drinks it of course became a priority at some point to rid one's body of excess water. I was needing just such release in a big way, but the thought of an upholstered and nicely appointed men's room just didn't seem exciting enough. But a fountain and waterfalls, with monkeys screeching overhead—now, *there* was adventure to suit the most daring swashbuckler.

As it happened I wasn't the only one with floating eyeballs. Larry, David, and Willie were also ready for a potty break. All of us being pissed as a newt, I persuaded the boys to take a short hike with me to the Hawaii Kai. Arriving at the restaurant's entrance with lush foliage framing the magnificent water feature, we all unzipped, whipped out, and relieved ourselves in the colorfully lighted water.

It was just after four a.m., but this was the city that never sleeps. There wasn't much difference between the traffic flow now and the traffic flow at midday. Cabs, limousines, buses, cars, and pedestrians were crawling past—and it took only moments for drivers, passengers, and passers-by to notice that some of the bushes in front of the Hawaii Kai were moving. And yelling. And waving. David, Larry, Willie, and I were the moving bushes, and we were foaming up the crystal clear water in the fountain quite nicely. Vehicles honked while people shouted encouragement and waved. Whistling, howling, noises of all kinds—all to let us know they were with us. Even the damn capuchin monkeys seemed to be egging us on. I don't know, but I suppose at least some of our spectators and cheerleaders had done or imagined doing something similar to what we were doing.

I never found out whether our shenanigans in the dawn darkness of Broadway helped or hurt Hawaii Kai's bottom line, but I'm pretty sure management had to replace the monkeys.

| New York Alley Rhythm |

In September, 1961, Joey Marasciullo (a.k.a. Joey Brooks) was our drummer, having come on board when Don Martin left to pursue a different path. Brooks had been with us for a few months, and I figured he'd be with us for a good while longer. Maybe permanently. We'd even spent money for official photos with him in the group. But it wasn't to be. Joey got other offers and decided to leave us and return to Brooklyn. But he'd stay with me till I could find a replacement, he said. Respect to Joey for that. This is how it was supposed to be but too often wasn't. I had to deal more than once with the abrupt exit of a musician. Sometimes they left after a show and never showed up again. I'd even had them leave right in the middle of a song. Musicians are a strange breed of cat. I should know.

About a week passed and I had no leads. Time was getting tight, and it was a simple fact that we couldn't make our music without a drummer. And then one night I stepped outside the Pep between sets. I heard an intriguing sound and followed it to find a colored guy "playing" garbage cans with drumsticks. Now, this was a sight not commonly seen right outside the Pep—or anywhere else, for that matter—so I granted the man my attention. After a few minutes it was clear to me that this guy could flat-out play a mean trash can. I approached him.

"Man, you can play those cans," I said. "How are you on the real thing?"

"I'm okay, I guess," he said.

"I need a drummer, man," I explained. "How 'bout auditioning?"

"I'd like to, man," he said, "but I can't lay my hands on a kit just now."

"We've got drums you can use," I said. "And if you make the cut I'll buy you a kit. Just hang around till closing, and then we'll see what you got."

After we finished up I asked Carl Lattimore to lay down some sound on his keyboard so I could see and hear how my new friend handled real drums. The answer came quickly. He and Carl made a great sound together. The man could play the drums. I knew I'd found what I needed. What I wanted.

"What's your name, man?" I asked.

"I'm Willie," he said. "Willie Davis."

"Well, Willie Davis, you're hired. Welcome aboard." We shook hands; each knew he'd found what he needed.

Willie joined the band. After a few days of rehearsal, I knew I'd found the missing piece of our puzzle. We were hot. We were damn hot. Brooks was out, Willie was in. True to my word, I bought a set of drums for Willie, and he paid me ten bucks a week for ten weeks till I was paid back for the kit.

If ever you're looking for a drummer, don't ignore alleys or trash cans.

| Down in Flames with James Brown |

In 1972 I decided to try my hand at concert promotion again. My efforts with Lois and her cousin Gene had gone sideways in 1968, but that smoke had cleared. Time to try again—this time, in my hometown of Passaic.

The Capitol Theatre in Passaic stood at the corner of Monroe Street and Central Avenue. Once a vaudeville house and then a movie theater, the Capitol was transformed into a rock concert hall in 1971. The 3200-seat venue quickly became a popular tour stop for top-name bands in the seventies and eighties, including the legendary Rolling Stones, the J. Geils Band, Humble Pie, and many others. I chose the Capitol as the site for two concerts that I would organize and promote.

My first would be an R&B show, and I signed the great James Brown to headline. Surely it would be a sell-out. Passaic was a multicultural town, and I knew James had many fans on both sides of the aisle. I paid James his fee of five grand in advance and set about to do the work required for a killer show.

I promoted the concert using the name "Joe Soul," but that didn't help anything. I don't know what went wrong. Bad timing, maybe. Stars misaligned, perhaps. Maybe I zigged when I should have zagged. I just don't know. What I do know is that it all went sideways, and we didn't sell enough tickets to populate a kindergarten shadow play. But I didn't throw in the towel right away. I held on, hoping that last-minute ticket sales would surprise me, and all would be fine. But that miracle didn't happen. On the day of the concert, I accepted what was. I knew what I had to do.

I went into the Capitol in the afternoon before the show was to begin. The band was in the middle of sound check, and James was sitting a few rows back from the stage. I sat next to him, and I guess the look on my face told him something. "What's going on, Joey?" he said.

"It's not good, James," I said.

"Not good?"

"No, man. Not good. The show's a bust."

James grunted softly, leaned back, and looked straight ahead to the musicians working on stage. "You're right, man," he said. "Not good."

I'd no idea what to say. Nothing seemed right. A terrible mix of dismay and embarrassment had stolen my words, but I did my best to explain.

"I don't know, James," I said. "I don't know what went wrong. We just didn't get the sales we'd hoped to get. We've gotta cancel."

After a moment James turned to me and said, "Joey, we know each other a long time. Man, we go clear back to the Pep and Big Wilt's. I'm sorry this happened. I won't let you eat the whole thing." I didn't know what he meant by that last part, but I soon found out. Before leaving Passaic James returned half of the five grand I'd paid him in advance.

The second was to be a Latin show. Passaic was home to many Puerto Ricans and Cubans, and I was sure we could put together a show that would appeal to our Latin friends. I hired the now-legendary Cuban entertainer, Celia Cruz. Anywhere else and any other time, she'd have packed the joint. And I hired the best Latin players in Northern Jersey and New York. Still, it just didn't happen. Even my Latin promoter pseudonym, "Joey Diaz," couldn't save us from another disaster.

Certain that these shows would turn a healthy profit, I backed them with everything I had, including my Lodi home. The home where so many family memories had been made. The home in which I'd auditioned and hired the great Jimi Hendrix only a few years earlier. Foreclosed, and gone.

I'd known Joe Durante since we were young men. His father owned a washing machine business, and his family was wealthy compared to mine. Some time after the Capitol Theatre calamity, Lois and I were having dinner with Joe and his family. Talk came around to our difficult circumstances.

"Joey," Joe said, "I'm moving down to Florida. Why don't you bring your family and move down there too?"

Florida? Florida. Well, why not? I had nowhere else to be just then, and I'd often thought about living there.

Joe knew we were broke. "You can stay with me till you're back on your feet," he told me.

Cue the U-Haul. Lois and I packed it full, piled everyone into the car, and headed south to Florida—with a fat bankroll of fifty bucks in my pocket. True to his word, our compassionate friend let Lois, the kids, and me live in his house for a year. Rent-free. And that wasn't all the man did for us. Joe owned a nice Italian restaurant in Apopka called "Little Joe's." Not that he was little. Joe was well over three hundred pounds—with a heart of equal size. We ate at his restaurant every night for free. And Little Joe was one helluva cook.

And Joe's help extended beyond room and board. He also managed to book me for a few gigs in and around the Orlando area.

Perhaps Mr. Shakespeare had Joe Durante in mind when he penned this: "He that is thy friend indeed, He will help thee in thy need . . ."

Thank you, Little Joe.

| THE Gigolo of Hotel Pierre |

One night in December, 1961, I got hit on by a chick at the Pep. She was a real looker, but I knew what was what. If experience had taught me anything, it was how to recognize a hooker. And that's what this chick was—high-class, but a hooker. I knew she knew I knew, but still she pushed. I was intrigued. It was known that I didn't pay for it, so I was a bit puzzled as to this lady's endgame. Smiling sensually and acting just saditty enough to be interesting, she slipped a business card into my hand. "Meet me after you're done here," she said softly. Then she turned and walked away, trailing behind her a fragrance even the smoke-filled lounge couldn't defeat. It was as fresh and crisp as the air after a light rain.

I decided I needed a bit of inside help here, so I approached Joe Danna, showed him the card, and explained the situation. Seeing that the card Miss Enigmatic had given me read "Hotel Pierre," Joe knew what was up.

"That joint's high-class, Joey," Joe said. "*Real* high-class. It'll cost you."

"So what should I do here?" I asked.

"Don't know, man. Whatever you want, I guess," Joe said.

If you've learned nothing else about me during this read, you should know by now that I don't shy away from adventure or intrigue—and here was certain intrigue. When the show finished, I hailed a cab and instructed the driver to take me to the Hotel Pierre. The cabby smiled at me over his shoulder, dropped the flag, and drove into the New York morning.

Arriving at the Pierre, I paid the cabby and entered the lobby to find the woman waiting for me there. She was gorgeous, and the pure sex in her lips as she placed a cigarette between them and drew in the smoke—well, just that, all by itself, was enough to bring a grown man to his knees in tears.

With the slightest hint of anxiety in my step, I approached her. Intent on being absolutely clear about things, my first words to her were, "I don't pay for this, you know." The lady ignored my greeting altogether, took me by the hand, and led me to the elevator.

Neither of us spoke as the elevator climbed to her floor, nor as we walked to her room. Inside, I saw one fine place. My trysts and one-nighters at the Pep were often played out in the near-shabby rooms of the adjoining Knickerbocker Hotel. This room wasn't that. Danna was right: This joint was class. High-class. I could see that this working girl had connections to some very wealthy john who wanted his girl to have the best. I didn't care about any of that at the moment. By now I was hornier than a rabbit on his honeymoon and wanted one thing only.

We spent the better part of the night getting it on in just about every way imaginable till fatigue got the better of my libido, and I fell asleep. I felt an eerie sensation as I slept—as if I were being watched. But I managed to sleep through the night—or morning, to be accurate. As usual, I awoke sometime after noon. I swung my feet to the floor and sat on the side of the bed, rubbing the sleep from my eyes and stretching. I was thinking to shower and get out of there, but the lady sitting next to me on the bed had other notions. I was more than happy to oblige. We started the whole thing over again, and it played out just as it had a few hours earlier. When at last we were spent, I headed for the shower to get myself cleaned up, dressed, and ready to leave.

"It's been great, baby," I said to the woman, as I emerged from the bathroom suite. "Gotta run now, but it's been great."

Approaching me and placing an open hand on my chest, she stood on her toes and gave me a light kiss on the cheek. "It certainly has been that," she said. "Hang on. I've got something for you."

She stepped to the bureau and slid open a drawer. She reached in, pulled out a healthy stack of hundred-dollar bills, and returned to me.

"Just a little something," she said, offering me the bills.

Well, I was so confused I didn't know whether to say thank you or you're welcome. *She* was offering *me* money. I'd figured to be the one expected to cough up the cash. This was a new one on me. I mean, yeah, I was good. But good enough to get paid?

"What?!" I said. "What's this?"

"Nothing, sweetie. Just a tiny little thank you for your time and trouble," she said. "Believe me—you're worth it."

"Uhh, I can't say I don't appreciate this," I explained, "but no. No thanks. Can't take it."

I didn't take it, and she didn't argue. I left, still a bit confused.

The two of us met once more, a short time later—but there was nothing there. I simply told her it was time for me to move on. Again, she didn't argue.

| An *Asterisk* Kind of Year |

On a day in early December 1961, I got a call from Dorothy Kilgallen, an erudite personality in the print and broadcast media. "Joey," she said, "would you be so kind as to make an appearance on my New Year's Eve TV show?"

I'd seen the lovely Miss Kilgallen many times on the television show *What's My Line?* and was always impressed by the near-cryptic way she homed in on the guest's profession. I wouldn't miss this opportunity to join her. I accepted without hesitation, and she seemed genuinely pleased that I had.

I arrived at her New York studio around ten p.m. and was directed to a waiting area where I was to sit till show time. Around 10:30 p.m. a gentleman walked in and sat on the couch next to me. Being a devout New York Yankees fan, it took me only a moment to recognize him as Roger Maris—the same Roger Maris who, in the past season, had made Big League history by belting sixty-one home runs, breaking Babe Ruth's long-standing record of sixty round-trippers in a season. How ironic that Babe's mark of sixty homers was broken by Roger's sixty-one, in 1961. And there he sat, this history-maker—on the couch right next to me, larger than life. We introduced ourselves to each other and chatted while we waited to be called in to the show. He couldn't have been nicer. I admit to being more than a little star-struck, but he seemed as excited to meet me as I was thrilled to meet him. Whoda thunk it?

The three of us had an absolute blast ushering in the new year together. Dorothy was a most gracious host, asking so many questions of Roger and myself. We both spoke of how very special 1961 had been for each of us—for Roger, a record-breaking season; and for me, a number-one international hit record. I lip-synced "Peppermint Twist" as millions of viewers looked on.

The time went far too quickly for me, and it was all over before I knew it. I said my farewells to the two of them, but to this day I still can't believe I didn't get Roger's autograph. But I made two amazing acquaintances that night. I'd never forget meeting Roger Maris, a true baseball hero and genuinely swell guy—and Dorothy's and my paths would cross again three short years later, in a very important way.

By the way, if you turn 1961 upside down and flip it over lengthwise, it's still 1961. Just sayin'.

| Stooges and a Speargun |

While touring in Ohio in 1965, we were staying at a Holiday Inn. The blowing snow outside kept us indoors and bored, but Joey Dee and the Starliters never stayed bored for long. Someone always found a way to break through the doldrums, and this time it was Larry. He disappeared for a couple of hours and returned with scuba gear in tow. That's right: *scuba gear.* From a nearby dive store, he'd rented mask, fins, tank with regulator, wet suit—even a speargun. See, Larry had discovered something at this Holiday Inn that the rest of us had somehow overlooked: an indoor pool. And now it was time for a little adventure. I mean, if excitement wouldn't come to us . . .

At the pool we took turns using the gear. I don't remember who was the first in, but I remember my turn. You don't forget the first time you strap on a tank, slip on a pair of fins, pull on a mask, wrap your lips around a regulator, sink below the surface of the water, and not come up. Weird. Very weird, to breathe underwater. It's just not natural, and it takes a minute for your brain to convince you that it's okay not to panic. After that it's downright fun.

Each of us took a turn—even Willie. Yep, Willie donned the gear and jumped into the deep end of the pool, just like a pro. He plummeted to the bottom like a rock—as if it were just another day at work, doing demolition diving for the Navy.

Never mind that Willie couldn't swim. Not a lick.

From the bubbles rising to the top we could tell our man was breathing—but the bubble streams were coming up fast and furious. That wasn't good. That meant distress and panic. All the rest of us jumped in, fought our way to the bottom of the pool, and somehow managed to wrangle a thrashing Willie to the surface and out of the pool. Other than wide eyes and a bit of hacked-up pool water, he was fine. But I don't remember any follow-up dives for Willie that day.

But the rest of us had a gas taking turns pretending we were Mike Nelson on the CBS series *Sea Hunt* for a few hours. As for that speargun . . . well, we couldn't get it to work. Not that we didn't try. But the spear was jammed in the firing mechanism and wouldn't eject.

But we weren't finished with the thing yet.

Having had enough diving, we left the pool and took all the gear—including the stubborn speargun—to Larry's room. And then the mission began: We'd free the spear from the restrictive firing mechanism.

Setting the butt of the gun on the floor with the spear pointed at the ceiling, the bunch of us surrounded it with our heads directly over spear's tip. Each of us had his own idea as to why the little pecker wouldn't release the spear, and each of us began to take action to resolve that problem. We thumped the trigger, slapped the shaft, hammered the handle. We tapped the tube. We batted the butt against the floor. Pushed the pointy spear. Pulled the pointy spear. Larry kicked the gun. Moe banged the gun. Curly twisted the gun.

Nothing. We were confused. As we took a moment's break, looking at each other and figuratively scratching each other's heads . . .

Zzzzzziiiiiiippppp! Schlunk!

The spear released, shot right through the midst of our huddled heads, and sank about six inches deep into the ceiling. It happened too fast for us to actually see the spear fly to the ceiling and stick, but now we stood looking upward, stunned, our gazes fixed on the shaft's twangy vibration. When at last it was still, our collective gaze dropped slowly till we found each other's flabbergasted faces—wide-eyed, jaws sagging.

How could it be that at least one of us wasn't dead right now—or had a pierced ear anyway?

Boys will be boys. Again.

| California Bits and Pieces |

Early in 1962 we took a stab at Tinseltown—the great Southland of California, starting with a gig at the world-famous Romanoff's in Hollywood for the impressive fee of five grand, a hefty fee in those days. The place was jumping with the creme de la creme: Hollywood greats such as Frank Capra, Jack Benny, George Burns, Gracie Allen, and Cesar Romero, each of whom I met. When we did a sound check and discovered a broken PA system, it was no less than director Frank Capra himself (*It's a Wonderful Life*, *It Happened One Night*), who ran interference for us and had the system replaced.

On the corner of Hollywood and Vine, we played an outdoor concert at the behest of the one and only power columnist, Hedda Hopper, who, with the stroke of a pen, could make or break any Hollywood personality. Hedda then graced us with a five-star review that kicked off our six-week gig at the Crescendo, a West Hollywood club that featured the best in jazz, rock & roll, comedy, and folk music. During our first week of that gig, we lost Larry and Carl to Nick Venet of Capitol Records—a little bit of sweet payback for him for my having chosen Roulette instead of Capitol to record "Peppermint Twist." Looking for a replacement for Carl, I auditioned a few keyboardists before deciding to ask my old friend Billy Callanan to rejoin us—which he did. Forty years later I'd learn that one of those I auditioned and passed on was Bruce Johnston, who of course went on to the Hall of Fame as a member of the legendary Beach Boys. Man, did I miss that one! Whenever I see Bruce, he thanks me for not hiring him. I tell him he's welcome, and we both laugh. My old pal Rogers Freeman also rejoined us to replace Larry, and we were good to go once again.

While in Hollywood we stayed at the Beverly Hills Hotel. One day, as I was going out to purchase some sundries, I saw Larry Fine of the Three Stooges. He had his hair slicked back, but there was no mistaking that face. I walked up to him and said, "Mr. Fine, it's a pleasure meeting you in person."

"The name's Larry," he said, grasping my hand to shake it, "and you're Joey Dee, right?" He had that great smile on his face that I'd seen so often on the big screen. I thought it was incredible that Larry Fine knew who I was. Though brief, this was an exciting visit with one of my comedy heroes. I was surprised to see that I stood four inches taller than he—but, to me in my childhood, he was a giant.

For the first three weeks at the Crescendo, we worked with Don Rickles, the one-of-a-kind, in-your-face, take-no-prisoners comedian who'd say *literally* anything to anyone anytime and anywhere. And how did one work with such a man? *Carefully*, that's how. Very *carefully*. If you think this man turned off that Master of Insults persona when he wasn't in front of a camera or on stage, you're very mistaken. You couldn't be thin-skinned, and you had to be able to give as good as you got. I should know; we shared a dressing room with the abusive clown prince.

"Hey Dee," he'd say, "I have regards to you from Frankie the Nose and Funzie. You'll be dead by morning."

"Up yours, Rickles!" I'd say, and we'd both laugh. Back-and-forth banter with Mr. Warmth—there was nothing like it.

Don had an arranger/pianist/right-hand man named Key Howard. Anyone who wanted Don had to go through Key—except us, of course, because he had to see us in the dressing room every day whether he wanted to or not. One night David and I glimpsed Key helping Don put on his pants.

"What's the matter, Rickles?" we taunted. "Can't pick up your own pants?"

"Fuck you, you little guinea pricks!" he yelled.

"Fuck you twice, you bald-headed bastid!" we yelled back. Then we all laughed like hell.

It went this way for three weeks. Just about wore me out, but I enjoyed every minute with Don. The next three weeks, however, weren't so great. We shared the dressing room and the stage with a folk music trio called the Limeliters. The guys were very popular, and one of them, Glenn Yarbrough, later went on his own to record the hit, "Baby, the Rain Must Fall"; but rock & roll and folk music go together like orange juice and toothpaste. I always found folk music to be quite prosaic. For me this was a long three weeks.

Now, I had no Hollywood representation—just my old friends Don Davis and Jolly Joyce. But they managed to land a commercial for me while I was there, for Vaseline Hair Tonic. My mop of wavy black hair made me the perfect pitch man for the product. I also made an instructional record on how to do the Peppermint Twist, which was packaged with the product to promote it. I was paid the handsome sum of fourteen grand for the short afternoon's work. Now, anywhere I can knock down fourteen *thousand* bucks for a couple hours' work, that's where you'll find me. Even after the commissions I paid out, it was a helluva paycheck.

Perhaps the highlight of the trip for me was an appearance on the TV show *Here's Hollywood*, hosted by none other than Helen O'Connell herself. I'd loved her since I was a kid on Washington Place, listening to her flawless voice lilting from my radio. Helen's version of "Green Eyes" never failed to take me out. Meeting her, I found that Helen was special, just as I knew she would be. She proved a most gracious host as well, full of questions about my family and me—asked in a way that told me she truly cared. After the interview Helen kindly gifted me a beautiful brown leather bag to thank me for being on the show. For the next forty-five years or so, I never went to a gig without it. When at last it became worn and frayed and no longer strong enough to withstand the rigors of the road, I gave it honorable retirement. It resides now on a shelf in my office, standing proudly among other prized possessions such as my shoeshine box and hard hats. But the stories behind those treasures are for another day.

The time the guys and I spent in California was magical. In those days California was what it was supposed to be. I pity those who know only the California of today, which in so many ways is no longer California at all. Perhaps one day it will be again.

| A Flight to Remember |

Late in 1962 we were booked to play a fine supper club in Pittsburgh called the Twin Coaches. The whole area was socked in by a snowstorm, and all scheduled flights had been canceled. But there was a large commission at stake for him here, so Don Davis decided to fix the situation by trying to talk me into letting him hire a private plane to get us to the gig. He succeeded.

I'd like to say Mrs. DiNicola didn't raise any foolish kids, but maybe there was this one . . .

Don disappeared for a time and returned to report that he'd arranged everything. We were to go immediately to Idlewild (now JFK) Airport, he said. The bunch of us piled into two taxis and soon found ourselves there, expecting to find—at least I was—a nice aircraft large enough to not only seat all of us but to give us a fighting chance at withstanding the storm and actually landing in Pittsburgh. Alive.

Now, I guess I have my pessimistic side, just like the next guy. But mostly I consider myself an optimist. I generally look on the bright side of things and expect the best of people and situations, and I usually figure things will turn out just fine, no matter how bleak they may appear at a given moment. But I've gotta say, those two little Piper Cubs that Don hired to fly us through that blizzard just sorta made me gulp. And there was nothing I could do to prevent the name *Buddy Holly* from popping into my head.

But the Cubs were all Don could get; nothing larger was available. It would be Willy, Billy, and Rogers in one; Don, David, Sam, and I in the other. It was nonnegotiable that I would fly with Sam. See, Sam Taylor, Jr. had fought in Korea, where he had survived two tail-spinning helicopter crashes. So, whenever we had to travel by air, I always made it a point to find a seat next to Sam. I figured that if the good Lord had wanted to take Sam in a crash, he'd have already been dead. So I hitched my trailer to his wagon, figuring it was the safest thing to do. Hopefully, it would turn out that this short flight of three hundred fifty miles would do nothing to weaken my faith in Sam's mojo.

Don had the perfect system for coping with this mind-bending situation: He simply turned off his hearing aid and fell swiftly into a sound sleep. And Sam seemed relatively inured to any impending danger. I suppose surviving two helicopter crashes might steel one's nerves a bit. But David and I were in full panic mode as the pilot taxied the Cub into position for take-off after the other plane was airborne. We were white-knuckling the seat arms, and neither of us was talking. I wanted to close my eyes, but I couldn't remember how to do it. So I just stared in wide-eyed silence as the plane gathered speed and climbed, being enveloped in a perfect combination of white and black in which nothing was visible. It took a moment or two for my neurons to start shaking hands again, but when they did, I thought to myself, *How can this guy possibly see where he's going?*

Right on cue the pilot took out a paper map, opened it a fold or two, and traced it with the tip of his finger. It was like he was a tourist driving on Route 66, checking the map to see how far it was to Albuquerque.

David saw the map when I saw the map. He looked at me. I looked at him. Somebody whimpered, but I'm not sure which of us it was.

"I've never been to this particular airport before," the pilot said with an odd smile. I guess he saw us seeing him and thought he'd explain to us why we should be reassured by seeing him look at the map.

Waste of effort. We weren't reassured.

All through the flight he kept putting on the light to refer to that damn map. While we dropped and rose with every tiny air pocket in the sky between New York and Pittsburgh, I feared that he, sooner or later, would put that light on, look at the map, and say *oops*. Or *uh-oh*. Or *dammit*. He never did, but still it was the longest short flight I ever took.

When at last we landed in Pittsburgh, we were surprised to find that the other plane hadn't yet arrived. While I waited, that name Buddy Holly popped into my head again—but now I had time to think about the whole story, complete with Ritchie Valens and the Big Bopper—and a replaying of the hellish story seemed now a frightening possibility. I nearly worried myself sick for thirty long minutes until the plane came into sight at last, touched down, and landed safely. The guys wasted no time deplaning, eager to tell me that their flight was at least as nerve-wracking as ours had been. Their pilot was drunk, they said, and they had to make a stop somewhere for gas. Nice. A drunk pilot flying a plane that's running out of gas. Stuff right out of a sit-com. Or *The Twilight Zone.*

Of course, with all the delays we were running late for the gig. We piled once again into a couple of taxis and high-tailed it to the supper club. But I guess we couldn't get our tail high enough. When we arrived at the Twin Coaches, we learned that the owner had given up on us and pulled the plug. He canceled the show and refunded the ticket sales. And he threatened me with a lawsuit. Bonus.

We found a hotel for the night. Although we were worn to a frazzle, we stayed up all night talking about our harrowing experience. It was unanimous: There's no business like show business. Having reached that agreement, Willie decided he needed to take a nice, long, hot shower—which he did. The only problem with that was the water spraying from the showerhead. It smelled like rotten eggs. And the putrid odor was so strong that it seeped out into the hallway and permeated the entire floor. We were all gagging on the stench and begged Willie to turn it off, but to no avail. He kept showering and singing for over an hour.

A fitting conclusion to such a night.

| Joey Dee and the "Starry Night"-liters Unplugged |

In 1962 we were in great demand everywhere, often booked for large charity functions at venues ranging from the Plaza to the Astor to the Museum of Modern Art. That's right. The Museum of Modern Art. MoMA. Home of Van Gogh's *Starry Night*, Monet's *Water Lilies*, Dali's *The Persistence of Memory*, and other such masterpieces. An odd place, you might think, for Joey Dee and the Starliters to play rock & roll.

If that's what you're thinking, be advised that legendary dance instructor Arthur Murray agreed with you.

Here's how that went.

In April, 1962, someone representing MoMA called our agent Jolly Joyce to book us for a fundraising concert there. I don't know who *did* the MoMA event planning, but I know who *didn't* do it: museum director James Rorimer. Mr. Rorimer sort of . . . well, he *hated* the idea of rock & roll at MoMA. But somebody farther up the food chain thought it was a great idea, and Mr. Rorimer was persuaded to concede that one. In fact, I'm not absolutely sure we'd been booked to play there till we actually showed up on premises.

For this gig we could use only Carl on organ, Willie on drums, and myself on sax and vocals with David and Larry. We entered the hallowed halls of the very distinguished Museum of Modern Arts and were told where to set up. While we were being miked, I talked with the sound guys about the irony of this whole thing. I mean, there we were, surrounded by masterworks of Van Gogh, Monet, Dali, Chagall, Matisse, Picasso, and so many more masters—and in three months from then the iconic *Campbell Tomato Soup Cans* of our Pep regular Andy Warhol would be hanging there—and we were getting ready to play "Peppermint Twist." Talk about a confluence of arts.

And so we played. We were good, and we were received well. The patrons of the arts loved us and danced like nobody was watching. I wasn't surprised. We'd charmed the Beautiful People at the Pep; now we'd charmed the arts crowd at MoMA. You just couldn't stop good rock & roll.

We were into our third number—"Money," I believe it was—when Carl's Leslie speaker went silent. And a Lowery organ with a dead Leslie speaker doesn't do anyone much good. We had to stop playing, of course, and do some fiddling and jiggling to try to get our sound back. If we couldn't find and fix the problem, we were screwed. Everyone was chipping in, trying to find the source of the trouble. Even Jolly was wandering around, just looking for anything that seemed odd or out of place. And he saw something: an electrical plug on the floor that looked like it didn't really want to be on the floor. He reached down and plugged it into the wall receptacle above it and . . . voila! The Leslie came to life. Relieved, we regrouped and jumped back into it.

Sitting next to the speaker and the little plug on the floor that didn't really want to be on the floor was renowned television dance instructor Arthur Murray. See, Mr. Murray couldn't shake his old-school notion that such music just didn't belong within such venerated environs. It was just too darned loud, he thought. And if it was too loud for him, certainly it must be too loud for everyone else. When he noticed the plug within reach, he decided to save the day. But, as I said before, you just can't stop good rock & roll. Delay it, maybe. But stop it? Never.

After the show Arthur's wife Kathryn approached me. She thanked me for an enjoyable concert and apologized for her husband's behavior, assuring me that it didn't represent her feelings in the least. Kathryn was a fine, classy lady.

I was told later that the fundraiser was a great financial success. I didn't have to be told that it was a social and musical success. I saw that on the faces of the people as they danced and smiled and enjoyed themselves throughout our performance. I like to think that the bold and groundbreaking creators of the masterworks that surrounded us that day would have enjoyed our performance too, and that they would have been the first ones to hit the floor dancing, had they been there. Their lives and their works are testament to their cutting-edge spirit. They pushed envelopes. They challenged boundaries. Certainly they'd have been fans of rock & roll and the Twist—and of Joey Dee and the Starliters.

| BOREDOM AND BURNS |

Even with all the girls and the sex on the road, the boys and I found ourselves bored from time to time, when we weren't performing or rehearsing. Such gaps in attention had to be filled with something besides sleep, so we found things to satisfy our need for stimulation when none presented itself. Take the experiments in aeroballistics for instance.

Apparently, David and my nephew Johnny had, at some time in the past and without my knowledge, received a grant to do research in aeronautics and flight sciences, and they decided to use our offstage time for experiments.

Not really.

But even without grants, they were determined to test their ideas. Lorenzo's in Syracuse had a large basement dressing room, where the boys' research yielded a fun little item sure to liven up even the most boring moment.

The *Flaming Doohickey.* That's what those mad scientists developed. Or, if you prefer more scientific nomenclature, the Flaming *Doodad.*

These two frustrated flight engineers developed a technique—even today a classified secret—that allowed them to turn a ball of foil into a mini-rocket which, when lighted afire, took off at whatever trajectory it chose. It could run up your arm, into your face, into your hair. It might bounce off your nose, your eye, your ear. The hot little orb could threaten other, more precious parts of your body. After perfecting the Flaming Doohickey in Lorenzo's dressing room, the boys broke it out whenever they were feeling coltish. And I just have to say, you haven't lived till you've seen a room full of drunk musicians and go-go girls running into and over each other, seeking cover from flaming foil balls ricocheting around the room. And all of this begging the question, *Why are we are we doing this shit?* So, whenever the boys got to feeling playful, we all had to be alert and stay on our toes—and watch our balls and anything else that was near and dear to our hearts.

Boys will be boys. Again and again.

| Tito Mambo |

Being on the road never bothered me. I was a blooded road warrior. I'd drive five hundred miles overnight to make the next gig and never break a sweat. But as good as I was at making jumps, I wasn't the champion. Joe Terry, Frankie Maffei, and Billy Carlucci of Danny and the Juniors made the biggest jumps ever. I've known them to drive nonstop from Palm Springs to Chicago to do a gig. On one road trip their van broke down. Joe bought a new van with his credit card and made the gig. Yep, road warriors for sure. While those boys were arguably the best at beating back the road to get the job done, the road was a fact of life for all of us musicians out there trying to do our thing.

And there was great diversity among acts we met on the road. One of my favorites was a man called Tito Mambo. I believe his band was called the Messiahs of Soul when we worked together, but it might have been the Upsetters or the Men of Chantz. Whatever his band, Tito made it happen. He had long black hair and beard, making him look a bit like most people's mental picture of Jesus of Nazareth. And he played that appearance to the hilt. Plus he could scat and make the most interesting noises ever. If you're interested listen to his single of "Black Pepper" b/w "Jungle Farm 7." You'll hear what I'm talking about.

To advertise a gig Tito and his group would drive around town in a 1952 Cadillac hearse. Tito lay in a coffin strapped to the car's roof, sitting up suddenly to surprise people and wave to them as they passed. I've often wondered just how much psychotherapy was later required by passers-by who happened to be looking at the coffin in the moment when Tito sat up.

To say the man's show was unique is an understatement. At the beginning of his act the club was dark as night—except for the spotlight that illuminated a coffin center stage. The band was on stage but hidden by darkness as they stood at the ready. All at once the coffin's lid flew open as the band began playing the Bobby Lewis hit "Tossin' and Turnin'," and Tito popped up from the coffin singing, "I couldn't sleep at all last night . . ." The startling illusion was enough to send the unsuspecting audience to the same therapists who treated the psychologically abused pedestrians who saw Tito sit up in that coffin on the roof of the hearse. I can't prove that. I'm guessing.

I worked with Tito in 1967, at a place called the Tiger Tail in Revere, Massachusetts. His closing number was the Isley Brothers tune "Shout," just as mine was. During that closer he whipped the audience into a frenzy then jumped off the stage and ran outside. The mesmerized crowd followed him out the door to see, I suppose, just what the hell this psycho was up to. He was headed for the Atlantic Ocean directly across the street from the Tiger Tail. He jumped into the water, splashed around a bit, came out, and ran back to the club, with the audience close on his heels. Back on stage he grabbed the mike to finish the number.

I was—ahem—shocked that he wasn't electrocuted.

Tito was an honest person; his stage persona was simply an extension of his personal lifestyle. Some have granted Tito the title "First Hippie," and I wouldn't argue that point, based on my occasional visits to his home.

In Tito's place stood several huge marijuana plants, and everyone who visited enjoyed their magic leaves—except me. But the man's *human* guests weren't the only ones who enjoyed those potted pot plants. Tito had a large Labrador retriever that loved to nibble the plants' leaves. The dog was pretty much always stoned.

| SIZE MATTERS |

In 1974 I met Alvin Morse at a jai alai game in Florida. He didn't know who I was, and I didn't know he could sing. A minor comedy of errors led to a close friendship. Some months later—we had both learned who each was—I invited Al to sing with the Starliters, and he happily accepted. It would be my very great pleasure to work with Al as a Starliter from then until about 1982 and then off and on for some years after that. Greater than that pleasure, however, was the great privilege of becoming fast friends with him and his family, and it remains so today. Our families are in this thing together.

Not long after Al joined us in the mid-1970s, we played Bachelors III, a night club in Utica, New York. Al had written a song called "Shine Your Flashlight," and a friend in Orlando created an outfit to match the song's theme. It was a white jumpsuit (pay attention, Elvis) with a bejeweled jacket featuring strategically placed diamond studs for sparkle. And the jumpsuit fit tightly. Now, when I say it fit *tightly*, imagine having to smear its inside with the world's slipperiest polytetrafluoroethylene, a synthetic fluoropolymer of tetrafluoroethylene—I think I sprained my keyboard—to get yourself into it. Tight. *Tight* suit.

When Al took the stage that night, he was wearing said suit—sans underwear. Please don't ask me how I knew that. In any case he was rocking that sparkly garment that fit so tightly that his leg hairs raised Braille-like bumps in the fabric. But that wasn't the worst of it.

Now, I've no idea what caused the problem. Perhaps Al saw something in the audience that piqued his libido, or perhaps he was recalling some past encounter or imagining a future one. Whatever the source of inspiration, Al became aroused. And in that tight jumpsuit, it showed. Boy, did it show. Bubba, our bass player, noticed it—keep your eyes on your work, Bubba—and slowly sidled up to me.

"Joey," he whispered, "take a good look at Al."

I did. Damn.

I knew what had to be done, but I couldn't do it till after the song had ended. When it did, I moved close to Al.

"Al," I said, "you need to get off stage for a minute and get yourself under control. Mr. Johnson's showing, man."

Al couldn't have been completely surprised by what I was saying to him. I mean, he must certainly have known he'd gotten aroused. I think he just didn't realize how obvious it was to everyone else. But he didn't argue. He stepped off into the wings, and we played a tune that covered his absence.

A stage worker approached me after the set.

"Mr. Dee," he said, "you're wanted in the office. Right away."

I reported as instructed and found an unhappy manager.

"Joey," he said, "what the hell was that?"

"What was what?" I asked. I knew. I just hoped he meant something else.

"Damn, Joey! The man had a hard-on!" he said. "His joint looked like a python trying to crawl out of those damn pants."

"Oh *that*," I said. "Yeah, I took care of that. No sweat."

"No sweat for *you*, maybe," he said, "But *lots* of sweat for *me*. And we can't have it again. You tell Morse he's not to wear that jumpsuit again. Something a little looser. Maybe sweat pants or something."

I assured the man that I'd take care of everything. "You don't have to worry," I told him. "I'll talk to Al and make sure he understands."

I met up with Al backstage. He hadn't yet changed out of the jumpsuit.

"Al," I said, "you can't wear that outfit again."

"What's the problem, Joey?" he asked.

"Problem?! What's the problem?! Damn, man," I said, "you were flashing a bone the size of Vermont, and the audience found it a bit distracting." I paused a moment, then said, "Well, to be honest, only the guys didn't like what they saw. The chicks were diggin' it."

Those men! Envy is such a wasted emotion.

| Largest, Hottest Crowd Ever |

The largest crowd we ever played was at New York City's Central Park in August, 1962. It was estimated at just over one hundred thousand. Bo, David, Sam, Willie, Wild Billy, and I took the stage that day to play some fierce rock & roll. What we saw from our vantage point was a vast sea of humanity. People upon people upon people. Anyone standing in the audience couldn't have swung a dead cat without hitting a dozen people. If an artist had done a stage dive, we'd have had only moments to retrieve him or her before issuing a missing person's report.

Now, it's important to note that we were in the dog days of summer. August is not typically known as a crisp month in New York, and the temp on this particular day was right around the century mark—and who knows what the humidity level was. Truth be told, the event probably should have been canceled; I was amazed that it wasn't. When we performed that afternoon, people were sweating buckets and passing out left and right. But not to worry, people. Joey Dee and the boys had first aid to offer. We were given citrus fruits to throw out into the audience when we saw persons in distress. Now, this was an ironic twist: Usually, the *audience* throws fruit at the *act*.

Having gotten through our performance—we were puddles—we struck a beeline to the dressing area and the canopies placed there to shade us, and giant fans to cool us. But neither helped very much. It was just too damn hot and humid. To play a gig like that one, you needed total commitment to your music and to your fans, and you needed fans—no pun intended—that were totally committed to your music and to you. We always found that in New York City.

| Mutiny in the Parking Lot |

In 1967 we were doing a week in Youngstown, Ohio. I don't remember the name of the venue or even the members of the band except Bobby "Rod" Rodriguez and my brother-in-law Eddie Barbato. Bobby Rod had told me that he was planning to leave the band after this gig, and that the other band members—except Eddie—would be going with him. Even though Eddie wasn't going with Bobby, I knew he was unhappy and planning to go his way as well. I didn't blame anyone for wanting to leave; I wasn't paying very well at the time, and gigs were hard to come by. Lois and I were sad that the band was going to call it quits, but we knew far too well that musicians came, musicians went. C'est la vie. But it was always extra hard when they jumped ship en masse.

My manager at the time, John Gomez, wasn't as nonchalant about the situation as I was. Nor was he a trusting soul. When he got wind of the planned exodus, he worried that the boys might leave before the gig ended. That wouldn't be good. As a preemptive measure he hired a couple of guys—*bodyguards*, if you'd like to put a positive spin on it—to help the boys be where they needed to be and remember their obligation. One was an ex-pug called Big Louie, a friend of mine who was plenty intimidating just being in the room. But his .45 caliber semi-automatic could add that little extra touch of *I-mean-what-I'm-saying-to-you* when he needed it.

The boys finished the gig.

But the week wasn't an easy a one. For anybody. Lois and I were preoccupied with worry about the changes coming after the gig. The boys lived with the threat that hung over them like a heavy cloud. If you were a betting man, you'd have to figure it a sure bet that, by week's end, the boys were bound to have a suppressed feeling or two that would need to be vented. And you'd have won money.

We'd played this gig in tuxedos, figuring that the extra bit of class would cover some of the holes that were in our sound at the time. Of course, the pervasive tension punched additional holes in that sound—and when all the holes were summed, even the tuxes weren't able to cover them all. Still, we wore them. And when he got back to the motel after the final curtain had dropped, Eddie couldn't get out of his monkey suit fast enough. He ripped it off piece by piece as though he were ridding himself of some other-worldly parasite that would suck the life from him. And then he stood looking at the pile of wool, rayon, imitation satin, and pleats that lay in a crumpled heap on the floor. As he gazed, that heap became the repository of the past week's anxiety, stress, frustration—and suppressed rage.

Eddie threw on his street clothes, grabbed the pieces of tuxedo and a bottle from the nightstand, then headed out the door and into the parking lot. Throwing the clothes onto the asphalt, he doused them with vodka from the bottle, pulled a match from his pocket, struck it, and dropped it onto the jumble of cloth. The mound burst into flame.

All the motel rooms opened to the parking lot, so the other guys saw what Eddie was doing. It was only moments after the torching that they all spilled from their rooms, clutching their tuxedos as they ran. Into the flames went their offending formalwear, combining with Eddie's to complete this fiery shrine to their indignation.

Lois and I watched as the boys laughed and danced around the bonfire, releasing, I suppose, the pent-up feelings they'd been forced to contain through the course of a difficult week. While I'd never have held it against them that they were moving on, I was hurt that it all was ending this way. I saw this insurrection as a personal slap in the face, and I don't know what stopped me from giving Eddie a beating that night. He had one coming—but he was family. Still, family or no, Lois was angry enough with him that she didn't speak to him for years after that night. I mean, family has to be respected both ways, and Eddie had clearly disrespected it first.

But time has a way of healing. Lois and Eddie eventually made amends, and Bobby Rod and I are friends today. I mean, why not? If we dissolved family relationships and friendships with every little argument or misunderstanding, we'd all die alone and wasted.

TWENTY-SEVEN

LOVES OF MY LIFE

The placement of this most important chapter turned out to be a difficult issue for me to decide, and I grappled more than a little with it. Logic and reason told me that the most important thing in any sequence of things should lead out that sequence—meaning that this would be the first chapter of this volume. Somehow that just didn't work. But, on the other hand, to nest it somewhere among lesser chapters seemed to me disrespectful, as though I were treating its subject matter as any ol' detail of my life. At last I came to see that the end of the book is this chapter's proper and rightful place, given that its substance is what remains real and most valuable to me, after all else has been said and done.

| Joan Wuthrick |

Years before Joe Durante graciously housed and fed my family after we lost our Lodi home in 1973, he'd granted me an even greater favor. See, Joe played trumpet in those days and had a band in Hackensack. One summer he invited me to sit in on a gig at the public pool. I agreed and played with his band. No matter whether we played well that day or not, I still remember it as the greatest gig of my life. See, that's where I met her.

Joan Wuthrick of Hackensack.

To my eyes this fifteen-year-old was the most beautiful girl in the world, and in a flash of lightning I fell head over heels for her. She had amazing blonde hair, dazzling green eyes, and a body to evoke the envy of any Greek goddess. It took me a while to get to her, but I did; I was determined. We enjoyed several dates and eventually began going steady. Now *there's* a term that seems to be gone with the wind: *going steady*. In my day going steady was a very important thing. It meant this girl could wear my high school ring on a dainty chain around her neck, or wrap layers of adhesive tape around the bottom of it till it fit on her petite finger. In either case others would know she was "taken." I was in heaven.

I invited Joanie to my gigs, and she usually managed to find a ride to them. She'd dance with my friend Junior Giunta while I performed—and let me tell you, my girl had the moves.

Joanie showed up once wearing a poodle skirt—the rage du jour—and a multi-layered crinoline petticoat. Her wardrobe left me to ponder what it would take for me to get underneath all that damn clothing.

Joanie always felt I had too many girlfriends, and I did—so we eventually broke up for a while. But I never took back my ring, figuring she was just a phone call away from being mine again if I asked. That's called eating your cake and having it too. It's a shaky philosophy. Looking back, this all seems to have been a foreshadowing of things to come for us. But neither of us had a crystal ball handy at the time, so it went unnoticed.

Despite the temporary disruption in our relationship, everything worked out. On August 10, 1959, Joanie and I stood before Judge Garofolo at Hackensack City Hall and recited our vows. This wedding was no great affair; it was a small ceremony with only family in attendance. Afterward Joanie and I honeymooned at a dumpy hotel on Route 46 in Clifton, only a few miles down the road.

The apartment we'd secured wasn't yet ready to occupy, so we moved in with my mother. That first while was a bit tough, considering that we had only the single bed in my old bedroom, and our room shared a wall with my mother's room. But there were no in-law problems. Joanie got along famously with my family—she loved them, they loved her. In Joanie's words, "Joey's family is the kind of family every girl [would be] lucky to be in. We loved each other, and I was lucky to have them in my life. They always loved me."

My sister Angie and her husband Neil Gylling bought a farmhouse in New Hampshire and kindly invited us to stay with them until our apartment was ready. We accepted. This turned out to be a bit of a struggle for my bride. In her words:

"Well, I'm a city girl, and this farmhouse was from a ghost story. No bathroom, just an outhouse. After I used the toilet Angie asked if I'd flushed it. I told her I couldn't find the flusher."

The whole experience was a nightmare for Joanie. If you think about it, you may conclude that if the house had an outhouse because it had no bathroom, then it must have been an interesting proposition to take a bath. That wasn't a problem, really. See, there was this large rain barrel outside . . .

Yes, all that and animals too. We had to contend with all manner of farm critters roaming through the house at will. When Joanie complained about this, Angie simply laughed and told her to not pay any attention to them. Again, from Joanie: "Oh?! Try sleeping and looking up to see two eyes looking down at you, and you don't know who they belong to."

Well, I couldn't just continue enjoying this luxurious living forever. I mean, I had to work and make some money. I left to play a gig in the City, leaving Joanie to stay at the farmhouse for another week. When I returned, she immediately and energetically threw her clothes together into a suitcase and informed me that she wouldn't stay there any longer. I couldn't blame her. She'd been as stalwart as anyone might have expected through these first days of marriage. Fortunately, just a short time later, my mother informed us that the apartment was ready for us.

I have such wonderful memories of our early years together. Joanie and I were deeply in love and soon brought into the world two wonderful boys, Joey and Nicky. Sadly, regrets are scattered among those wonderful memories. How I wish there were fewer regrets and more wonderfuls. And there would have been, but for my very many poor choices.

Given how much I loved my Joanie, it's difficult to understand why I felt a need to cheat and run around with other women. And so soon after marriage. But if you've gotten this far into the book, you've read many confessions of my errant libido. The truth is, I cheated on Joan more times than I can count—or even remember. All the while, she continued to heed the counsel of our mothers. *Just look the other way*, was their advice—and she forced herself to do that for as long as she could.

Ironically, I was insanely jealous of my wife, despite all the stuff I was pulling. It must be one of life's great ironies that the same men who are willing to flirt, date, and otherwise engage "other" women are the same men who jealously guard their own "turf." I was certainly one of those men. What's sauce for the gander, I thought, was most definitely *not* sauce for the goose. It wouldn't be long before the words Johnny Taylor sang became real to me: "Who's making love to your old lady while you were out making love." Yeah, payback would come for me, and it would be the proverbial bitch.

Even though Joanie knew about my shameless shenanigans, and I knew she knew, it was nevertheless particularly awkward when I was caught red-handed. On one of my nights off in 1962, I told Joanie I needed to relax—what balls I had to even say such a thing—and I was going to play cards with the guys. I knew she wanted me to stay home, but I ignored that unspoken plea and went ahead on like the ass I was. I met my friend Tony Bonura—brother of Sal, of the Choo Choo Club—and we drove into the Pep to see what was going on.

Girls—that's what was going on. We found a couple of unescorted, good-looking chicks, and we threw our best lines at them. Easy peasy. Now, Tony was a newlywed himself, having just married Cathy. One of Cathy's friends saw Tony and me and gave her a call. "Guess who I just saw at the Pep?" she asked, and the answer made it clear to Cathy that there'd been no card game that night. Cathy scooped up Joanie and the two of them drove to the Pep, moving like Speedy Gonzalez at the Olympics. They double-parked, left the car's motor running, and stormed into the club before the bouncers could give me a heads-up. Joanie found me and closed in. She tapped me on the shoulder, and I turned.

"What are you doing here, Joey?"

The blood sank from my face to my feet faster than a dumbbell in a swimming pool. Through nervous laughter I stammered, "Uhh . . . well, I . . ." Having suddenly been taken mute, Tony was no help at all.

"You'd better take your ass home right now, Joey," Joan said. She didn't give me an *or else*, but I knew there was one she was saving for a surprise.

Tony and I paid the check, left the girls without so much as a "see ya," and raced toward home. I dropped off my partner-in-crime at his house.

Joanie arrived home before I did. I guess she wanted to welcome me properly. And welcome me she did. She threw every dish in the house at me. She may also have borrowed a few from the neighbor. And she had mighty good aim. A few of the flying saucers bounced off my sconce, and I was seeing stars—but I couldn't even feel angry about it. Hey, this is the kind of thing you've gotta expect when you're caught red-handed at such shenanigans. I was wrong, plain and simple, and I got what I deserved. Well, actually, I deserved much worse, but Joanie was a patient person, and she loved me. Go figure. She and both our mothers knew I was a chronic philanderer, as did I. What makes my behavior so inexplicable was, Joanie was far better looking and in general lovelier than any of the women I used to cheat on her. It just didn't make sense, but still I did it. Over and over again I did it.

Remember the barmaids David and I met at the Pep—the ones who worked for Matty the Horse at the 49er Club? Here's the rest of that story.

The relationship between Cheri and me lasted quite a while, and I think she fell in love. But she eventually learned I was married, and perhaps you can guess what happened next. Now, I don't claim to know much about the female psyche or how it works in a situation such as this. Or maybe it's not a gender thing at all but simply a human thing: You get hurt, you tend to want to return the hurt. Whichever of those is true, Cheri found my phone number and called Joanie to explain the wonders and magic of the affair she and I had enjoyed. Having not been privy to the conversation, I've no idea how Joanie handled this, but she certainly confronted me when I arrived home that night.

I denied everything.

I'm sure Joanie didn't for a moment buy my story, but we managed to go forward anyway. It was another rotten thing I'd done to her, I know. All she wanted was to love me, be my wife, and raise our children in a happy home. I wanted that too; I simply couldn't control myself or keep it in my pants.

Joanie accompanied me on our first tour of Europe in 1963. She telephoned her sister Ida every day to see how our boys were doing. When she made her daily call from Paris, her nephew picked up the phone. Asked how things were, he answered that everyone had chicken pox. Joanie's maternal impulses kicked into high gear, and the needle on her guilt-o-meter shot to the top and stuck there. There she was, thousands of miles and many hours of travel away from her sons when they needed her.

I was busy doing interviews and recordings. When I got home that night, Joan told me she had to fly home immediately to be with the boys. We got her a ticket, and she arranged to have her father pick her up at the airport when she arrived home. Because of a severe blizzard in the Northeast, the plane was unable to land right away. After two hours of circling it was cleared for landing. Joanie's father met her as planned, and the two of them drove directly to Ida's to collect Joey and Nicky. Joanie carefully—and thoroughly—bundled the boys in coats and blankets and took them home.

The boys were settled in when my sister Mary and her husband Shuffs dropped by to deliver fan mail. They were the presidents of my fan club, so the mail always went to them, and from them to me. As you might suspect, much of it—too much of it—was from girls telling of my escapades with them. With Joanie's eyes being the first to see the mail this time instead of mine, I was caught once again at my incessant game of cheating. I've thought so often about all the times Joanie had to withstand the emotional impact of my infidelity, and I've pondered how I'd have felt had roles been reversed. It's a difficult mind-swap to pull off, and my struggle always leads me to the same conclusion: I'd never want to endure what I inflicted so many times on her.

Some time later Joanie visited the doctor when she wasn't feeling well. The doctor confirmed that she was pregnant. Knowing, I suppose, how things were going to end, this wasn't good news for Joanie. In her words: "I didn't want another child with [Joey]. I had enough. I didn't take care of myself and ultimately lost the child. It was a boy. I never told Joey about this until 2010. It was very sad, with a lot of crying, pain, and lost feelings for Joey."

By 1966 Joanie had taken enough from me. She decided she no longer wanted to look the other way. Instead, she'd have a different life. Being encouraged by my mother to get out and have some fun—yes, my mother changed her point of view as well—Joanie began seeing a guy from Lodi named Mike Fricchione. I suppose she decided that life with him would be more stable than life with me. In any case Joanie announced that she wanted a divorce and moved out, taking the boys with her. Just like that it was over. I could hardly fault her for tiring of it all and finding a way out. She'd tried so hard for so long, but she simply couldn't overcome the problems of our marriage—ninety-nine percent of which were my fault.

I was leaving for a gig when Joanie told me she wanted a divorce. I noticed a huge box of her shoes shoved up against the wall in the hallway.

"What's with all the shoes?" I asked.

She answered, "I'm leaving them for all the girls you said would love to be in my shoes."

Oh! the pain. It was a dagger through the heart of a man who still loved his wife and sons—but, sadly, not enough to keep them.

Our divorce became official on July 20, 1967. By then Joanie was living in Park Ridge, New Jersey. Lois Lee had come to live with me in my Lodi home. Despite the awkwardness of it all, Joanie was always friendly with Lois. I wish I could say

Joanie's and my relationship was equally friendly, but no. It became contentious after the divorce. We didn't communicate with each other for years afterward, nor did I see the boys. I hated the disconnection from my sons, but I deserved it. My finances and income were so bad that I wasn't able to pay any child support. Joan stayed in touch with my brother Al's wife Kathy and was always close to her. And to my mother. Mike would often pick Mom up and bring her to see Joan and the boys. "I divorced your son," she told Mom, "but I still love you." And the two of them remained close throughout my mother's life. But with anything having to do with Joan, I was persona non grata.

| Lois Lee |

By 1964 the price of Joey Dee and the Starliters had outgrown the Pep's budget. Many groups were brought in to play for the house, and some were very good. My favorite was Johnny Maestro and the Crests, who had scored big with hits like "16 Candles," "The Angels Listened In," and "Step by Step." Johnny would later become the lead singer for the Del-Satins, and, in 1969, he'd lead an eleven-piece band called the Brooklyn Bridge to a number-three chart hit with the Jimmy Webb tune "The Worst That Could Happen" and other chart hits. When Maestro played the Pep with the Crests, the band consisted of himself, Roger Valdez, John Torri, Bob Hirschliefer, and a very beautiful and talented Lois Lee. Johnny not only sang lead; he also played bass guitar. Now, Johnny Maestro playing bass while singing was tantamount to Karen Carpenter playing drums while singing. I mean, with voices like theirs there was simply no need to play an instrument. Nothing should distract in the least from the beauty of such a voice.

Johnny once paid me a great compliment. "Joey, you're a great entertainer and a great dancer," he told me. "I wish I had that. And, by the way," he continued, "how do you work out like you do for an entire show?"

"Johnny," I replied, "if I had your voice, I wouldn't *have* to kill myself on stage every night."

"Man, we'd make a great entertainer, you and me," Johnny said. "If we could combine our talents, we'd be the complete package."

Johnny Maestro's voice and Joey Dee's stage presence. I wish!

After Johnny and the Crests moved on, the Pep went in a new direction, developing a stage show with dancers and singers. The production was effectively choreographed, well rehearsed, and nicely staged. Lois didn't move on with the Crests when they left the Pep. Instead, she auditioned to be the lead female singer in the Pep's new show. She got the job. Of course.

Whenever I had a break from the road, I always returned to the scene of the crime: the Peppermint Lounge. One night I was enjoying the show, good company, and a few drinks—and particularly enjoying Lois Lee's rendition of "Fever," the Peggy Lee signature tune. Lois's voice was strong and beautiful—like a combination of the stylings of Bette Midler and Janis Joplin. And she was a very good comic, with the timing of the great Totie Fields. The difference between Lois and the other three? Lois was better.

But there was something just a bit odd about her performance that night. Given that the general attitude of the song "Fever" is sultry, sexy, sensual, it seemed out of character that Lois would be laughing while singing it. But laughing she was. Not continually, but now and then. I wasn't sure what that was about—perhaps it was comedy that eluded me, or . . . well, I didn't know what or there could be. After the show the singer walked past me, and I spoke to her.

"Excuse me," I said, "but you're a great singer. You don't need to fall back on comedy while you're singing. You should be more serious."

Miss Lee responded with a smile and walked on. I didn't know then why she didn't speak to me, but it was because she was starstruck. I say this only because Lois told me some time later that she went into the dressing room and promptly announced to the girls, "Joey Dee spoke to me!" In my mind that wasn't something for anyone to get too riled up about, but I'm certainly glad it caught her attention. Lois told me something else as well: The reason she'd been laughing while singing "Fever" was that the male dancers were sucking on her toes and fingers at various times during the performance. Learning that, I withdrew my initial faulty judgment, now being impressed that she was able to get through the song at all.

Another of Lois's talents was preaching. You read it right. *Preaching*. Lois Lee preached. When the timing was right, she'd take off on one of those wild rampages like some smile-plastered-on-the-face star of an early Sunday morning "Come to Jesus" show. She had the voice, the stylings, the face, the gestures, the energy, the drama. Sometimes she'd drop suddenly to the floor and pound it like a pulpit. Brought the audience to its collective feet.

Lois and I began dating after that. She lived in the Morris Park section of the Bronx but had a place in the City. I went there often to be with her, especially when

I'd been drinking hard—and that was more often than Bill Russell pulled down a rebound.

After Joanie left me, I asked Lois to join me in my Lodi home, and she did so. Even though I loved Lois very much, the next years would turn out to be quite a bumpy ride for us. And you won't have to think very hard to guess who caused most of those bumps.

I was still disappearing into the City, telling Lois I was going to play cards. Yeah, I played cards all right: strip poker with my bimbos du jour. Given that such sleeping around had cost me one family already, one might think I'd try a different tack in my second act. But no. At that point in my life it seemed to be true that some things simply weren't going to change. I was the same old Joey with the same old modus operandi.

Lois called Joanie one day. My sons Joey and Nicky were preparing to visit me, and always before they visited, Joanie and Lois talked by phone to finalize plans. They were never uncomfortable speaking with each other. On this occasion their conversation wasn't only about the boys. Lois was pissed at me. "Joan, I came home and found Joey sleeping in our bed with two nude women," Lois said.

"So what's new?" Joanie asked. "What did you do?"

"I smacked them on their rear ends and told them to get out," Lois said.

"Well, Lois," Joanie said, "I appreciate your dilemma, but what are you telling me for? It wasn't *my* bed the three of them were in. *My* bed was round, and I sold it before I left." Then she added, "What goes around comes around, Lois. And like they say, you made your bed, you lie in it."

In lean times, when I wasn't making much money gigging, Lois had to hold everything together. She always managed to do that. She took care of bookings, interviews, bookkeeping, and performing. All I had to do was show up; she handled the rest. And besides running the household and the music business, she did whatever else it took to keep us vertical with noses out of the water. When we lived in the Bronx and paying gigs were few and far between, she took a job as a secretary at a firm on Wall Street. Rain, sleet, or snow, she commuted daily to and from the job by train. No kind of inclement weather got in her way, even though she had only a flimsy spring coat to wear, which her mother had lent her. She wouldn't spend what little money we had on a good coat. And her shoes were nothing to brag about either.

Don't think I wasn't doing my part. I was drinking a bottle of booze every day, and, like any dues-paying alcoholic, I didn't wait till evening to get started. V.O. was my morning juice and my afternoon tea. I smoked four packs of unfiltered Lucky Strike cigarettes a day. I was a chimney. I smoked so incessantly that I was accused of smoking in the shower. I was freeloading off Lois's parents, with whom we were living at the time. To be fully transparent here, I was a bum. I was a disaster just waiting to happen. I knew I had to lose the booze and the butts or I'd be dead soon or kicked to the curb—or both, and neither possibility appealed to me. So, in 1983 I stopped drinking. I stopped smoking. I wasn't kicked to the curb, and I'm not dead yet. Hell, I've even managed to hang onto my lungs and liver.

I constantly wonder why I had the good fortune of two such amazing companions in my life. Of all people surely I was least deserving of such love, support, patience, and long-suffering, and yet I was blessed with it. If only I'd seen that as clearly in past years as I see it now.

Lois was an incredibly talented singer/comic. She took command on stage like no one I ever knew. She walked out there and simply owned it. Those lucky enough to be in her audience always knew they were seeing greatness—it burst from her like the sun's corona during a total solar eclipse. She came by her talents honestly, her parents being Lou Bart and Harriet Lee, once known as the "Sweethearts of Broadway."

Lois was a major part of our act—supremely talented, with a voice that could make angels buy a record. And she was a trouper. At a 1969 gig at Trude Heller's in the City, the stage was already being heated up by Ronnie Grieco, Joey DuVol, myself, and a kickin' rhythm section anchored by Perry Smith on drums. But when Lois took the stage, it exploded. Never mind that she was seven months pregnant. Didn't slow her down even a little bit. The audience seemed as *nervous* that she'd miscarry or deliver on stage as it was *happy* to see and hear her perform.

Lois and I did some sweet music together, including a 1972 recording of "Storybook Children," a Billy Vera/Chip Taylor song produced by Johnny Maestro. Finding a copy of that Steady Records 45 won't be the easiest thing you've ever done, but it'll be worth your time and money. Trust me.

Lois once turned down the opportunity to audition for the part of Fanny Bryce in the Broadway musical *Funny Girl*. Of course, Barbra Streisand played that role to the hilt, and it set her legendary career in motion. But Streisand should be happy that Lois didn't compete for that role. Lois was funny and in control on any stage, and she'd have given Babs a run for the money. It's interesting to contemplate the directions lives and history may have taken, had Lois auditioned and won that part.

Lois and I married on her birthday, February 12, 1973. We did this because my mother didn't like the idea of us living together unmarried. She wanted our children to have a mother and a father. Yes, we'd made good music together, Lois and I—but our children were infinitely better work.

In spite of all I put her through, Lois never left my side—of her own accord. She died of lung cancer on September 7, 2003. Along with the entire family I was devastated. I always thought I'd be the first to go. Since her passing I've done many shows in her honor for the American Cancer Society, and I think of her so very often. When Lois died, a piece of me died too. And I'll be forever haunted by the thought of the glorious career she might have had—without me.

| Joan Wuthrick Part Two |

It's not over till the fat lady sings. Not to insult or belittle anyone's body size or type, but that's the opera-inspired saying. And for Joanie and me, that lady hadn't yet sung.

Some time after Lois passed I went to a birthday party for my son Nicky at his home in Bristol, Pennsylvania. Of course his mother, who had divorced Mike Fricchione, was there too. Joan and I spoke and got caught up a bit, and I asked her out to dinner.

"Are you crazy, Joey?" A predictable but unwelcome response.

"No. Well, I don't *think* I am," I said. "Why not go out? It's a dinner. When we get back to Jersey, we'll go out. We'll have a nice dinner. It couldn't hurt." I was staying with my brother Al in Jersey.

And we did it. We returned to Jersey and went to dinner. I was glad to be with Joanie, and she didn't stab me with a fork or anything. Taking that as a good sign, I asked her out again. She said yes. After that I asked her out again. And again. And again. She said yes to every invitation, and forks were never brought into play. I was emboldened.

"I'd like you to move to Florida," I said.

"Florida?! I've never lived anywhere but Jersey," she said. "Don't know if I'd like living in Florida. It's not Jersey."

"You're right," I said. "It's not Jersey. But take a chance. It could be good."

Joanie thought about it. "All right," she said. "I'll take a chance."

Joanie joined me in Florida in 2005. In 2007 we flew to Las Vegas and remarried on November 25. Again it was a simple ceremony with a few dear friends present. My old friend and drummer Tony "Dutch" Sciuto and his lovely wife Rita honored us as cumare and cumpare (matron of honor and best man). Tommy and Edda DeVito were also there, as was Ray Ranieri, another longtime friend. Following a brief but poignant ceremony, we shared a wonderful celebration together with dinner, reminiscing, and laughter. Soon after the celebration Joanie and I returned to our home in Clearwater.

In 2011 we started and ran a business for several years called Joanie's Metal Recycling. I'd had an interest in such a business for many years, and it seemed to be the right time to do something about it. And just like that, I'd come full circle from doo-wop to heavy metal. I found myself doing things I'd spent my entire life avoiding: getting dirty, lifting heavy objects, and getting up early in the morning. Funny how it all works out in the end. Ironic as hell sometimes, but it works out.

Together again, Joanie and I have enjoyed so much with our children Joey, Nick, Jamie, Kim, Ronnie, Jason, and Louie; our grandchildren Jade, Nicky, Vinnie, Mikey, Joey, Isabella, Ana, Justin, Jonathan, A.J., Jakob, John Paul, Heather, and Sammy; and our great-grandchildren Madyson, Keona, Bralyn, Aria, Dylan, and Kylan. How unspeakably proud I am of each and every one of them as I watch them travel their own life-roads and find their own interests, passions, and successes. Some have followed after music as Lois and I did. Some are even Starliters. My son Ronnie, my daughter Jamie, and my grandson A.J. work with me in Florida. When we're up North, my oldest son Joey, a keyboard player, works with us as well. And in Atlantic City or at Mohegan Sun in Connecticut, we get the whole gang together—and even throw in Jacob, another grandson, on drums. For me, working with my children and grandchildren is simply a dream come true.

For the record: I'm beyond happy to have family on the stage with me, but they're not there because they're family. I hire them because they're good at what they do on stage.

So, there you have it. I've got my Joanie. I've got my children, grandchildren, great-grandchildren. When I perform, I've got family on the stage with me, playing the rock & roll music I love, to audiences I love and who love me in return.

It's funny. Or ironic. Or something. In my early years of rock & roll stardom and the worldwide fame, wealth, and shenanigans that came with it, I thought life just didn't get better than that.

But it did. I found the balance, and it did.

Epilogue

I've omitted many important personal memories and experiences from this work. Its length otherwise would be greater than anyone but the most committed reader would tackle. Perhaps the same might be said by anyone who puts pen to paper to detail a rich life of many years. Nonetheless, the experiences shared here are pieces of the tapestry of my life—a tapestry woven of blessing, love, regret, accomplishment, opportunity, failure, fame, rejection, adventure, error, success, wealth, poverty, satisfaction, friend, and family.

To have lived a life so full as mine seems unlikely, but so it is. I've been helped along the way by family, friends, even foes—and I've helped others find their way. So many amazing artists passed through the Starliters on the way to their stars. From my band emerged seven inductees to the Rock & Roll Hall of Fame, one to the UK Music Hall of Fame, one to the Hammond Hall of Fame, three nominees and two inductees to the Songwriters Hall of Fame, one Academy Award winner, and countless others to satisfying and high-profile careers, and not only in music. I never felt upstaged when I proudly showcased and encouraged talent. My goal always was to produce a sound and a performance that would be enjoyed and remembered. I never cared who carried the ball—as long as the team scored. Jealousy and envy were never in my nature.

I've had my share of acclaim. I've been inducted into the East Coast Musicians Hall of Fame, the Las Vegas Entertainers Hall of Fame, and the Mohegan Sun (CT) Wall of Fame. Thanks to the efforts of my friends Vincent Capuana (late trustee, Passaic Board of Education) and Mark Auerbach (Passaic City historian), the auditorium at my old junior high school in Passaic is named for Joey Dee and the Starliters. At the corner of Washington Place and Columbia Avenue in Passaic, you'll find Joey Dee and the Starliters Square—also thanks to Mark and Vinnie. Gold records and other awards, such as the prestigious German Bronze Lion, hang on my office wall. I value all such recognition; it validates my career to an extent. But its importance pales in the light of my friends' and family's successes, which mean more to me than plaques or statuettes bearing my name.

All I've accomplished in my career has been without regard to color, creed, or culture. I rest comfortably within the ability God granted me to see people as they are rather than as societal stereotypes. Deep in my heart I believe Joey Dee and the Starliters helped move the world away from racial prejudice and further along the road toward acceptance, tolerance, and respect for all. But it's turned out to be a longer road than we thought it to be, and we haven't yet reached its end. I sometimes wonder, as perhaps you do, *What the hell's taking so long?!* It might even be argued that we've backtracked a bit. Perhaps so. But I have faith. I have faith that enough understanding and tolerance are scattered among the rising generations to bring us out of this funk and move us again with renewed energy in the right direction. Please, God—may it be so.

On the personal side of my life, I'm bewildered by an amazing mix of pleasant memory and painful regret. I feel intensely the blessing of family, and most of all that of having walked through life with two women whom I love and by whom I've been loved. Sadly, the cheer of that good fortune is diminished some by stinging memories of the infidelity, dishonesty, and disrespect I too often inflicted on them. This was a personal failure of giant proportions—one that could never be camouflaged or made right by professional accomplishment. To quote a very wise man, "No other success in life can compensate for failure in the home."

Sometimes, when I was with a girl, a sober thought came to me: I had a loving wife and children waiting for me at home, trusting. While my beautiful Joanie and then Lois was there changing diapers, I was on the road—changing girlfriends. The thought broke my heart, but life at the time was life at the time, and next day that thought was gone. But now, when I think back on how I was then, my heart breaks all over again, and I wish I could take back so many of the things I did. Pain that comes from memories of infidelity, broken promises, and bruised love is bitter. We can do better moving forward, but there are no do-overs for past opportunities missed or muffed.

In recounting my years on the way to the top, I realize that every step I took toward rock & roll stardom was a step away from being a good husband and a good father. I wish I hadn't strayed so far, but I'm glad I found my way back.

There's so much more of the tapestry of my life I'd like to share, and perhaps I will—but not today. Right now, let's just get back to making music.

And thank you kindly for your time.

Love, Joey

J. Kevin Morris is the author of *Daddy's Diary: The Adventures of an Everyday Father* (Cedar Fort 2013) and *Strangely Normal: The (Mostly) True Tales of an Incurable Oddball* (Cedar Fort 2011). He is retired after 42 years as a school psychologist, public school administrator, and executive director of a private not-for-profit family disabilities services agency.

Made in the USA
Las Vegas, NV
29 November 2024

12923130R00174